UNDUE PROCESS
THE NCAA'S
INJUSTICE FOR ALL

Don Yaeger
Foreword by Dale Brown

Sagamore Publishing Inc.
Champaign, Illinois 61824-0673

© 1991 Sagamore Publishing, Inc.
P.O. Box 673
Champaign, Il 61824-0673

Editorial production, supervision
 and interior design: Susan M. Williams
Cover and photo insert design: Michelle R. Dressen
Cover photo: Brian J. Moore
Editor: Sara Chilton
Proofreaders: Brian J. Moore, Phyllis L. Bannon

Printed in the United States of America

10   9   8   7   6   5   4   3   2

ISBN: 0-915611-34-1
Library of Congress Catalog Card Number: 90-62973

To Allison, whose love, support and encouragement made this all possible.

CONTENTS

FOREWORD

This is a profoundly sad and starkly illuminating book. Sad, because it is an account of a system gone awry in heaping injustice after injustice upon one part of our society. Illuminating, because it casts a strong light upon dark places that all of us knew existed but few of us even dared whisper about.

How strange that, in our macho business, courage has not been in abundance!

It almost seems impossible that, in the freest country in the world, we tolerated an organization like the NCAA. Is it because we were indifferent, intimidated, uninformed, selfish, loyal to the system, left out, or didn't know how to change a system that has failed in its mission?

Thank God it's all finally out on the table—spelled out in this book—which may be our only assurance that it doesn't happen again.

Finally, this is a book of hope, because Dick Schultz, an ex-coach and ex-athletic director and a man with both common sense and sensitivity, has taken over the leadership of our organization. And there is hope because members of Congress, coaches, college presidents, faculty, chancellors, athletic directors, conference commissioners and even the media have begun to speak out about the immediate need for reform.

There is no question that the system needs change. This honest review of the NCAA makes a precise, step-by-step case for that change and should help speed up the process.

All of us must now work together and forget the past. It takes courage to admit our mistakes, but, as Robert F. Kennedy said: "Each time a man stands up for an idea, or acts to improve the lot of others, or strikes out against injustice, he sends forth a tiny ripple of hope, and crossing each other from a million different centers of energy and daring, those ripples build a current that can sweep down the mightiest wall of oppression and resistance.

"Few are willing to brave the disapproval of their fellows, the censure of their colleagues, the wrath of their society. Moral courage is a rarer commodity than bravery in battle or great intelligence. Yet it is the one essential, vital quality for those who seek to change a world that yields most painfully to change."

Dale Brown

Louisiana State University
Baton Rouge

PREFACE

"Don't you feel a little funny defending cheaters?" a colleague asked when I began work on an investigation of the NCAA enforcement program in mid-1988. "Everybody you're talking to is a confirmed cheater." There begins the Catch-22 of a project like this. The only people who understand the abuses of NCAA "justice" are those who have gone through it; but afterwards, their credibility and motivation are suspect. The folks who haven't gone through an investigation—and are therefore more "credible"—don't understand the problem and have nothing to say. And the NCAA doesn't see a problem at all. Pleased with its 100 percent conviction rate, it has no reason to complain. So whom do you believe? The answer became clearer over time. If only a handful of those who had suffered through an investigation questioned the quality of the NCAA's work, they could be dismissed. When the same complaints, though, came from dozens of schools, the pattern was troubling. Maybe there was something to this chorus of complaints. Maybe someone should listen.

How do you raise those issues without "defending cheaters"? Just tell the truth. Tell the truth, and it becomes easy to understand why many have felt slighted. Tell the truth, and you wonder whether the NCAA should be counted on to tell us who is cheating in college sports.

Is the NCAA enforcement program any more credible than those it accuses? In the late 1970s, a congressional subcommittee that had spent two years investigating the NCAA responded with a resounding "no." In late 1990, several congressmen suggested the answer still was no. "The NCAA needs to stop being a schoolyard bully with petty grievances against schools," U.S. Representative Tom McMillen, of Maryland said after the organization placed tiny Upsala College on five years' probation. McMillen called on Congress to investigate again the NCAA's practices. The NCAA, according to the *Chronicle of Higher Education*, dismissed McMillen's comment as election-year rhetoric.

This book is not intended to defend cheaters. It *is* intended to better explain the impossible predicament facing those under investigation and suggest remedies. An improved and fairer NCAA, after all, benefits millions of fans, thousands of players, and coaches. We get into journalism hoping we can make a difference. This is my attempt.

ACKNOWLEDGMENTS

There are literally hundreds of people who should find their names here for the help they provided in pulling together this book. Some, though, have asked to be left in the background. Public mention of their aid could lead to retribution, they believe. I thank them.

Topping the list of those whose names I must mention are my former colleagues at the *Florida Times-Union*, the Jacksonville, Florida, newspaper that was my home from 1986 until 1990. It was the *Times-Union* that first agreed to this monstrous project of investigating the NCAA. The result of that work was published in October 1988. Editors Fred Hartmann, Mike Richey and Mary Kress proved instrumental, not just in agreeing to take on a project of such magnitude then, but in allowing the fruits of that labor to grow into this book two years later. Many of the more than 250 interviews conducted for this book, dozens of which were tape-recorded, were originally done for the *Times-Union* series. I also need to thank *Times-Union* investigative reporter Mark Middlebrook, whose idea this project was in the first place and whose editing of this book has improved the work immensely.

To help bring focus to a project that so easily can become blurred, I followed paths cut by many journalists before me. I have attempted meticulously to note their work throughout the book. Where no such mention is made, the research was done either by the *Times-Union* or myself. Those who will find their work reflected here include Jack McCallum, Robert Sullivan, Bruce Selcraig, Douglas Looney, John Steinbreder, Alexander Wolff, William Reed, Rick Telander and Curry Kirkpatrick of *Sports Illustrated*; Mike Lopresti and Steve Wieberg of *USA Today*; Chuck Flynn, Bob Asmussen and Loren Tate of the *Champaign-*

Urbana News-Gazette; Douglas Lederman of the *Chronicle of Higher Education*; Bob Gretz and Billy Reed of the *Sporting News*; David Davidson, Mike Fish and Furman Bisher of the *Atlanta Journal-Constitution*; Ric Bucher of the *San Diego Union*; Doug Bedell, David Casstevens, and Jeff Miller of the *Dallas Morning News*; Doug Tucker and John Nelson of Associated Press; Ron Green and Kevin Quirk of the *Charlotte Observer*; Chuck Abadie of the *Hattiesburg* (Mississippi) *American*; Allen Sack of the University of New Haven; Mike Littwin of the *Baltimore Sun*; Bill Campbell of the *Monroe* (Louisiana) *News-Star*; Armen Keteyian, formerly of *Sports Illustrated* and now with ABC News; David Whitford of *Sport*; Peter Alfano and Bill Rhoden of the *New York Times*; J. D. Reed of *Time*; Mark Blaudschun of the *Boston Globe*; David Elfin of the *Washington Times*; Gene Seymore of Copley News Service; Richard Hoffer, Alan Greenberg, Mike Downey and Danny Robbins of the *Los Angeles Times*; Patrick McManamon of the *Palm Beach Post*; Mike Fitzgerald of the *Honolulu Star Bulletin*; John Henderson of the *Las Vegas Review Journal*; Steve Carp of the *Las Vegas Sun*; Frank Deford, Phil Taylor, Scott Ostler and Jeffrey Marx of *The National Sports Daily*; John Camp of CNN; Ron Higgins of the *Shreveport Times*; Dave Dorr, Jeff Gordon and Jim Thomas of the *St. Louis Post-Dispatch*; Larry Donald of the *Basketball Times*; Ray Didinger of the *Philadelphia Daily News*; Ed Sherman and Robert Markus of the *Chicago Tribune*; Kent Pulliam of the *Kansas City Star-Times*; Jud Magrin, Jack Hairston and Tom Lyons of the *Gainesville* (Florida) *Sun*; Robert McCormick and Roger Meiners of *Fortune*; Liz Clarke of the *Raleigh* (North Carolina) *News & Observer*; Ken Hambleton of the *Lincoln* (Nebraska) *Star*; Loel Schrader of the *Long Beach Press-Telegram*; Clark Francis of *HoopScoop*; Tom Boggie of the *Schenectady Daily Gazette*; Bob Faw, CBS Evening News; John Dorschner of the *Miami Herald*; Alvin Sanoff and Joannie Schrof of *U.S. News & World Report*; and Melissa Isaacson and Brian Schmitz of the *Orlando Sentinel*.

The bookshelf proved valuable as well. There, the books *Raw Recruits* by Alexander Wolff and Armen Keteyian, *Tark* by Jerry Tarkanian and Terry Pluto, *Don't Count Me Out* by Bruce Hunter, *Vitale* by Dick Vitale and Curry Kirkpatrick and *The Hundred Yard Lie* by Rick Telander were helpful.

Thanks also to the folks at Sagamore Publishing: Joe Bannon, Peter Bannon, Joe Bannon, Jr., Michelle Dressen, Brian Moore and Sara Chilton. A special thanks goes to Susan Williams, who showed uncommon patience while teaching me a great deal about publishing. And the book couldn't have been done without Mary Scott Gilbert's research assistance. Last, but very certainly not least, I must recognize Peter Dunbar, Lester Abberger and Robert Bryan, for their work as advisers in the writing.

LIST OF PLAYERS

S. DAVID BERST   A former baseball coach at his alma mater, MacMurray College in Jacksonville, Illinois, Berst went to work as an NCAA investigator in 1972. After spearheading the investigation of University of Nevada–Las Vegas basketball coach Jerry Tarkanian, Berst was promoted to the NCAA's top investigative job.

STEVE MORGAN   A lawyer, Morgan was hired to handle the NCAA's legislative services department. He became associate executive director and serves as Berst's boss.

WALTER BYERS   In 1951, at age 29, Byers became the NCAA's first executive director. He served in the job for 36 years, building the organization from nothing to a staff of 145. He officially severed his ties with the NCAA in August 1990 after two years as a paid consultant.

DICK SCHULTZ   Hired in 1987 from a national list of candidates, Schultz became the NCAA's second executive director. Schultz spent most of his first year travelling, giving speeches and interviews, something Byers never did. He is a former football and basketball coach and athletic director at the University of Virginia.

JERRY TARKANIAN   After fighting the NCAA in court for 13 years, the University of Nevada–Las Vegas basketball coach lost his final appeal to the U.S. Supreme Court. His team turned around and won the 1990 national championship.

DALE BROWN   The outspoken basketball coach at Louisiana State University, Brown once called the NCAA investigative staff "Gestapo bastards." Shortly thereafter, the NCAA investigated his basketball program. He continues to rail against NCAA rules.

J. BRENT CLARK   A former NCAA investigator, Clark left in 1977 and became the star witness in a congressional investigation of the NCAA. His testimony led congressmen to express outrage at NCAA tactics.

DOUG JOHNSON   Another former NCAA investigator, Johnson directed investigations of LSU and Florida, among others, before going to work at the University of Miami. He calls schools that are bothered by NCAA sanctions "whiners and complainers."

RON WATSON   Now an assistant athletic director at the University of Oklahoma, Watson was an NCAA investigator for 16 months. He quit, he said, just as he was beginning to get good at his job. His short stay at the NCAA is common for the poorly paid investigators.

D. ALAN WILLIAMS   A University of Virginia history professor, Williams serves as chairman of the Committee on Infractions.

CHARLES ALAN WRIGHT   One of the nation's leading constitutional law experts, Wright served two terms on the infractions committee. The University of Texas law professor was committee chairman for one term.

LONNY ROSE   While a law professor at the University of Kansas, Rose was asked to become assistant athletic director for compliance. His work with the NCAA led him to found SportsMasters, a Kansas City company that represents universities and coaches under NCAA investigation. He left Kansas in 1990 to teach at the University of Miami.

JOHN WEISTART   A law professor at Duke University, Weistart is considered a national expert in the area of sports law. He has written extensively about the need for reform of the NCAA.

1

IN THE
BEGINNING

A HISTORY LESSON

The afternoon was typical for late fall in the Northeast with conditions so cold that watching football was nearly as painful as playing it. Dark clouds hung heavy, occasionally letting loose with a drizzle, temperatures were in the low 40s and the wind-chill was below freezing. Still, a standing-room-only crowd of 3,000 had converged on Ohio Field just outside New York City for the game all had waited for, the season-ending rivalry between Union College and New York University. As predicted, defense dominated the early going and the big game was a scoreless struggle when, midway through the 35-minute first half, New York University quarterback Thomas Rust took the snap at his 30-yard line and tossed the ball to the Violets' rugged right halfback for a sweep off left tackle. When Samuel Hayden dashed outside, all that stood between him and the game's first touchdown was Harold Ransom Moore, Union College's star linebacker and tailback. Both players lowered their heads and, according to newspaper accounts, met in a "devastating" clash. Moore held the slightly larger Hayden up long enough for the rest of his Union College teammates to bury the ball carrier. The touchdown was saved.

As the *New York Times* reported on its front page the next day, "There was a pile of men on the field, with Moore at the bottom of it. Seeing that somebody was about to be hurt, the referee blew the whistle."

It was too late for Harold Moore. While Detective Sergeant Thomas Darcy rushed onto the field to unstack the human mass, an eery silence fell over the crowd on that chilly afternoon, two days after Thanksgiving in 1905. Darcy, one of 13 police officers whose duty it was to prevent violence in the charged-up rivalry, found the 19-year-old Moore lying flat on his face unconscious. The boy's father, William Moore, who had traveled three hours from the family's home in Ogdensburg to watch the season finale, ran from the bench to his only son's side. Right behind him were Doctors Chester F. B. Whitney—NYU's team physician—and John Nunn. Whitney, after lifting Moore's head and peering into his steel blue eyes, told police the player was suffering from a cerebral hemorrhage and was in critical condition. The police borrowed a fan's car and strapped Moore's limp body to a makeshift gurney of wooden slats padded by clothes and rugs. During the ride to Fordham Hospital, Dr. Whitney injected strychnine over Moore's heart in an effort to revive him.

NYU went on to win the game, 11-0. Play resumed after Moore's teammates were told his condition wasn't serious, according to the Union College student newspaper, the *Concordiensis*. As soon as the game was over, several Union players rushed to Fordham to check on Moore. Doctors told the players that while Moore had yet to regain consciousness, "his chances for recovery were excellent," several players told the student newspaper. Relieved, the players went on to their traditional postgame dinner with their rivals. It wasn't long before that relief was shattered. A call from the hospital announced that Harold Moore, a modest, studious boy who was emblematic of all one could expect from a student-athlete, was dead. Ernest Dann, the football team's captain, broke into tears and staggered from the banquet hall. Most of his teammates followed.

There aren't any statistics available in the archives at Union College that show the on-field importance of Harold Moore to his team. There is no clue what his yards-per-carry average was or how many solo tackles or assists he made in his two seasons. But in the history of college football, Moore's death had staggering implications, setting off a string of events that would change forever the face of college sports. He was the 18th player to be fatally injured during the fall of 1905, a sobering figure that caused a nation to rethink the value of college football and made several college leaders consider banning the sport altogether.

Few college sports fans have ever heard of Harold Moore. According to the student newspaper, he had been nicknamed "Blue" by his classmates at Union College because he "always had a sunny nature." Moore, who had played the year before without ever leaving a game, was eulogized by H. L. Towne, Union's athletic director, as "one of the guttiest players who was ever on the team and one who did not know what it was to fear." The college's dean praised him "as a splendid scholar."

Union College doesn't even play New York University in football any more. In fact, while Union College has gone on to become a small-college Eastern power, NYU hasn't fielded a football team in years. Yet many believe that Union College's loss that day on a football field in Morris Heights, New York, was the nation's gain.

It was the response of NYU Chancellor Henry Mitchell MacCracken that may have paid Moore his greatest tribute. Just hours after he watched the boyish Moore carried off his team's home field, MacCracken canceled classes at NYU and sent a telegram to Harvard President Charles Eliot.

"May I not request, in view of the tragedy on Ohio Field today, that you will invite a meeting of university and college presidents to undertake the reform or abolition of football," MacCracken asked of his Harvard peer. No game was worth losing the likes of "a fine young man like Harold Moore," MacCracken told reporters.

Eliot, however, was not yet ready to listen. Perhaps it was because football at the major institutions was so financially successful—Yale's nationally ranked team, for example, had a reserve account worth more than $100,000 (the equivalent of about $2 million today). Or perhaps it was because the rivalries among Harvard and the other prestigious football schools were so popular—that year's game against Yale had drawn 45,000, including Harvard alumnus President Theodore Roosevelt. Whatever the reason, Eliot told MacCracken he was not ready to lead the fight for changes in the game. He wired back, "I do not think it expedient to call a meeting of college Presidents about football. They certainly cannot reform football, and I doubt if by themselves they can abolish it."

MacCracken's was hardly the first call for reform. Before the 1905 season began, a concerned President Roosevelt had invited several college coaches—including those from Harvard, Yale and Princeton—to the White House to discuss the dangers of this game that was growing in popularity. Pressure was mounting across the country for a radical change. Several state legislatures even considered bills that would have outlawed the game. And although none of the bills passed, the message was clear. Roosevelt took it upon himself to make it crystal: Either reform the game or it will die, the President said. The coaches told Roosevelt that it was too late to make any rule changes for the 1905 season, but they promised to use their influence to pass rules aimed at cleaning up the game during the December meeting of their cliquish rules committee. In the meantime, the coaches told the president they would work together to keep the season "as safe as possible."

Safe it was not. In addition to the 18 fatalities, another 149 players suffered serious injuries during that season. On the same day that Harold Moore died, Douglas Carter of Columbia was seriously injured in a game against Penn. He was paralyzed in both arms and was left with little feeling in both legs after a tackle made on his first run from scrimmage. According to wire reports, he entered the game after Columbia's starting halfback, Van Saltz, left the game with a broken toe. Over in Cambridge, Harvard's David Hurley also was paralyzed from the neck down in a game that day.

The problems weren't only at the collegiate level. That November afternoon on which Moore died and Carter and Hurley were injured, the *New York Times* carried stories about Carl Osborne of Rockville, Indiana, and Robert Brown of Sedalia, Missouri. The 18-year-old Osborne was killed during a game between Marshall and Bellmore high schools. An autopsy showed he was tackled so hard that one of his ribs had been driven into his heart. Brown, 15, was paralyzed below the neck by a blow he delivered during a game. Across the country young men were dying playing the game of football.

The image of college football was so bad it spawned one of the most popular plays of 1905. *The College Widow*, a story about the quirks of college athletics and the violence of football, was, according to the *New York Times*, a critical success.

On December 4, Roosevelt brought Harvard representatives William Reid and Herbert White to the White House to underscore his interest in reform of football. An avid football fan—he was the first president to use football analogies in his speeches—Roosevelt told them the 1905 season had damaged the game's credibility. He suggested that, at the next meeting of the Intercollegiate Football Rules Committee, the group consider "reduction of gate receipts, if not their elimination; the restriction of training methods; and the broad question of eligibility to prevent solicitation, importation and employment of players."

The Intercollegiate Football Rules Committee—formed in 1894 by Harvard, Princeton, Pennsylvania and Yale—met three days later in Philadelphia and snubbed President Roosevelt, reneging on its promise to clean up the violent game. The committee passed no significant rule changes, prompting outcries from college administrators and spectators alike, and leaving the future of college football in doubt.

Still troubled by visions of Harold Moore being carried from Ohio Field, NYU Chancellor MacCracken expressed outrage over the lack of commitment by the large schools to cleaning up college football. If the big boys won't police themselves, he said, maybe it was time for someone else to do it. MacCracken sent invitations to like-minded presidents at other football-playing schools, asking that they join him for a meeting at New York's Murray Hill Hotel. Together, they would decide the game's fate. Although the meeting was not sanctioned by the rules committee, thirteen presidents accepted the invitation and met briefly on December 9, 1905, to pass a resolution declaring their intent to reform the game. They also agreed to return three weeks later to hear ideas for change.

For this December 28 meeting, 62 colleges sent representatives. The nine-hour meeting ended with the creation of a formal organization, the Intercollegiate Athletic Association of the United States.

No one knew it then, but that group had formed what seven years later would become the National Collegiate Athletic Association, today the most powerful sports governing body in the nation. On January 12, 1906, the rules committee of the new association met with the Intercollegiate Football Rules Committee and together the two groups drafted new rules for the next fall's season. The forward pass was adopted, loose balls could no longer be kicked, hurdling—the act of literally flinging a small back over the line of scrimmage—was eliminated, a one-yard neutral zone between the offensive and defensive lines was established, the length of the game was cut from 70 to 60 minutes, first-down yardage was increased from 5 to 10 yards, in the hope that more teams would spread the field and run wide rather than diving haphazardly into the line, and, most importantly, the committee required that at least 6 of the 11 offensive players be on the line of scrimmage, ending dangerous "mass momentum plays."

In one afternoon's work, the group rewrote the rules so substantially that, in 1906, the game was, according to observers, both safer and more exciting. "I must say that football has been greatly improved this year," admitted Harvard's President Eliot after the season ended. "It has less injuries and is much more openly played."

The success all but guaranteed the future role of the IAAUS —and later the NCAA—as the rule-making authority for college football. "I firmly believe the IAAUS will finally dominate the college athletic world," said West Point's Palmer Pierce, the first president of the association.

He had no idea how accurate those words would become. Today's NCAA controls the lives of more than 250,000 college athletes and thousands of adults who make their living off college athletics. As California Representative John Moss said during a congressional investigation of the NCAA's enforcement program some 70 years after Palmer Pierce's prediction, "This is a private organization, responsible to no one outside itself, with powers normally reserved to governments."

For the fans at Union College, there was no 1906 football season. It was canceled after Harold Moore's death. Throughout that year, students wore black armbands, both as a remembrance of "Blue" Moore and an expression of their hope that college football would become safer, allowing them to field another team in 1907. Harold Moore's death, they hoped, would be the nation's gain. "He will not have died in vain if his death results in the reform of athletics," Union College President Andrew V. V. Raymond said. "There can be no question that a game that calls for so many victims each year in spite of every precaution and safeguard that may be taken is a wrong one."

THE MAN WHO BUILT THE BEAST

It's axiomatic in sports that teams take on the personality of their coaches. Indiana University's basketball team is a reflection of its fiery coach, Bobby Knight, as were Bo Schembechler's Michigan football teams. And Penn State plays conservative football worthy of its buttoned-down coach, Joe Paterno.

For 36 years, the man calling the signals at the NCAA was Walter Byers. Walter Byers *was* the NCAA. And the NCAA, from the day in 1951 when he walked in the office, took on the personality of Walter Byers, a cowboy-boot-wearing, tough-talking man who was as competitive as any coach in the country. To understand Byers, and the NCAA under his leadership, consider this story of how he spent his evenings after coming home from the NCAA's offices in Mission, Kansas.

"He loved to read," Betty Byers, his second of three wives, said. "His favorite book? Oh, it had to be *The Godfather*. He read *The Godfather*, well, he read it several times. I think we had to buy him a new copy because he enjoyed it so much. He would always go back and read portions again, check on it over and over. I really think that it fascinated him. I really feel that part of his personality, too, is that he wondered how the Mafia really worked and was kind of fascinated by how strong or how powerful the Mafia could be. I think he wondered how someone could become that powerful. He saw something of himself in that. Reading *The Godfather*, I think that had something to do with power. He felt that he had that much power. I mean, his office or the whole NCAA was run rather like the FBI. You just got that feeling. Yes, I think that tells you a lot about Walter Byers."

That also tells you a lot about the NCAA that Walter built. And build it he did. Before Walter Byers, there really was no NCAA. For the 40 years following that 1905 gathering of college leaders, NCAA conventions proved to be little more than an opportunity for athletic directors to catch up on gossip and distribute resumes. The NCAA's bylaws during those years—although they espoused the virtues of amateurism and encouraged schools to play virtuously—didn't even provide for punishment if the rules were violated. Membership in the NCAA was not contingent on adherence to the rules.

Then came World War II. No one paid much attention to college athletics during those four years. But when GI Joe started coming home, college teams became filled with former soldiers, in school on the GI bill.

"The GIs began to flock into the colleges and that's when you began to get the real good teams, not one or two of them, but a lot of them," said Arthur Bergstrom, who was hired by Byers in 1956 as the NCAA's director of enforcement. "And then, when the GI money ran out, or schools ran out of GIs, these colleges wanted to keep up the same level that they'd had. Then they really began the intense recruiting. They began to have tryouts, which were against the rules."

About the same time, commercial air flight became widespread. Lucrative postseason bowl games were spreading more quickly than Communism. Suddenly, schools were recruiting outside their region and offering more than an education in return for an athlete's talent. Suddenly (although many correctly argue it wasn't that sudden), schools were "cheating." It had to stop.

So, in 1948, the NCAA convention adopted the "Sanity Code," which prohibited NCAA member institutions from "inducing" athletes to attend their schools by offering lucrative scholarships. To be eligible for financial assistance the student-athlete had to show financial need or academic excellence, not just athletic ability, the code said. To enforce the Sanity Code, a Constitutional Compliance Committee was created. From day one, the committee had problems.

Three years later, in the spring of 1951, the committee reported to the NCAA membership that the code had been a failure. Six schools had been found by the committee to have violated the code, but the membership had refused to mete out the only penalty the code allowed—expulsion from the NCAA.

The Sanity Code was repealed, but the concern NCAA members had for potential rule violators continued. The annual convention created another committee to "develop and recommend proposals for new enforcement rules and procedures." And, the convention decided, if the NCAA was going to get tough, it needed a leader. The organization, which had no office and no staff, hired an executive director. Enter Walter Byers, a 29-

year-old assistant in the Big Ten Conference office, who was looking to make his mark on athletics.

"The truth is, there really weren't a lot of people interested in the job," said John Fuzak, retired associate dean of the College of Education at Michigan State University and a former NCAA president. "There were some other good people working for conferences, but they weren't interested. I mean, it was really just being executive director of a group that sponsored meetings once a year and that was about it. There wasn't much to the NCAA and I don't think anyone foresaw the future."

If there wasn't much to the NCAA before Walter Byers, there wasn't much else when he left. Without a doubt, the NCAA became king of the athletics hill, growing from 278 member schools in 1949 to 802 in 1989; from a one-person staff hidden away in the corner of the Big Ten Conference office in 1951 to a 160-employee conglomerate housed in a seven-story, 154,000-square-foot glass-and-granite building in Overland Park, Kansas, in 1990. The NCAA's hand-to-mouth existence in 1951 has given way, less than four decades later, to a $98-million annual budget (including $273,074 for maintenance of its own $1.7-million airplane). It was under Byers's direction that the basketball television package grew from a $190,000 afterthought in 1966 to $32 million in 1986. And in 1989, a new NCAA television contract expanded the worth of that basketball gold mine to $1 billion over seven years.

Byers clearly wanted to be the Godfather of college sports. In his zeal to make the NCAA the dominant force in amateur athletics, Byers worked ruthlessly to eliminate, or at least weaken, his competition. Over the course of Byers's tenure, the NCAA did battle with the Amateur Athletic Union, the United States Olympic Committee, the Association for Intercollegiate Athletics for Women and, to a lesser extent, the National Association of Intercollegiate Athletics. Generally he won, and it rarely was pretty.

In the early days, Byers launched a two-pronged attack on the AAU and the USOC. He wanted the NCAA to have increased influence in the selection of America's Olympic teams. But the USOC gave the NCAA and the AAU an equal number of votes on Olympic matters.

"During that time I really was the swing vote on every major issue," said Colonel Donald Hull, then the Department of

Defense's representative on the Olympic board of directors. "If I went with AAU, Byers would give me a little hell but he didn't jump on me too tough because there could be something else coming up pretty soon and he needed my vote. He wanted to control the whole thing, and when he couldn't, he kept USA teams weak internationally. He worked his membership and passed rules that wouldn't allow the NCAA athletes to participate in anything but NCAA-sponsored events. Now that was strictly, absolutely 100 percent a power play to kill the AAU. He'd say the athletes may be abused or misused by professional organizations or something, you know. He said he was protecting the athlete. All he really was doing was maintaining his power base to try and kill the AAU. What he did, it's sort of like Hitler, who got and misused power."

Byers's venom extended to the NAIA when that group of small colleges asked for the opportunity to have its players participate in the Olympic basketball trials, Hull said.

"Byers appeared before us [the USOC board] and he said the NAIA all-star team couldn't beat—what was the college we all used to laugh about? Podunkville or something—that they couldn't beat any single college team. He really killed their ability to play, he said they didn't belong in the Olympic tournament. He sort of hung himself by overdoing his bitterness. Then the first game, the very first game, the NCAA champion that year was Ohio State and the NAIA beat their ass. NAIA all-stars beat Ohio State with the great Oscar Robertson and one of the greatest college teams that there ever was. Well, they kicked Ohio State's ass but good. That made poor old Byers so pissed off he left the tournament and went home. He just sneaked out that night and took off."

Years later, when the AAU offered Hull a job as he prepared to retire from the military, Byers called him with a little career advice. "He told me I'd wish I were back in the Army in three months because there would be no AAU in three months," Hull said with a laugh. "We hung in there, no thanks to Walter."

There was little interest in women's intercollegiate sports through the first 20 years of Byers's tenure. Then Congress decided in 1972 to pass Title IX, forcing colleges to spend increased money on women's sports. And, like a shark smelling blood, Byers zeroed in. The AIAW, its importance and financial strength bolstered by Congress's action, negotiated its own television contract for women's championships. AIAW leaders also began talks with Byers about granting equal status to women's athletics, allowing each NCAA member university one vote for men's athletics and one vote for women's athletics at its convention. The idea would have significantly changed the way the NCAA did business—since 90 percent of those voting at conventions are men—and could have opened the NCAA's financial coffers to the burgeoning demands of rapidly expanding women's programs.

That wasn't exactly what Byers had in mind. He countered with a different offer. How about just folding up your tent and joining the NCAA altogether, Byers suggested. And, more importantly, we'll leave the voting procedures just as they are. AIAW leaders balked.

Byers wasn't finished. Over the next six years, he talked the NCAA leadership into underwriting a series of championship events for women. That finally happened in 1981-82. The NCAA events were scheduled at the same time as the AIAW championships, forcing schools to make a choice. As bait, the NCAA offered to pay the expenses of the schools competing in its championships. Many of the most successful AIAW schools opted for the NCAA championships. That was the end of the AIAW, although the organization didn't officially die until it lost its lawsuit against the NCAA in the mid-1980s.

"It was an antitrust suit. The analogy would be, you have a big supermarket like the NCAA and a little bakery like the AIAW," said Donna Lopiano, women's athletic director at the University of Texas and a founder of the AIAW. "Now the little bakery, it makes great bread, great whole-wheat bread. And the supermarket decides it wants to get rid of this little competitor and invites everybody that shops in the supermarket, that buys at least a dollar's worth of food, to take home a free loaf of bread when they check out. Now how long is the little bakery going to last if they can get a free loaf of bread at the supermarket? What the NCAA did was offer to pay the championship expenses, travel and per diem of all the women's sports, funded by the men's championship money. It cost the NCAA $3 million that first year and they earned roughly $500,000 on women's sports. But they were willing to take the loss to run our little bakery out of business. Walter Byers, he's certainly a predator when it comes to competition."

While Byers worked hard at running his competition out of business, he, like the Godfather, worked just as hard to remain an enigma. Stories of his attempts to avoid the spotlight are legion. Friends and family say he has been known to register in hotels under assumed names, and he instructed his children, employees and friends never to divulge his home phone number or whereabouts while on the road. Some call him paranoid. His ex-wife said Byers preferred to call this quirk a "fear of being vulnerable. And I don't think he liked ever being vulnerable. I think that was probably his main fault," Betty Byers said.

Byers managed his anonymity so adroitly that most sportswriters and broadcasters didn't know what he looked like. "He sat through the press conferences before the basketball finals this year and no more than six reporters talked to him," Dave Cawood, NCAA assistant executive director for communications, told the *Charlotte Observer* in 1984. "That expresses his manner. He doesn't try to let anyone know he's there. Until recently, he probably hasn't averaged more than half a dozen in-person interviews a year and one phone interview a month, primarily because people think he won't talk."

Sports Illustrated, which was unsuccessful in its first two attempts at writing profiles about Byers, finally completed in 1986 one of the rare well-done stories on his life. In that story, writer Jack McCallum described Byers as "a Wizard of Oz, an invisible button-pusher hiding out somewhere on the Kansas plain."

"Does he really exist?" McCallum quoted the Reverend Timothy Healy, president of Georgetown University, a dominant basketball power that had gone to the Final Four three of the previous four years, as asking. "For all I know, he's a figment."

"Walter in a sense was his own worst enemy because of his personality," said Wayne Duke, Byers's first employee and later the commissioner of the Big Eight and Big Ten conferences. "He does run things close to the vest, maybe too close to the vest. He instilled a basis of values in me and some of the other people who worked for him. Walter would say: First things come first; take care of your homework and things will take care of themselves; don't get your name in the newspapers, you'll just get in trouble, stay out of the newspapers; performance commands respect. I heard those words over and over from day one. Walter operated on those credos and I think those would apply to the NCAA."

Said Arthur Bergstrom: "His idea was that if you do your own homework and do a good job, you don't need the public relations."

Byers built his dynasty, friends and coworkers said, on three pillars: football on television, the basketball tournament and enforcement. While the greatest success financially was the basketball tournament, the greatest means of gathering power was with enforcement, his colleagues said.

"In 1955, Walter had this idea, and the NCAA agreed, that the president of each member institution would sign a statement saying that his institution would abide by NCAA rules and regulations," said Bergstrom. "That was in '55. The enforcement program was really strengthened when it became necessary for each president to sign that statement saying that his institution was in compliance. At the time I'm talking about, nobody said much about the NCAA. About the only thing they ever knew much about was at the end of the basketball season there was that little ol' NCAA basketball tournament. Otherwise, you hardly ever heard of it. Then when the NCAA began to take action against the violators, then the ears did perk up and people began to pay attention. I think it was the most important factor in stepping up the stature of the association."

"Walter built the power of the NCAA on enforcement," said former Pac-10 Commissioner Wiles Hallock, another of Byers's one-time employees. "Before the NCAA was involved in an enforcement program, it didn't have any power. It was a scheduling organization. They conducted a few championships. But as far as the power was concerned, it wasn't there until Walter started working enforcement."

When he started, he started big. Byers's first case was the point-shaving scandal at the University of Kentucky. He personally investigated the case that eventually led to the NCAA's first sanction—a one-year ban on Wildcat basketball.

"That's where the NCAA made its mark," Wayne Duke said. "With Walter Byers principally behind the effort, they suspended the University of Kentucky basketball team for a full year. I think the Kentucky action just indelibly stamped on the public that the NCAA meant business. It was first thing out of the box, so to speak, and it gave the NCAA clout."

As the NCAA's strength continued to increase, Byers's star continued to rise. Within the organization, he proved to be a master at manipulating the bureaucratic monstrosity that is the NCAA. It is a given in studies of public administration that, as organizations grow rapidly in size and complexity, the amount of responsibility and authority that eventually flows to staff grows proportionately. That fact increased Byers's strength within the organization, both friends and enemies said, that and his longevity. Byers and his top staff held their positions many times longer than key elected NCAA officers from member institutions.

"Since elected and appointed representatives of the member schools change often, it became easy for Byers to make them depend on his staff, especially in the area of operations," said former Nevada Representative Jim Santini, a long-time critic of the NCAA. "The area of operations, i.e. how rules are followed and enforced and punishment meted out, is the central core of power in an organization which uses the issuance of punishment as its means of obtaining desired actions from its members."

Byers didn't just outlast volunteers within the organization. His 36 years at the NCAA's helm was 5 years longer than Clarence Campbell ran the National Hockey League, 12 years longer than Judge Kenesaw Mountain Landis ran major league baseball, 16 years longer than Avery Brundage ran the International Olympic Committee, and 19 years longer than Maurice Podoloff ran the National Basketball Association.

There were other unique aspects to the NCAA that bolstered Byers's influence, as well. "The reason Byers became so powerful is that the NCAA is made up of all these disparate groups—rich schools, poor schools, big schools, little schools, revenue schools, nonrevenue schools—and they're all covered under the same NCAA blanket," said Nebraska Senator Ernie Chambers. "When that happens, you have people facing different situations who are required to conform to the same rules. That creates divisions among them, and since they're all so divided, there is no way to get a consensus among them to do anything that'll override the agenda set by Byers and the NCAA bureaucracy—and he knew this."

University of Miami sports law professor Lonny Rose, who has both studied and done battle with the NCAA's enforcement program, agreed with Chambers's assessment. "Despite the representation of Walter Byers that the membership made the rules and he really had no power, there is a tremendous amount of power in the staff. There is no question that schools or conferences propose legislation but that legislation is edited by the staff, and then there are interpretations, which are made by the staff. The staff doesn't have to pass a rule if it is empowered to interpret the current rules any way they want to. One of the things I learned early on as an assistant athletic director [at the University of Kansas] and that I use now is that, whenever you get an opinion from the NCAA legislative services staff, I confirm it in writing. There were times where, very frankly, if I wanted an opinion that was favorable to my facts, I knew who to call. Depending on who I got on the telephone over there and the relationship I developed with that person, I was able to get an opinion that was in my favor. A lot of it was personal credibility. But very honestly, the staff has a lot of power. They take positions that strengthen or destroy a rule. As with every bureaucracy, there may be policy guidelines established by the electorate, but the implementation of that policy is done by the staff and that is a very powerful duty. The power can only land in the hands of the staff. There is a very small group of people that hold it all. Walter Byers was no dummy. He knew he had the power because of the NCAA structure. He just never talked about it."

Former NCAA president Wilford Bailey concedes that NCAA members allowed Byers and his unelected staff to assume increased power. "I think frankly, for too long, the membership probably let things sort of coast along and evolve without enough attention by the membership," Bailey said. "And I think it did develop into what the membership feels is too much of an arbitrary, autocratic, authoritarian activity controlled and dominated by a small staff in the national office in Kansas City."

Byers often wielded that influence by ensuring that the NCAA's most important committees were stacked to his liking. The NCAA Council, the major decision-making body within the organization, has 44 members. Half are appointed by various other NCAA committees and half are elected from an NCAA-backed slate of delegates. Veteran NCAA watchers can remember only one time—the 1983 election of San Diego State University Athletic Director Mary Alice Hill to the Council—when the NCAA-backed slate wasn't rubber-stamped by the convention. "I think once a person was on a committee, Byers may have had some influence with them to make sure that other people that he felt were capable and talented were chosen," said Wiles Hallock, one of Byers's closest friends. "I think he influenced everything that went on in the NCAA, he really did. He had great influence but it was always a very subtle influence. Number one, he was always prepared to argue whatever he believed in better than anybody else. I mean he was an extremely intelligent man. And he is terrific one-on-one with people. I've never seen anybody, one-on-one, get the best of him. And so he exercised his influence through other people that had clout within the association. That was part of his mental discipline. He knew exactly how he was going to go about doing the various things and he got the right people to help him do them."

"I guess the thing that's left over from Walter that always somehow made an impact on me was that he didn't even trust you to say the right thing in the microphone at the convention," said Donna Lopiano. "He would have it all written out for you. For example: Let's say the NCAA Council is going to sponsor 40 or so amendments at a convention. And they pick out different members of the council to formally move the adoption of each amendment. Well, every one of those people are provided with a script of exactly what to say at the microphone. And it was absolutely dumbfounding. Everybody had a perfectly typed piece of paper and they just stood there and read it. He made people dependent on the organization. That was considered, and I think still is probably considered, as, 'Gee, thanks a lot for doing my work for me.' I mean he literally made them dependent. The members didn't run the NCAA, Walter did. Walter controlled information in a very precise way and just let people in on certain pieces. He manipulated very well, I thought."

One of the best examples of a Byers-manipulated powerplay came in 1984, when nearly three dozen university presidents suggested it was time that they take control of the NCAA. The group proposed a Board of Presidents that would have veto power over NCAA convention actions. If it had been approved, the board would have taken control away from the labyrinthine committee structure within which Byers was used to working. Quietly, behind the scenes, Byers worked his network of athletic directors and killed the presidents' proposal. "We worked pretty hard on behalf of that [Board of Presidents] legislation," said Robert Atwell, executive director of the American Council on Education. "Walter didn't like it. But he figured they couldn't fight something with nothing. And so they had to come up with something of their own. That something was the Presidents Commission, an advisory commission, which is all the Presidents Commission is. I thought it was a very clever strategy on Byers's part. So in that sense, Walter kind of kept the power with those who had been running the NCAA for a long time. Is it tough for an outsider to get something across? Absolutely. It is a highly competent group, but it's paid to advance athletic interests. We failed because most athletic directors and faculty [athletic] representatives felt threatened by our proposal. He [Byers] played off those fears. He is a very shrewd, very able man. He is a very understated man, not a charismatic figure particularly. But in him you had a very effective, quietly effective, administrator and a very shrewd negotiator."

Added Texas's Donna Lopiano: "I believe that Walter Byers set up the NCAA Presidents Commission to fail. Structurally, within the organization, a Presidents Commission makes no sense. They're nowhere. They're out of touch with the membership, they're out of touch with the Council, there is no interaction with expert bodies of the organization and they meet once or twice a year. That's all he wanted them to do."

To complete his mission, Byers surrounded himself with an incredibly loyal staff, so loyal some wondered if they were clones of the master. "Byers only hired people who would tolerate unquestioned obedience to rules," Lopiano said. "Walter didn't want human beings. He wanted robots. I've always just kidded the heck out of the NCAA staff because of not being able to have a cup of coffee at your desk. Well, it was—it's not fair to say Hitleresque, but it was almost that kind of structured mentality."

Though Lopiano may have joked with NCAA staff members about not being able to have coffee at their desks, it was no laughing matter in Mission, Kansas. One of Byers's first decisions as the staff size increased was to create a booklet called *NCAA Office Policies and Procedures*. By his retirement, the book was more than 100 pages long. Among the regulations:

■   Male administrators are to wear suits or sport coats and slacks, shirts and ties. Women administrators and nonadministrative employees are to wear dresses, suits, skirts or slacks and blouses. All blouses must cover the waistline and below at all times.

■   All office drapes, including thermal drapes, are to be drawn at the time the occupant leaves his or her office for the day.

■   Smoking is not permitted except in the lunchroom during lunch periods.

■   Employees must leave behind their copy of the *NCAA Office Policies and Procedures* upon termination or resignation.

"The staff was living in an ivory tower," said Louisiana State University basketball coach Dale Brown. "The NCAA was guarding its offices with the same mentality that existed at Dachau and Auschwitz—we're just following our Führer's orders, heat the ovens. It was cold and calculated."

The long list of rules—and long hours of work—seldom brought complaints from the NCAA office staff. And if they did gripe, it was never to Byers or top NCAA officers. Former Committee on Infractions chairman Charles Allen Wright once said, "It may be true that the NCAA office is run like a plantation, but if so, the slaves seem happy with their lot."

"Everybody was very, very loyal to him and they knew that if they spoke out of turn or if they did something wrong, that was it," said Betty Byers, who became closer to some NCAA staff members than even her husband did. "That's why few people would ever say anything negative about the NCAA or Walter."

That shouldn't shock anyone, since Byers's loyal office staff was well known for its penchant for falling in line behind the leader. In fact, as *Sports Illustrated* once noted, "Byers has achieved something most corporate managers can only dream about: an office staff that does not whisper about him at the water fountain. Of course, under his buttoned-down, over-regulated, nose-to-the-grindstone administration, Byers has a staff that wouldn't dare whisper at the water fountain."

The greatest controversy during Byers's reign came when some suggested he was using his influence for his personal gain as well. In November 1985 the *Washington Post* reported that, in the seven previous years, the NCAA had arranged more than $600,000 in no-interest mortgage loans for its staff, the largest loan being the $118,000 provided to Byers. The long-term no-interest loans were provided quietly to Byers's inner circle of top managers: $71,000 to Associate Executive Director Ted Tow,

$71,500 to Associate Executive Director Tom Jernstedt, $58,000 to Controller Louis Spry, $55,000 to Assistant Executive Director William B. Hunt, $54,000 to Assistant Executive Director Ruth Berkey (whom Byers would later marry), $49,000 to Assistant Executive Director Dave Cawood, and $46,000 to Associate Executive Director Steve Morgan. The *Post* questioned whether the loans were proper, especially given the NCAA's delicate role as guardian of integrity. NCAA officials defended the practice, pointing out that the loans were mentioned in the fine-print footnotes to the NCAA's annual report. Still, the *Post* reported, the loans were a mystery to several prominent NCAA officials, including then-president John Davis and secretary-treasurer Wilford Bailey. The loans "cause enough questions to be raised that we would want to determine whether or not there were conflicts of interest," Davis told the *Post*.

Additionally, the *Post* reported that Byers and Spry, the NCAA employee most closely involved with investments, received low-interest loans at rates of 7 percent and below from United Missouri Bank of Kansas City, the only bank at the time authorized to receive unlimited deposits from the NCAA, which then had an annual cash flow in excess of $40 million. Byers borrowed $455,000 on the low-interest plan and Spry had received another $51,000, according to the *Post*. Banking officials throughout Missouri pointed out that the Byers-Spry low-interest loans represented "preferential treatment" at a time when interest rates for United Missouri's best customers had soared to above 16 percent. After the article was published, a troubled Byers disputed the *Post*'s facts and figures. "The basic article that appeared in the *Washington Post* represents an unfortunate collection of half-truths and misleading innuendoes designed to carry forward the preconceived story line of the writer," Byers said in a December 1985 issue of the *NCAA News*, the organization's in-house publication. He said his loan had an outstanding balance of about $244,500 at the time and — in a curious assertion—said it was not a "personal" loan because the money actually was borrowed by the Byers Seven Cross Ranch, Inc., the company Byers established to manage his sprawling getaway ranch about 115 miles from Kansas City.

Charles Allen Wright told *Sports Illustrated* that the NCAA loans "constitute a perfectly legitimate fringe benefit for keeping upper-level staff people." Part of the NCAA's official rationale for the loans, according to an NCAA Executive Committee document, was that "it would be less expensive to benefit the executive director by such a loan rather than to tender him a corresponding salary increase." But Wright considered the bank loans "the more questionable thing. That doesn't look very good. I'd feel better if Lou and Walter borrowed their money from somewhere the NCAA doesn't keep its money."

That isn't the only allegation that Byers traded on the NCAA's vast wealth and business holdings for his personal gain. Ernest J. Straub, Jr., a Kansas City developer, sued Byers in 1987, alleging that Byers agreed to sell him a piece of NCAA land if Straub did extensive remodeling to Byers's house for cost only. Straub said Byers worked a similar arrangement with Straub's best friend, James Dent, an architect who had done design work for the NCAA's two office buildings. In exchange for Byers's promise that he would get future NCAA work when the association built its new NCAA building, Dent designed an addition to Byers's house at no cost, Straub said. The deal was that Straub would do the work on Byers's house and then have the opportunity to pay fair market value for a lot near the NCAA's offices. Court records show Straub delivered, doing the work for cost. After the work on Byers's home was complete, Straub asked Byers to make good on his end of the deal. Byers kept putting him off.

"I finally went to his office one day and told him that it didn't look like I was going to get to buy the property," Straub said recently. "I told him I was going to send him a bill for my time. Oh, did he get mad. So then he says, 'You bill me today.' I sent him a bill for 10 percent of whatever the expenses were and he refused to pay it. Now, there are three parties who knew about this agreement—me, Dent and Byers. Before the case ever got to trial, Dent died. Now it was Byers's word against mine. He was saying I did all that work for cost because I'm a nice guy. My lawyer said there was no way of winning the suit without a third party. We dropped the lawsuit.

"When I read all this stuff in the newspapers about schools being sanctioned because they gave a kid an airplane ticket or $200 or he sold his football tickets for $100, or something like that, I get sick," Straub said. "They [the NCAA] come down on the schools and put them on probation and all that jazz and he [Byers] is behind all that. I thought, Jesus Christ, that's the kettle calling the skillet black. You know if they're going to sanction people, to me, they've got to get straight themselves. You know, when you're playing with the kind of money that organization is playing with, power and money corrupt."

Byers enjoyed the NCAA's largesse right to the end. When he finally severed his ties with the organization in August 1990, the NCAA handed him the keys to a new Chevrolet Caprice Classic as a going-away gift.

But when it came to sanctioning people, the NCAA under Byers was merciless. Byers, a stern disciplinarian, often dismissed those complaining about the NCAA's investigation of seemingly picayune violations with the statement, "A rule's a rule." "We don't write the rules," he told reporters. "We just see that they are applied. A 'no' to an institution is not a 'no' from the NCAA staff but from the members."

There was no gray with Walter Byers; everything was black and white. He learned that from the man who was his first great influence, Avery Brundage, the original guardian of amateurism. While Byers was still a public relations assistant in the Big Ten office, he used to chat with Brundage. The Big Ten, and later the original NCAA office, were headquartered in Chicago's LaSalle Hotel, which was owned by Brundage, then a member of the International Olympic Committee. "Avery used to come in at two in the afternoon and work till midnight," Byers recalled in a rare interview. "We'd get in violent arguments about what the colleges were doing. There was nothing that would stop him from giving us his monthly lecture on how professional he thought the colleges were getting." Brundage believed that the day colleges began giving scholarships based on athletic talent, the athletes became professional. They were being paid—no matter that it was a free education—to play. It was Brundage, Byers's friends and associates say, that taught Walter to be unflinching in his defense of the NCAA's rules.

"You're always tempted to make exceptions to every rule, and while there could have been exceptions in certain cases, Walter's answer was always 'no,'" said Wiles Hallock. "He didn't let his heart get involved in the individual cases that came up. He was tough. He knew the enforcement program is what gave the NCAA its power. And once you started granting exceptions, you lost power."

"We applied the rules the best way we knew how," said

former enforcement chief Bergstrom. "If you want to read the rules, they were black and white; any deviation, [Byers] felt, called for some kind of remedial action. One thing we tried not to do in the application of the NCAA rules was accept excuses. Apply them as they were and let the chips fall where they may."

Said his ex-wife, Betty: "No, there wasn't much gray with Walter. That's probably what made life a little hard. You know, it's a little hard to live with someone that doesn't ever forgive and forget."

If forgiving was difficult for Byers, forgetting 1984 was impossible. In one year, the NCAA suffered major defeats at the hands of the U.S. Supreme Court, which had limited Byers's treasured football television monopoly; the rival College Football Association, whose challenge led to the Supreme Court's decision; and the district court in Nevada, which had ruled in favor of University of Nevada–Las Vegas basketball coach Jerry Tarkanian in his well-publicized due process lawsuit. As the problems mounted, Byers deflected them in brilliant fashion. Rather than admit he might be losing control, he went public with his concerns that individual universities were not helping the NCAA in its efforts to keep college sports clean. As quoted in newspapers and magazines across the country, Byers said some athletes were getting as much as $20,000 a year in illegal payoffs, that his personal investigations indicated about 30 percent of NCAA schools cheat, and suggesting the time may have come when perhaps schools that do not wish to abide by the rules should form an "open division" with the power to set its own rules. Byers's outspokenness was so strikingly uncharacteristic that it shocked the collegiate sports world, which is precisely what he intended to do. By going public, he attempted to shake the schools from their sleep, mustering the firepower the NCAA needed to police college athletics.

As was the case most of his life, Byers's timing and foresight were right. He shocked enough college presidents that they called a special NCAA convention and gave the NCAA even more power: the ability to shut down an athletic program—the so-called "death penalty"—on those caught cheating twice in five years.

If Byers said his piece for a reason, it fit perfectly in his life story. Everything Walter Byers did, it seems, was for a reason. Born on March 13, 1922, and reared in Kansas City, Byers grew to be an all-city center in football at Westport High in 1938. He went one year to Rice University in Houston, hoping for a chance to play college football. But Owls coach Jimmy Kitts sent him home, saying Byers, one day to become the biggest man in college sports, was "too small." Byers then transferred to the University of Iowa, where he majored in English and minored in journalism. He got a job at the student newspaper, the *Daily Io-wan*, and there met Marilyn McCurdy, the first of his three wives. Byers was only 9 hours short of graduation when he dropped out of Iowa and enlisted in the Army. His decision to quit college created one of the many ironies of Byers's life: Although he was the top man in intercollegiate sports for almost four decades, heading an organization that spends hours at each of its conventions talking about graduation rates, Byers never earned a college diploma. He was eventually discharged from the Army because of an affliction known as "wandering eye." The disease had required him to wear glasses since he was younger than two years old and, he said, allowed him to see out of only one eye at a time. Because he wears wire-rimmed glasses, the ailment was not particularly noticeable to most who hadn't known him since his youth. His friends and family say he doesn't like to talk about his eye condition, but back in 1958 he joked: "The Army was afraid I'd shoot the wrong person. When I went to the Navy and Marines after that, they just laughed at me."

Once discharged by the Army, Byers took a job with United Press (as it was then called) wire service in St. Louis. United Press moved him to Madison, Wisconsin, Chicago and finally to New York City, where he was editor of the foreign sports desk. Once he moved out of journalism, Byers never looked back. The only vestige of his career in the media was the vintage Royal typewriter on which he wrote his office memos. After sitting in New York for more than a year, Byers decided he wanted to go home—the Midwest. So in 1947 he took a job as assistant to Kenneth L. (Tug) Wilson, commissioner of the Big Ten and secretary-treasurer of the NCAA. Four years later, the NCAA broke off from the Big Ten into a separate organization. Byers got the job as executive director on October 1, 1951, and one of his first actions was to move the NCAA headquarters to a more central location, the Kansas City area, which, not coincidentally, was also his birth-place.

Byers and Marilyn were married in 1946. They had three

children: Ward, who now lives in Yukon, Oklahoma; Ellen, a law professor at Washburn University in Topeka; and Frederick, now a lawyer in Temperance, Michigan. In 1971, Marilyn filed for divorce. Six years later, Byers married Betty Sooby, whom he had met through his son, Ward, a classmate of Betty's son, Brad. The boys were fourth graders in Shawnee Mission public schools. Byers required Betty to sign a prenuptial agreement, preventing her from seeking alimony or property settlements in the event of divorce. That event came in December 1982, when Betty, too, filed for divorce. Byers's third attempt at marriage came after his 1987 retirement, when he wed his former assistant, Ruth Berkey, whom he had hired in 1979 as supervisor of the NCAA's foray into women's championships. Berkey was the first and only woman Byers promoted to his inner circle at the NCAA.

Byers gave up golf, smoking and Scotch in an attempt to focus more of his energy on his work. He once had a battle with alcohol, but beat it back alone. Afterwards, he limited his drinking to a couple of light beers in the evening and perhaps a dollop of Drambuie. "When he'd come home, he'd either read or just relax and watch television," said Betty. "He didn't play golf or tennis and he was not interested in sports at all, not actively anyway. We did play tennis once in a while. I play tennis a lot and he would join me once in a while but not often."

He spent his free time, which never extended beyond three days at a stretch, at his Seven Cross ranch in the northern reaches of the Flint Hills in Pottawatomie County, halfway between Topeka and Manhattan. The ranch covers more than 6,960 acres, about 3,000 of which are owned by Byers; he leases the rest. "I'm a legitimate cowboy," he said in a 1984 interview. "I'm not a dude, I've shoveled horse stalls plenty of times." With the help of a ranch foreman and two other ranch hands Byers keeps about 1,100 head of cattle, the majority suckling calves and yearlings. There are 61 miles of fence on the gently rolling property, and Byers and the hands put up 2,000 bales of hay annually. He is mostly a self-taught rancher, but it may be hereditary. Byers, Texas, a small town just north of Wichita Falls, was named after Walter's grandfather, who once owned a 35,080-acre ranch between Wichita Falls and the Red River. Walter's father, Ward, a Kansas City real estate man, was the one who purchased the original 774 acres of the Seven Cross ranch back in 1924. Walter inherited the property in 1968 after his father's death.

"It was amazing, really, what happened to him when we went out there," Betty said. "He would become an entirely different person. I mean, strictly a cowboy or a rancher. He can change that easily, change his personality, change his clothes, change the way he talks. It was just that dealing with the foreman and with anybody out there, he became country folk."

On the ranch, the usually dapper Byers would wear blue jeans and cowboy shirts, occasionally donning a dress shirt that was frayed at the collar. He loved his aging quarterhorse, Levi, his western hat and his Tony Lama boots, which he sometimes wore with spurs. The ranch was not just his refuge from life at the NCAA, it served as an important link between him and his family. In the early 1980s, his three children purchased a 500-acre addition to the ranch known as Four Corners.

Byers's highest level of athletic competition was in high school. His coaching career began and ended with the junior ice hockey teams on which his sons played. Some of his closest friends believe that the 5-foot-8-inch Byers's lack of athletic success—especially given his rejection for being "too small"—was a driving force in his desire to succeed at the NCAA. "I think that the physical problem, his physical stature—he is a relatively small person—and then the fact of the discharge, the eye situation—in his world of intercollegiate athletics they made for some kind of a complex, " said Duke.

Added Wiles Hallock: "Walter had certain personal mannerisms that I think turned people off. You know he's not very big, and he was always sitting around people who were big, mostly former athletes. There's a certain arrogance about him that people saw sometimes when he dealt with the media or anybody in certain situations. I really don't think he realized that this was the case."

Possibly the most shocking thing Byers did in his 36 years at the NCAA was announce his decision to retire. He always joked that he was from "the George Meany school of retirement," a reference to the late labor leader who retired at 85. But once again, Byers's timing apparently was right.

"Walter, throughout his time at the NCAA, held cards too close to his vest," said Donna Lopiano. "Whoever has all the information can run the beast, and Walter ran the beast. I don't think he was a particularly sharing—believer in participatory democracy—kind of guy. I think if he had not left, the NCAA would have really been in danger of falling apart. It became a prehistoric beast, and there was a time you could rule that way. Not any more."

Added the American Council on Education's Robert Atwell: "Walter towards his last days as head of the NCAA really did come to understand that things were a bit out of control. It was like Dwight Eisenhower discovering the military-industrial complex in his last months of the presidency."

Byers himself conceded in a 1990 interview with the Associated Press, "Time and circumstances have passed the entire system of intercollegiate athletics by. The management structure has become bureaucratic and unresponsive. I include the NCAA in that."

Woven throughout comments from those who both revered and despised Byers are two common threads: a unanimous respect for his intelligence and confusion about his overwhelming desire for privacy. Not even his closest friends—none of whom ever were invited to his ranch—feel like they can say they know Walter Byers.

"He was an iron-fisted, dominating, intimidating personality," said former NCAA investigator J. Brent Clark, who crossed Byers when he left the NCAA in 1977, and was the star witness during congressional hearings into the NCAA enforcement program. "I'd compare Byers to J. Edgar Hoover at the FBI. He was a kid in Chicago who built the organization from a little service organization. He built that thing into an empire. I have always, not admired, but respected Byers's business acumen."

Most who have worked for Byers share the same regard for Byers's intelligence, but all felt they were kept at arm's length. "I met him the first day I was hired, first day on the job," said former investigator Ron Watson. "My superior in enforcement introduced me to him and I think I lasted in his office about 22 seconds. He asked me to tell him a little bit about myself and as I started, he patted me on the back and said, 'Thank you very much for coming,' and escorted me to the door. That's when my superior laughed and told the rest of our crew that I may have survived in his office less time than any of the others, about 22 seconds. I saw him two other times, once in the elevator and once downstairs. As he was coming in, I was leaving the building. If I told you he ever said more than a 'hi' I would be lying."

Even though they didn't see him, Byers's employees knew he was there. "I saw him twice. Once when I came in, once when I left," former investigator Marcia Morey said. "He runs a tight ship. He knew every move that was going on in that building." Added former investigator Tom Yeager, "His presence was always felt, every instant of the day, wherever you were."

Those former employees shouldn't feel slighted, Byers's closest friends said, because he treated them just the same. "I don't know that there's anybody who feels he totally opened up to him," Hallock said. "I don't think anybody is really personally close to Walter."

"He never became a friend of any of his office help or anybody connected with the NCAA," Betty Byers said. "I tried to change that and that was one of our big disagreements because I did have friends in the NCAA. He would always argue that when you become friends, that you relinquish some of your power. He thought it was very poor policy. I can't think of anyone who can say they know Walter Byers. Maybe I could say I had the privilege of knowing him. But I'm not sure he really wanted me to."

What people did know was the NCAA. And they knew it was powerful. The Godfather would have liked it that way.

2

HOW THE GAME IS PLAYED

MARIST COLLEGE

There were three things the folks at Marist College weren't used to before 1984: a winning basketball team, national attention and being called cheaters.

They adjusted to the first two rather quickly. But nothing incensed the students and faculty at Marist's ivy-covered campus in Poughkeepsie, New York, more than having their integrity questioned by the NCAA, an organization whose investigation they called "sloppy" and whose tactics they branded "un-American."

"The case against Marist College is unprecedented in the history of the NCAA because of the many mistakes and the misconduct of the NCAA staff in its handling of this investigation," Marist officials wrote in their appeal to the NCAA after being judged guilty of 14 rules violations. "From the very beginning of this case, [NCAA] staff provided incomplete and/or inaccurate advice to college officials, have not been forthright in admitting these errors, and have attempted to fabricate a major case against Marist College to cover up their own inappropriate activities."

The NCAA staff didn't take too kindly to that level of disrespect from such an upstart. "I thought that statement was wholly inappropriate," David Berst, the NCAA's director of enforcement, said after reading Marist's appeal.

Others apparently weren't so sure Marist was far off base. Don DiJulia, assistant vice-president and director of athletics at St. Joseph's University in Philadelphia, was a member of the NCAA Council that heard Marist's appeal. He said he sided with Marist in its attempt to have its penalty reduced, but his position lost in a close vote.

"I'd say it can arguably be stated, yes, that there was a breakdown of the entire [NCAA] system on this one," DiJulia said. "Sometimes things get unnecessarily blown out of proportion because they aren't handled properly. We need to keep things in proper perspective. In this case, it was three years after the fact that the case finally was heard. There are problems like this when the process is not able to move more swiftly. There are many unfortunate cases like this one. You just don't hear about them."

In the early 1980s, the Marist Red Foxes were a fledgling Division I team hoping to play big-time basketball in the 3,200-seat James J. McCann Recreation Center, just a jump shot from the Hudson River. President Dennis Murray believed his 3,000-student school, which was founded in the 1940s by the Marist Brothers, had taken a major step towards the big time when, in March 1984, a committee appointed by Murray selected a new coach. Mike Perry, who had spent the previous 10 years bouncing around Europe coaching club teams, was a successful junior college coach at Ulster County Community College when last he drew Xs and Os in America. "They made a big deal about it with a press conference in the president's office," said Brian Colleary, who later was hired as Marist's athletic director and in 1989 became athletic director at Duquesne University. "They invited everyone in upstate New York, had sandwiches and everything. This was the real thing."

Shortly after being named coach, Perry attended a game in the Netherlands where that country's national team was playing. Sitting in the stands was Rik Smits, a Dutch kid who sidled up to Perry and said he wanted badly to play college basketball in

America even though he had just begun playing the sport 18 months earlier. Smits just happened to be 7-foot-1-inch tall at the time—and still growing.

So while Perry dined on a $38 order of frog legs at Divest Restaurant in Smits's hometown of Eindhoven and Smits's mother and father each enjoyed a rum and Coke, the new coach reeled in his first big catch. The 18-year-old Smits signed a national letter of intent, without reading a word of it. It should have been a marriage made in heaven: a new coach, a small college and a giant of a player with unknown potential.

Before Perry returned to the rolling hills of Poughkeepsie, he persuaded two other European players—Alain Forestier from France and Miroslav Pecarski from Yugoslavia—to ink commitments to his program. Everything seemed to be looking up when the players started flying in to begin classes. But then the real problems began.

Perry said he felt a "special obligation" to Smits, Forestier and Pecarski, because they were not only just beginning college, they were doing so in a totally new environment. So, for starters, he had assistant coach Bogdan Jovicic meet them at New York's John F. Kennedy Airport and drive them the 80 miles to Marist's campus. Jovicic, a native of Yugoslavia who had left his country for the freedom of America, admitted later that he stopped along the road and bought Whoppers and milkshakes for the players at Burger King. Perry also allowed the European players to call their parents from his phone, signed Smits up for the school's weight program two months before he officially enrolled and sent Jovicic to New York to buy winter coats for two players—with the players' money—at a tall men's shop, among other things. And since Smits, who wasn't a starter at Marist until his sophomore year, arrived when the dormitories were closed, Perry arranged for him to stay at the home of Thomas J. McKiernan, a member of the Marist College Board of Trustees, for four days.

All of those were NCAA violations, as were the drinks Perry had bought Smits's parents in Holland. Those, plus 6 other free meals or car rides for players, were the crux of Marist's 14 violations.

The total monetary value: $773.20.

Perry might have continued undetected, except for an allegation made in mid-September 1984. That's when he took Forestier to New York City and the two shared a hotel room.

Forestier claimed, days after they returned, that Perry made a homosexual advance during the weekend. Perry called the allegation "preposterous," saying Forestier was upset because Perry dragged him along rather than allowing him to stay in Poughkeepsie with his girlfriend. When Perry and Forestier returned, the player lodged a complaint with Joseph Belanger, Marist's foreign student advisor. "He was pissed off because I wouldn't let him shack up with his girlfriend," Perry said of the allegation. "I just wanted to prove to him that he wasn't going to be taking off every weekend to shack up with her. We had a season coming."

Little by little the tales of meals, phone calls and the purchase of a sport coat for a player began to come out. Belanger, a self-professed sports addict, had read enough stories about NCAA investigations to know the trips and gifts were violations. He called President Murray.

When Murray learned of the incidents, in late September 1984, he summoned Perry—who had never coached a game and had yet to conduct a practice—to his office. Perry made no bones about breaking the rules, arguing that if Marist really wanted to compete with the big boys, it had to play the game his way. "He seemed to indicate he would continue, that that was the only way you could get ahead, that the regulations were crazy," Gerard Cox, vice-president of student affairs, said.

Murray didn't buy it. Two days after Perry's 45th birthday and just 167 days after he was hired, Perry was fired.

Murray had been running his small school's sports program without an athletic director after Ron Petro—who also had been the school's basketball coach before Marist hired Perry—left in August 1984 to take the athletic director's job at the University of Alaska–Anchorage. With no one to turn to—Colleary wasn't hired until July 1985—Murray called the NCAA to report the violations Perry had admitted and to seek the NCAA's advice on how to proceed.

The NCAA sent an investigator to Marist College in February 1985. In two days, he investigated the violations Murray had reported and stated in his follow-up memo to NCAA officials that Murray was doing his best to address whatever problems may have existed.

Nine months later, working with a short staff report and Marist's internal investigation, the NCAA Committee on Infractions decided the Red Foxes should serve one year's probation. There were no sanctions, no scholarships lost. Still, Murray asked if that wasn't too harsh. The Committee on Infractions agreed, offering to let Marist off with a public reprimand if the college would promise to do a better job of policing athletics in the future. In the world of sports investigations, this was all small potatoes.

But in September 1985, a day before the public reprimand was scheduled to be announced, Murray received an anonymous letter detailing further rules violations. The same day, Smits received a post card telling him to transfer because Marist was "in trouble with the NCAA." The card was signed, "a friend." Marist later requested an FBI analysis of the handwriting on the post card to Smits. The conclusion: the writer was Perry, the former coach.

Murray's concern increased when he picked up the morning papers and read where Perry had told two reporters that during its "so-called investigation," the NCAA staff had never contacted him, even though he was at the center of most of the allegations.

"It's impossible that the NCAA could have investigated without contacting me," Perry told the *Poughkeepsie Journal.* "If they had asked me what happened, the investigation might still be going on."

"I probably committed 40 other violations," Perry said in a separate interview with the *Kingston* (N.Y.) *Freeman.*

So Murray called the NCAA again, this time asking them to put off announcement of the reprimand until "they did it right and talked to Perry," he said. Again, the NCAA agreed, sending investigator Anthony Constantino back to interview the former coach.

How did the NCAA miss interviewing Perry initially? Steve Morgan, the NCAA's associate executive director over enforcement, said the first investigator "couldn't find him. Besides, what would be more significant about talking to the head coach than any other principal in the case?" Perry doesn't believe it.

"Three days after I resigned, I went to Florida for a couple of weeks," Perry told the *Florida Times-Union* in 1988, days before he left for a new job selling novelties on Hawaii's Waikiki Beach. "Then I came back here [Kingston, New York, just across the river from Poughkeepsie]. . . . It wouldn't have been tough at all to find me. It's curious that the media never had a problem finding me and the NCAA couldn't."

From September 1985, when he requested a postponement of the reprimand announcement, Murray didn't hear again from the NCAA's Committee on Infractions for nearly two years. During that time, Perry was interviewed eight times by three different NCAA investigators. In those interviews, he detailed a laundry list of other violations he had committed during his short tenure, and admitted these were violations he had not told Marist officials about. One infraction included paying for Smits's flight from Holland, then hiding the expense in falsified hotel and meal receipts so Marist accountants wouldn't find it.

"Some of the violations [Perry] shared with the NCAA were things the college never could have uncovered," said Susan Roeller Brown, Murray's executive assistant. "Despite our good efforts at tracing records, he had a receipt that had never been submitted that showed he'd bought an airline ticket. He fudged his expense accounts to make it look like he had an expensive hotel bill. So here we had the NCAA saying in the Official Inquiry that the college had committed this violation, providing air fare to a student-athlete. They knew it because Perry had given them the receipt. We had to completely compile our response to the Official Inquiry without access to any of the documents, like the airline receipt, that he had kept and shared with them. The idea of trying to answer allegations without access to the same information the NCAA had really sets you up to be stooges."

"They were using Mike Perry to get the college that had fired Mike Perry for violations of rules," President Murray said. "And then they were allowing Mike Perry to bring out additional information that we couldn't possibly have known about. A disgruntled man used the NCAA to get back at those who fired him. He was masterful at it and they were complicit."

Murray took particular exception to what he viewed as the NCAA's attempt to help Perry once he started to talk. The president accused the NCAA of offering the coach free legal advice, producing a 1987 memo from NCAA investigator Stephanie Sivak that shows the investigator advised Perry he should tell his lawyer about falsifying college expense reports and begin preparing a defense, "as it possibly might be seen as a misuse of funds." Sivak wrote after an interview with Perry in

Fort Lauderdale that she "wanted Perry to be aware of the potential legal issue."

Eventually, the case that looked so simple—and which NCAA enforcement chief David Berst once wrote in a letter was filled "only with trivial violations" —dragged on for three years and involved seven NCAA investigators.

By August 1987, Marist was looking at two years of probation, a two-year ban from the NCAA tournament and two years of limited recruiting by assistant coach Jovicic. And, just for good measure, the NCAA also slapped Marist with the public reprimand the college had been promised earlier.

Wait a minute, President Murray told the NCAA. The college had turned itself in, a fact the *NCAA Manual* says should work in favor of the institution. The NCAA's response: You turned yourself in for violations A, B and C. Coach Perry, though, told us in those later interviews that he committed violations D through Z, as well. You can't get credit for turning yourself in for D through Z.

But, Murray countered, the NCAA would never have talked to the former coach and discovered violations D through Z if Marist hadn't pointed out the NCAA's "sloppy" investigative work and asked investigators to call Perry. And besides, the fired coach, who had committed the bulk of the violations and then built the NCAA's case, had refused to talk to Marist's attorneys, causing the school to twice ask for a delay in its infractions hearing.

"That was our mistake," Murray said. "Even though we're supposed to point out the errors of our athletic staff and our coaches, no matter how minor they are, when the [NCAA] started creating errors, we were just supposed to accept those and be quiet about it. I'm ready to admit we violated NCAA rules. We made mistakes. We admitted them. They didn't want to admit their mistakes, and that was troubling. The *NCAA Manual* says this is supposed to be a cooperative venture between the college and the infractions staff to seek the truth. But the only truth they wanted to seek was what we did. They never wanted to deal with their errors. Us pushing them to admit their errors just really increased tensions. If it had been a legal case, the prosecution of this case would have been thrown out as a joke because of the errors."

Murray took his concerns to anyone he could reach on the

telephone at the NCAA office. But the NCAA turned a deaf ear. Marist was stuck with the penalty. Marist officials' anger turned to rage a week later when UCLA, a program later found to have long been blatantly and repeatedly flaunting the NCAA's rules, was censured—no probation, no sanctions—for 10 violations, many of which sounded worse than those committed by Marist. The *Los Angeles Times*, in fact, reported that the total value of UCLA's 10 violations—including $2,300 of free rent provided by a booster—was over $2,600. Compared to the total of $773.20 in benefits Perry had provided his players, the difference between the penalties "is outrageous," Athletic Director Colleary said. The decision probably had nothing to do with the fact that UCLA, a big television draw, could still play in the NCAA tournament with its penalty, Colleary said facetiously. "To be perfectly honest, it drives me crazy," he told reporters. "We're looking for consistency from the NCAA and, frankly, we're not finding it. It is frustrating."

Colleary and Murray, though, thought the different penalties handed down to Marist and UCLA would bolster their planned appeal to the NCAA Council, which can reverse or restructure the infractions committee's decisions. But when they showed up for their appeal in January, they were given only 20 minutes to state their case.

"Presenting three years of an investigation in 20 minutes is hard to do," Colleary said. "And worse, the Council is supposed to make up its mind about something so important after hearing only 20 minutes on the subject. It was a disaster."

In their efforts to prepare for their appeal, Marist officials asked for a copy of the tape-recorded infractions committee hearing. They were told that the only way they could hear the tape was if they flew to Kansas City and listened to it in an NCAA office. Once there, they were told they could not take any notes from the tape verbatim. They couldn't have coffee in the room. No one could smoke. An NCAA staff member stood nearby to make sure none of those rules were violated.

"It was very intimidating, just being there," Murray said. "They did everything they could to remind you that they were in control. They were in charge. They set the rules and you had to live by them."

The appeal was denied, and Murray was left with a bad taste in his mouth. "During the whole process the NCAA continually tried to say that all of the little things Perry did allowed us an advantage when we recruited Rik Smits and that's why we deserved harsh punishment," he said. "But we were able to show that no other school in the country was interested in or had ever heard of Rik Smits. Hell, Rik even has a letter that he wrote to ABA/USA [Amateur Basketball Association of the USA] asking how to contact American college coaches. So how could we have had an advantage? Or rather, who did we have an advantage over? Now, try to explain that to the Council and you've used up 10 of your 20 minutes and that was only one little part of the case."

Once Marist used its appeal time before the Council to argue that no recruiting advantage was gained by providing a raw, gangly Smits with a winter coat, cheeseburger and fries, the NCAA's Steve Morgan lit into the university. Afterwards, he told reporters he believed "some little things can make a difference in recruiting" and that the $773.20 in extra benefits spent on Smits may be the reason he spurned multimillion dollars from the NBA to stay in school. "The fact is, if Rik Smits said, 'I would still be here if none of those things had happened,' the fact is those meals, the transportation, the entertainment, more or less local transportation in various modes, those things are a factor in making it possible for him to be there," Morgan said.

January 1990 marked the end of Marist's probation. Smits, who played his four years at Marist, signed a multiyear contract with the National Basketball Association's Indiana Pacers as the second pick in the 1988 college draft. And the NCAA's leadership—while refusing to discuss specifics—is standing by its investigation of Marist.

"From our own perspective, though it started out as a case where the president tried to find out immediately what the problem was and treat it immediately, it developed into a situation where the president had not solved the problem entirely because there were violations that continued and there were individuals at the institution who weren't telling the truth," David Berst told a reporter in 1988. "That put the institution in the position early on of defending those individuals. The enforcement staff didn't accept that and we continued to look, and that created, in part, the adversarial relationship."

"Marist has been a lot of fun in this process," said Steve Morgan, who supervises the NCAA's investigative staff. Morgan wouldn't answer specific questions about Marist's complaints. He did say, though, that there was "nothing particularly better or worse" about the Marist investigation compared to any other NCAA investigation.

"That should scare a lot of people," Murray said, after hearing Morgan's comments. "And it should open a lot of eyes and ears. There's something wrong with this system."

If, as Morgan said, the Marist case is typical of the NCAA's investigative work, every president, athletic director and coach at an NCAA school should be profoundly concerned. It also should send up a red flag to every sports editor whose staff is covering an NCAA investigation at nearby Local U. Clearly, this is not a system without significant flaws.

Privately, many who have been through the NCAA wringer offer similar accounts. They say the only difference in the Marist investigation is athletics are such a small part of life at Marist that Murray and Colleary were more willing to speak out about their experience than administrators at larger schools. Marist officials were willing to open their records—records that even the NCAA says should be kept from reporters—to anyone willing to listen to the sad, sordid tale of their experience. At schools with more successful athletic programs, NCAA sanctions can cost millions of dollars. The fear of reprisal keeps a lot of jaws wired.

"The NCAA through the years has been very sensitive about any comments relative to their enforcement operation," said College Football Association Executive Director Charles Neinas, a former NCAA staff member. "The feeling is that enforcement is not fun and the NCAA would rather people not talk about it. There's just a general concern about adding to that difficulty by expressing concerns which may sound like criticisms."

Others who have been investigated say that the process left their credibility so damaged that any questions they raise will be viewed as sour grapes. Just as the complaints of prisoners who argue they have been wronged by the criminal justice system are summarily dismissed, so too are the concerns expressed by those who have been through the NCAA system. Despite the fact we dismiss most complaints from prisoners, there is no doubt that some have, in fact, been wrongfully accused, convicted and jailed. If a criminal justice system with so many safeguards can be wrong, how often does the NCAA enforcement program— which ignores such safeguards—miss the mark?

"Most institutions bow down without a whimper," said Erwin Ward, an attorney who represented Mississippi State University in its infractions hearing. "Those that stand up against the NCAA do so with trembling and continuing fears of retaliatory retribution—retribution that can be dispensed without warning by a powerful arm of arbitrary force." Even former NCAA president John Fuzak conceded that, after going through an NCAA investigation, "there are those who feel it unwise to express their concerns about what has happened and about their impressions of fairness."

For the folks in the mid–Hudson Valley area, Marist's battle with the NCAA ranks in sports lore right up there with the 1986 game in which the Red Foxes led highly-touted Georgia Tech late in the second half of their first-round game in the NCAA tournament. Rik Smits outscored future Detroit Piston John Salley 22-9 in that game. Smits fouled out midway through the second half with Marist down by only three. Once he was gone, Marist was soon to follow. Marist enthusiasts admit they lost to the Yellow Jackets fair and square. Not so with the NCAA.

"I'm a town judge. I've been a judge for 10 years," Marist attorney Paul Sullivan said. "Before that I was a prosecutor. I've worked in the Manhattan DA's office. I've worked as a prosecutor in the Duchess County district attorney's office. I've tried every type of case, from a misdemeanor to a murder case. And I have never, in my experience as an attorney, been confronted with such a kangaroo court as I was with the NCAA. They have everything stacked against the member institution. There is no way that you are going to go and appear in front of them, follow their guidelines and be treated fairly. It just can't happen. I still believe, if every member of the NCAA was confronted with this situation, if they had to go through an investigation, then they, too, would be repulsed by the entire system."

Murray's experience has led him to call for wholesale changes in the way the NCAA investigates its members. Particularly, he wants the NCAA "to recognize that people have rights." He knows the NCAA argues that it is not a court of law and isn't bound by the same requirements. But maybe that should change, he said. "With the stakes involved today in college athletics, it is fair, in my opinion, to ask the NCAA to recognize the rights of the accused," he said. "You're talking about reputations and careers of individuals, and in our case a very unfortunate consequence for an individual involved."

His reference there is to Bogdan Jovicic, the assistant coach. Jovicic knows how unbridled power can ruin lives — he watched it happen in his native Yugoslavia for three decades. But it was not until 1985 that he understood what abuse of power could do, he said. That's when he met his first NCAA investigator, who asked if he had purchased the Burger King meals for the team's European players. Jovicic said "no," then later admitted he had, explaining he didn't tell the truth because he was scared by the investigator's "FBI tactics."

"When I finally told them the truth they asked me questions like, 'Did you buy Rik a Coke,' " Jovicic said. "I said, 'Yes.' They asked if it was a big Coke or a little Coke. I said, 'Extra large.' They asked if it had ice in it or not. No joke. I had to tell them, 'Lots of ice.' "

Jovicic also denied that he had gone to New York and purchased winter coats for the three foreign players. He later admitted the violation, but was able to show that the players' parents had repaid him for the coats within a month after the purchase.

"I had three foreign kids on the team at that time," Jovicic said later in his still-rough English. "And their parents were thousands of miles away. They did not come with winter coats. I personally had a conversation with the parents over the phone and I suggested that I'm going to borrow them money to the kids to buy some clothing, and that I would be reimbursed later on, here or in Europe. For me, this is secondary. The priority should be getting those kids coats so they are not cold. It gets cold here in New York."

For his earlier refusal to tell investigators about the meals, the coats and the soft drinks, the NCAA branded Jovicic a liar, slapped him with an ethical violation of the NCAA rules, the worst possible violation in the eyes of the NCAA, and took away his right to recruit off campus. Jovicic couldn't believe it.

The morning after the NCAA's report was made public, he was found wandering aimlessly through the streets of Poughkeepsie, not far from Marist's campus. Members of the Marist athletic staff took him to nearby St. Francis Hospital. There, Jovicic was diagnosed as having had a nervous breakdown. He then attempted—with near-tragic results—to escape from the hospital through a window near his bed. He was on the fourth floor. Jovicic caught himself, but not before ripping a large gash in one shoulder.

Jovicic, who remained on the athletic staff at Marist, is bitter about the whole experience. "Where I come from, when you say 'communistic,' it can be a compliment," he said. "I would never damage the term *communism* by linking it to something as bad as this. A real communist would never act as the NCAA acted over us. A real communist is a real human being who can understand how things happen and then sometimes corrects the rules.

"They [the NCAA] don't treat members as human beings. They treat you as a violation number."

"As you can see," Murray said, "this very bad experience touched a lot of lives in very bad ways. Athletics at Marist, I have to tell you, is almost inconsequential to the overall life of this institution. I can't imagine what going through this must be like at a school where athletics has a more prominent place. Especially if the quality of the work [by the NCAA] is no better."

SACRED COWS

Brian Colleary's comparison of the penalty meted out for Marist's violations with the penalties slapped on UCLA just a few days later was another example of one of the longest-running criticisms of the NCAA's enforcement program—that there are some schools that will walk free after committing murder while others will go to Death Row for jaywalking. UCLA, in the days of John Wooden, and the University of Kentucky, in the days before Eddie Sutton, were long held out as classic illustrations of this argument.

If ever there was a man who helped finance the best college basketball program that money could buy, Sam Gilbert was that man. On the court at UCLA, John Wooden called the plays. Off the court, Sam Gilbert called the players. And when he did, he offered them everything from a scalper's price for their season tickets to help in arranging abortions for their girlfriends. Gilbert was a multimillionaire contractor from Encino who befriended Wooden and became a surrogate father and adviser to UCLA players for more than 15 years. He was, as the *Los Angeles Times* described him, "a one-man clearinghouse who has enabled players and their families to receive goods and services usually at a big discount and sometimes at no cost."

Among UCLA's dynasty of 10 NCAA championship teams —a feat unmatched in the history of the college game—players on seven different teams told the *Times* that Gilbert helped them get cars, stereos, clothes and airline tickets. He also purchased and sold their allotted season tickets. All of these, Gilbert and the players knew, were violations of NCAA rules.

Additionally, Gilbert arranged and paid for abortions for the girlfriends of Bruin players. According to the *Times*, he even told an NCAA investigator as much in 1978. "If a girl came to you pregnant and said she needed an abortion, what would you do?" Gilbert asked the *Times* reporter rhetorically. "If a boy came to you and said he needed to fly home for a funeral, what would you do?"

Gilbert said he told an NCAA investigator he paid for an abortion and financed a player's flight home for a funeral. He said the investigator told him the NCAA wasn't interested in those violations. "It [players getting women pregnant] happened often," former Bruin All-American guard Lucius Allen told the *Times* for a story in 1982. "If a ballplayer impregnated someone, there was always a hospital available. I never paid for it."

The *Times* also quoted Kareem Abdul-Jabbar as admitting that he had sold his season tickets through Gilbert for more than face value. Although it was not a violation at the time, selling players' tickets is against NCAA rules today. Scalping them for more than their face value, though, has long been a violation of law. Abdul-Jabbar also confessed to living in an Encino guest house at little or no cost during his junior year. The same arrangement was made by Gilbert for Bruin player Larry Farmer, who a few years later would be hired as UCLA's head coach.

Abdul-Jabbar was one of a half-dozen UCLA All-Americans that Gilbert signed to professional contracts, most while the players still were in college. In fact, it was the suspicion that Gilbert was representing Bruins Marques Johnson and Richard

Washington that first caught the NCAA's eye in 1976. Washington went on to play for the Kansas City Kings, but Johnson decided to stay in school. Johnson told the *Times* that, before he chose to remain at UCLA, Gilbert paid for his flight to Denver for negotiations with the American Basketball Association's Nuggets. Gilbert's relationship as an agent with the players, as well as his payment for Johnson's flight, are rules violations.

Gilbert told reporters from several papers that he did all of this out of the goodness of his heart. He never received a penny for the help he gave players. Besides, Gilbert told the *Times*, just because these acts were violations of NCAA rules did not make them wrong—at least in his mind.

Several players told the *Times* that Gilbert had little or no respect for NCAA rules, and made little effort to hide his disdain. Abdul-Jabbar said Gilbert told him the rules were racist. Brad Holland, a starting guard for the Bruins in the late 1970s, said Gilbert saw himself as the link that helped inner-city players live up to the standards of other students, something the NCAA should encourage, not discourage. While other students could hold a part-time job to earn spending money, NCAA rules prohibited players from doing the same.

"Sam's feeling is that athletes are working at a full-time job and not getting paid for their efforts," Holland told the *Times*. Another former Bruin All-American said, "Sam did a lot of things that were against the rules. But you have to remember that he thought he was fulfilling a need that the university was neglecting."

"He knows what the rules are and he thinks they're rubbish," said Keith Erickson, a star on UCLA's first championship team. "So he does what he believes is right."

There was one thing, though, that Gilbert did not have—a degree from UCLA. A graduate of Hollywood High School, Gilbert went to UCLA for three years before having to drop out for economic reasons. The son of a Lithuanian immigrant, Gilbert tried his hand as a boxer after dropping out of college. That didn't keep bread on the table, so while beginning his own real estate business in the evenings, he worked as a technician in a film lab at a Hollywood motion picture studio. It wasn't long before his work in real estate took off and, at the height of his career, Gilbert was worth in excess of $25 million.

The revelation of his rule-breaking relationship with a

generation of UCLA players was among the least of Gilbert's concerns in the years before his death in 1987. Federal prosecutors in Miami began investigating his business deals and discovered that on two occasions in 1985, Gilbert ordered his son, Michael, to deliver several large boxes to a bank president in Encino. Inside those boxes was $1.8 million in Miami drug money, which Gilbert referred to as his "Florida Sunshine." Prosecutors later discovered the transfers were part of an international money-laundering ring that, according to financial documents, memos and cashier's checks made public during a 1990 trial in Miami, was organized by the elder Gilbert and three Miami associates, primarily to build the $150-million Bicycle Club casino in Bell Gardens, California.

Federal authorities claimed Gilbert was the "West Coast architect" for a network that funneled $12 million from Miami to Los Angeles by way of the tiny Central European nation of Liechtenstein and the British Virgin Islands. As a result, they indicted Gilbert, his son and others on charges of conspiracy, racketeering and money-laundering on November 25, 1987, three days after he died of heart failure in his home.

During the trial, Charles Podesta, the courier who delivered the drug money from the dealers in Miami to Gilbert in California, testified he handed bales of cash directly to Gilbert "four or five times." Once, he even packed an Igloo cooler with $800,000, then sealed it shut, wrote "University of Florida–Gainesville Veterinary School" on top and told the pilot the cooler contained tissue specimen from his sick Rottweiler, Max. The tissue was bound for UCLA, where doctors would do an urgent biopsy, Podesta recalled telling the pilot.

The trial ended with the conviction of Michael Gilbert and the three Miami men who were associates of his father.

Wooden said after the 1987 indictments that reports claiming his friend and top booster was involved in laundering drug money came as "a complete surprise to me," describing Gilbert as "a friend to me and the university." That was an understatement.

Despite the fact he never graduated, Gilbert always saw himself as a Bruin. Erickson remembered Gilbert as one of the many boosters who stood outside the Bruin locker room during the early 1960s, handing oranges and apples to players after games. He was a bit player in what already had become a major charade—an "amateur" basketball program in which players were earning big bucks under the table.

In *The Wizard of Westwood*, a biography of John Wooden written by Dwight Chapin and Jeff Prugh, former Bruin forward Jack Hirsch told of boosters who paid players for their rebounding performances. Hirsch said players earned $5 for each rebound up to the first 10, and $10 per rebound above that. Although they had the shortest team in what was then the Athletic Association of Western Universities, the well-funded Bruins led the league in rebounding. "It was a helluva feeling to pick up $100 for a night's work," Hirsch said in the book. "Believe me, we went all out for rebounds."

Then, in 1967, Gilbert's role changed. The team's two stars —Kareem Abdul-Jabbar, then Lew Alcindor, and Lucius Allen— were feeling out of place in Los Angeles and were considering transferring. Another booster told athletic department officials that Gilbert might be able to help. According to then-assistant athletic director Bob Fischer, the booster told him Gilbert "had a lot of experience with minorities, with the black community."

Gilbert went to visit the two players, and they stayed. Allen said later that had it not been for Gilbert, he would have left UCLA that spring. How important was Gilbert to the success of UCLA basketball? Said Allen: "UCLA wouldn't have won any championships without athletes. And without Sam Gilbert, they wouldn't have had the athletes."

Through it all, Wooden claims to have known nothing about the lavish treatment Gilbert gave his players. "Maybe I had tunnel vision," the retired Wooden told the *Times* in 1982. "I still don't think he's had any great impact on the basketball program." The legendary coach did concede he was occasionally concerned, but not overly so, by the flashy clothes suddenly worn by stars Sidney Wicks and Curtis Rowe after they became close to Gilbert.

"There's as much crookedness as you want to find," Wooden told the *Times*. "There was something Abraham Lincoln said— he'd rather trust and be disappointed than distrust and be miserable all the time. Maybe I trusted too much." Or maybe, like the NCAA, he chose not to see what had become obvious to so many.

David Greenwood, another former All-American, said he was surprised when the media began "making a big deal" out of

Gilbert's relationship with players. The reason for his surprise: he thought everyone knew about it, thus it wasn't news. "Everybody knew what was going on," Greenwood told the *Times*. "Nobody was so naive. It was common knowledge in the whole town. We just felt it wasn't an isolated incident. It was going on at all universities."

So where was the NCAA during Gilbert's exploits? How could an organization that could find violations in Alabama A&M's soccer program not see the cars being driven by once-impoverished Bruins? Was someone asleep at the switch? Or was there a willful decision to let a media-darling university situated in a media mecca run rampant for the good and the growth of college sports?

Brent Clark says the answer is B.

Clark joined the NCAA's enforcement staff in July 1976 and, early the next year, started snooping around the UCLA campus in pursuit of the truth surrounding the contract negotiations Marques Johnson and Richard Washington were having with pro teams. Clark said he returned to NCAA headquarters with enough reason to believe that Gilbert, Johnson and Washington had violated NCAA rules. "Gilbert was well-known to the NCAA for years and years," Clark told the *Times*. "His name had appeared in print many times. I suspect he had been interviewed prior to being interviewed by me. He's about as colorful and provocative a figure on the fringe of college athletics as you'll ever encounter."

During a congressional investigation of the NCAA in 1978, Clark told the House Committee on Interstate and Foreign Commerce's subcommittee on oversight and investigations that he filed a memo suggesting an investigation of the Bruin program. But his supervisors at the NCAA "just sat on it," he testified. Clark told the committee that William Hunt, then his supervisor in the enforcement program and now the NCAA's director of legislative services, "called me aside and said, 'We're just not going after that institution right now.' " During questioning, Connecticut Representative Toby Moffett asked Clark why he thought Hunt would ignore such information.

"The conclusion I draw is that it is an example of a school that is too big, too powerful and too well respected by the public, that the timing was not right to proceed against them," Clark told Congress. He went on to say that it was his belief the decision was made "not to pursue the individual [Gilbert] since it would involve one of the NCAA's leading money-makers, a major basketball power. In this instance, politics and balance sheets seemed to dictate the NCAA take no action."

This was a case of selective enforcement, pure and simple, Clark said. As he later told the *Times*: "The bottom line, as Senator Baker said of Watergate, is what did they know and when did they know it. They [the NCAA] damn well knew all along."

NCAA enforcement chief David Berst called Clark's assertion "somewhat incredible," saying Clark "lives in a fantasy world." Clark, now an attorney in Norman, Oklahoma, is one of the few former NCAA investigators who no longer has ties to college sports. He said Berst is just upset that someone the NCAA can't threaten has gone public. "With all those staff members who go on to work at conference offices or at different universities, they couldn't be outspoken, they couldn't be open about what they saw," Clark told the *Florida Times-Union* in 1988. "But I left and decided that I had had my fill of college athletics."

Berst and a number of other NCAA staff members worked hard to discredit Clark after his testimony before Congress. First, they challenged his objectivity, since he left the NCAA and took a job with the congressional committee that was investigating the NCAA. Berst said Clark felt jilted by the NCAA because he was not promoted when another supervisor resigned. Then Berst and NCAA staff members disputed several of Clark's allegations— including his claim that Hunt called him off any investigation of UCLA—by claiming that no paperwork could be found in NCAA files to support Clark's comments.

"I'm not shocked by that, are you?" Clark said of the NCAA's actions. "That is just the way the NCAA works. Rather than taking what was said and looking for ways to improve, the NCAA decided to attack the bearer of bad news. Those things happened the way I said they did and one day they'll have to admit it."

But whether Clark did or did not file a memo, there is no doubt that the three-part series detailing Gilbert's UCLA ties, written by *Los Angeles Times* sports writers Mike Littwin and Alan Greenberg in 1982, contained enough dynamite to blow up the entire UCLA basketball program. Interviewed after the series had run, Berst said the NCAA had no intention of reopening its just-completed investigation of Bruin basketball that had resulted in two years' probation—tantamount to a slap on the wrist—for committing nine violations. He said that although NCAA rules allowed the enforcement staff to reach beyond a four-year statute of limitations to establish a pattern of willful violations that could bring major sanctions, the NCAA still saw no such pattern at UCLA.

The *Times* had 45 players, coaches and other boosters on the record detailing 15 years of blatant disregard for the rules, and David Berst could see no pattern.

Other programs have had, and will continue to have, their own Sam Gilberts. Despite its best intentions, the NCAA has not found a solution for the overzealous booster. What made Gilbert's story interesting, though, is that he operated so long and with such a high profile at a university whose athletic programs are so publicly celebrated. And while the Bruins were stringing up more title banners than any school in history, the NCAA was focusing its investigative attention on the football program at Ole Miss, the basketball program at Centenary College and other less than high-profile universities.

The NCAA's enforcement staff—no one else—determines which schools will and will not be investigated. The staff, after its decision to do some initial poking around, eventually takes a recommendation to the Committee on Infractions. If the committee likes what it hears, it allows the staff to continue its investigation with a formal blessing known as a letter of preliminary inquiry. The letter to the university says little more than that NCAA investigators soon will be on campus. It gives the school no clue as to what the school may have done wrong, and doesn't even say what sport is being investigated.

Any time such power is vested in a group of bureaucrats that is accountable to no higher authority, the potential for, and the perception of favoritism is inherent.

Berst, while stuck for an answer to why the NCAA didn't get right back into an investigation of UCLA in 1982, said he is tired of hearing that there is a group of schools that his enforcement staff won't touch. A dozen former investigators who once worked for Berst said the same thing.

"Over the years I was there, it would seem like the list of sacred cows the public felt we had would change weekly," said former NCAA investigator R. Dale Smith, now assistant commissioner of the Metro Conference. "It used to be USC, then it was UCLA, and then it was the Southwest Conference. Each time one of the schools that was supposedly on the protected list would come under investigation, the media would just change the list."

"I was never asked not to investigate something and I was never told to put somebody on probation," said former investigator Doug Johnson, now an assistant athletic director at the University of Miami.

Smith, who worked at the NCAA from 1979 until 1987, said the only case that can be made for selective enforcement is built on budget—not the school's budget, but the budget of the NCAA. "We were selective only in the sense that we only had a limited amount of resources to apply to a particular problem, and we had to take the ones we judged to be most important and serious and go after those first," Smith said.

Several former NCAA investigators said they decided what violations to chase much the same way as any other law enforcement organization: the tip that looks the most credible goes to the top of the list. "The problem is, you'll never get anyone to believe the NCAA on this one," said former investigator Mike Gilleran, who now is commissioner of the West Coast Athletic Conference. "Everybody likes to say it. No one can prove it. But for the same reasons those people who believe it can't prove there are sacred cows, the NCAA can't prove that there aren't. I guess every school would have to be investigated before people would stop thinking there are sacred cows. And even then, they'd say the favorites got off light on penalties."

Take, for example, the University of Kentucky basketball program. For years, the Wildcats were thought by coaches and fans to be on the protected list. Then, in 1985, the *Lexington Herald-Leader* published a series of articles in which 26 former basketball players said they accepted "$100 handshakes," other cash payments, clothing and extravagant gifts during their school years. The newspaper won the 1986 Pulitzer Prize for the series.

The *Herald-Leader* took a lot of heat for investigating and proving (all major interviews were on tape) what the NCAA couldn't. When the NCAA stepped in to follow up on the allegations made in the series, its investigators couldn't get the athletes to repeat their claims. Kentucky's only penalty was a public reprimand from the NCAA for poor handling of its internal investigation, furthering the widespread belief that the

'Cats could run wild without incurring the NCAA's wrath. In fact, the NCAA's most stinging criticism was leveled at the *Herald-Leader*. "One of the primary frustrations was the refusal of the newspaper that printed the original article to provide us any assistance in solving this case," David Berst was quoted as saying. Editors at the *Herald-Leader* asserted, correctly, that it was not the newspaper's responsibility to assist the NCAA in carrying out a thorough investigation. The *Herald-Leader* had checked and double-checked its sources and had printed everything the editors believed could be proven. The paper had lived up to its responsibility for fair and accurate journalism. Now the challenge to conduct a fair, accurate and comprehensive investigation fell to the NCAA. The NCAA failed.

NCAA investigators conceded they did not interview all the players who spoke with the newspaper's reporters, leading some to criticize the vigor of its inquiry. *Sports Illustrated* went so far as to sarcastically chide the NCAA for sending "the crack investigative force, presumably made up of Geraldo Rivera, Inspector Clouseau and Roger Rabbit," to probe the allegations made by the *Herald-Leader*.

NCAA Executive Director Dick Schultz conceded that when his enforcement staff comes up empty-handed in situations where reporters have been successful, it casts aspersions on the quality of the NCAA's work. "If you [reporters] can really find some evidence that that really took place and investigate that as thoroughly as you possibly can and you're successful, that makes the enforcement staff look bad, it makes the whole process look bad. In some cases it gives the impression of selective enforcement." People began to question whether the Wildcats had escaped punishment because they were subject to different standards.

Then, in an unexpected development, an Emery Worldwide Air Freight employee made a discovery that even the NCAA couldn't ignore. In March 1988, just five weeks after the first investigation ended, a package addressed to a Mr. Claud Mills "fell open" at Emery's service center in Los Angeles, the city where Mills's son Chris was the hottest basketball prospect of the season. Inside the package was a recruiting videotape that Kentucky assistant Dwane Casey was sending to the elder Mills. But when the package opened, there also happened to be 20 crisp $50 bills inside.

Casey said he knew nothing about the $1,000 and filed a $6.9-million defamation and invasion of privacy lawsuit against Emery. The NCAA found Kentucky guilty of the violation, although Emery later settled the suit with Casey for an undisclosed amount. The Committee on Infractions also confirmed the Wildcats were guilty of several other major NCAA violations, including aiding high school All-American forward Eric Manuel in cheating on his college entrance exams. Kentucky was finally slapped with a two-year ban from postseason play and a one-year loss of television appearances. But would all of this have happened were it not for a poorly sealed overnight package?

Some NCAA officials say they've long heard accusations of selective enforcement. In fact, however, some NCAA investigators say that the perception of selective enforcement may actually work against the schools, coaches and athletes supposed to be untouchable.

Former investigator Johnson handled a case in 1986 that gained national attention and underscored how ludicrous the NCAA rules can be. He prosecuted Indiana University basketball guard Steve Alford for appearing in a calendar printed and sold for charity. At the time, NCAA rules didn't allow student-athletes to pose for pictures later used for sale. The rule was changed in 1988.

"One of the reasons we had to rule him ineligible was selective enforcement complaints," Johnson said. "There had been two other players earlier that same month suspended for the same thing. And even though I thought it was a stupid rule, I couldn't just say this is Steve Alford, a clean-cut kid getting ready to play Kentucky on national TV. We had to do something."

Even Brent Clark, the former investigator, recognizes that things aren't as cushy for the previously untouchable programs as they were when he worked for the NCAA in the mid-1970s. "The gild is off the lily out there now," he told the *Los Angeles Times*. "They [UCLA] are vulnerable to past sins."

If selective enforcement is only in the minds of some sports writers and a few hundred thousand sports fans across the country, then there may never again be a dynasty like the one Wooden built in Westwood. Because no matter how hard Bruin supporters protest, there is little doubt that some of those banners hanging from the rafters in Pauley Pavilion wouldn't be there were it not for the NCAA's lack of interest in Sam Gilbert and the basketball team he helped finance.

A QUESTION OF ACCURACY

Deon Thomas exited the elevator on the 34th floor of the deserted Three First National Plaza building in downtown Chicago and wandered through the darkened halls of Coffield, Ungaretti, Harris and Slavin, one of the city's most prestigious law firms. He knew what was waiting for him behind the conference room door, but nothing could have prepared him for it. It was a sunny Sunday afternoon in August of 1989 and Deon would have preferred to have been five miles away, in the neighborhood where he grew up in the shadow of Chicago's business district. Instead, he had spent the morning driving from Champaign, where he would begin his freshman year at the University of Illinois three days later, to Chicago to face questions about his recruitment by the Fighting Illini.

Assembled around a table in the conference room were NCAA investigators Randy Rueckert and Richard Hilliard and the University of Illinois's special counsel Mike Slive and his law partner Mike Glazier, a former member of the NCAA's enforcement staff. For more than five and a half hours, they asked one question after another of Deon, who was one of the best high school basketball players ever to come out of Chicago. Most of the questions had to do with an alleged $80,000 offer made to him by University of Illinois assistant basketball coach Jimmy Collins.

Collins, who had driven Deon to the interview, waited outside the conference room. He had been told the inquiry would last about an hour, and as the questioning went on and on, he ducked his head in three times to see how Deon was holding up. Thomas, who would later be redshirted during his freshman year because of the allegations swirling around him, watched NCAA investigators jot down his answers on yellow legal pads. Those answers would become Deon's official statement to the NCAA.

This was the most important moment in Thomas's young life, and it all hinged on what those investigators chose to scribble down, on what they were able to remember of his sometimes rambling answers.

Missing in this courtroomlike setting was the one thing that a courtroom would have guaranteed Thomas: an accurate record of his statement. Because the NCAA rules prohibit its investigators from using tape recorders or court reporters, the statement that Deon Thomas gave—which would be used against him in any NCAA infractions hearing—is not in his own words. It is the written record of what two NCAA investigators believed they heard Deon Thomas say. These summaries are not in question-and-answer form and, as the few memos that have become part of lawsuits have shown, are filled with the investigator's opinion of what was said.

"I feel confident Deon is willing to stand or fall on his own words," said J. Steven Beckett, Deon's attorney. "I don't think he feels comfortable—nor should he—that the infractions committee will read his statement, but it won't really be his statement. Why not let him say it himself?"

There's a great irony in Deon Thomas defending himself to two NCAA investigators. Thomas was being questioned because Iowa assistant coach Bruce Pearl, who had lost the recruiting battle for Deon's services, had surreptitiously tape-recorded a phone call he made to Deon after the power forward from Simeon High School signed with Illinois. During the phone call, Pearl asked Thomas if he was happy with the $80,000 and the Chevrolet Blazer he received for becoming an Illini. Thomas said he was, although several people who have heard the tape said it was somewhat obvious that he was telling Pearl what he thought the losing coach wanted to hear.

What did Pearl do after talking to Deon? He sent the tape to the NCAA. So now we have the NCAA, which doesn't allow its investigators to tape, using a tape as its best source that Illinois had cheated in its recruitment of Deon Thomas.

"I'm using the fact that they don't tape to show the folly of their using a nonconsensual tape recording to accuse Deon," said

Beckett as he prepared for a meeting with the NCAA's infractions committee. "Bruce Pearl tape-recorded a conversation with Deon Thomas, unbeknownst to Deon, and here the NCAA is relying on it when they've got all these rules and regulations that won't let their own investigators get a consensual tape recording. Within the NCAA system, they ought to not utilize a tape recording in any way, shape or form, unless their system is willing to recognize that a tape is the most accurate way of taking one's statement."

It seems that the NCAA has no objection to the use of secretly tape-recorded telephone conversations during investigations. David Berst conceded the organization itself used that technique for years, despite the fact that recording without two-party consent is illegal in many states.

During a deposition taken as part of University of Nevada–Las Vegas basketball coach Jerry Tarkanian's lawsuit against the NCAA, Berst said that clandestine recording of telephone conversations from the NCAA's Kansas headquarters was "usual" and that the staff had a telephone system installed specifically so they could do so.

Sam Lionel, Tarkanian's attorney, queried Berst, who directed the UNLV investigation in the 1970s that led to the lawsuit, about the association's internal rules regarding taping telephone conversations.

LIONEL: Did you make tape recordings of any conversations you had with persons you interviewed or spoke to on the UNLV case?

BERST: Yes, tape recordings. Not in-person conversations but in telephone conversations, there would be some of those.

LIONEL: There were no tape recordings if it was not a telephone conversation?

BERST: That's right.

LIONEL: You didn't tell anybody, any of the people you mentioned that you were taping them, did you?

BERST: No.

LIONEL: Is that standard procedure not to tell?

BERST: Yes.

Berst went on to say there was nothing exceptional about taping telephone calls during the UNLV case because, at the time, that was standard procedure in many investigations. Berst said the practice continued through 1976, although minutes from an NCAA Council meeting in October 1976 show that Walter Byers and investigator Warren Brown assured the Council that the taping of telephone conversations by the enforcement staff had ended four years earlier, in 1972. Brown and Byers had to know that wasn't true. In a letter to Byers, former Big Ten Commissioner Wayne Duke complained that he had been taped "without my knowledge" by Berst or Brown as late as December 1973.

Associate Executive Director Steve Morgan said the NCAA's policy against recording has nothing to do with questions of accuracy. The organization does not want to tape because recording an interview might intimidate a student-athlete. "Student-athletes already are intimidated by being interviewed," Morgan said. "Taping has a little bit of a chilling effect, we feel."

How could Deon Thomas have suddenly felt more intimidated by the interview if the investigators used a tape recorder? And in this day of media exposure that reaches all the way into junior high schools, isn't the average college athlete well accustomed to having a microphone shoved in his face? If sitting in a room in the bowels of the athletic department being grilled by a couple of guys who look like FBI agents — and who, in some cases, once were FBI agents — isn't intimidating to a student-athlete, could adding a tape recorder really make it so?

Beckett doesn't think so. "Intimidation cannot be the reason they don't want to tape, because their whole enforcement program is built around intimidation," he said.

For an example, Beckett points to a mid–summer 1989 incident when two University of Illinois faculty members witnessed the kind of daunting interrogation that would have made any FBI agent proud. NCAA investigators Randy Rueckert and Bob Minnix showed up on the Illinois campus and wandered through the Intramural–Physical Education Building, where Deon Thomas was playing a pickup game on the challenge court. Playing on the adjacent court was Jim Anderson, a professor in the College of Education and chairman of the Illinois Athletic Control Board.

According to his statement, Anderson looked over and saw two similarly dressed men—both wearing polo shirts and blue slacks—watching Deon as he made his way up and down the court. Suddenly, one of the two men, later identified as Rueckert, began walking up and down the sidelines yelling at Deon while he was playing. Just as suddenly, Deon quit in the middle of the game and walked away. The two men followed. So did Anderson.

The still-unenrolled Thomas made his way downstairs to the weight room with the men following. From the top of the stairs, Anderson identified himself as a university administrator and asked the two men what was going on. Rueckert told Anderson that he and Minnix were from the NCAA and were actually on their way to Chicago when they decided to stop in and see Deon. As Thomas worked out in the weight room, Rueckert and Minnix watched through a glass door. Anderson stood back and watched them. When Thomas left the building, using a service door in the rear, the two investigators hustled out to meet him. There, they ran into Craig Stinson, then assistant director for campus recreation. According to a statement from Stinson, Rueckert began yelling at Thomas. "You're a liar," Stinson quotes Rueckert as saying. "You're going to talk to me. If you don't have anything to hide, you'll talk to me."

Minnix stepped between Rueckert and Thomas and, in classic good cop–bad cop style, told Thomas that Rueckert, a former Chicago prosecutor, "sometimes gets angry like that," according to the memo Stinson wrote describing the incident. Minnix then asked Thomas if he could leave Rueckert behind and come by later for a little one-on-one talk. On Stinson's advice, Thomas declined, saying all interviews should be scheduled through the university.

"Now, if you read Rueckert's memo of that supposed incident, none of that intimidation, none of the yelling that Jim Anderson and Craig Stinson witnessed, is there," Beckett said. "Rueckert doesn't admit to calling Deon a liar. If you read it, you'd think the two had a pleasant conversation at a dinner table.

"You want to know why they don't want tape recordings? That's why. Because in writing their memos, they can put every-thing in the best possible light for themselves. They can try and scare the hell out of kids, then make no mention of that and the

Committee [on Infractions] will believe the investigator acted like a true professional, not like some accusatory animal."

Former University of Florida football coach Charley Pell, who was fired during the NCAA's investigation of his program in 1984, agreed with Beckett, saying the NCAA avoids taping because the nightmare would be theirs. "I don't think they want a record of their questions," Pell said. "I think their questions are loaded, leading and unconstitutional. You've got your whole life, career and family hanging in the balance and you're stripped of any accurate reflection of what is asked and what you said. They take testimony without transcripts. That's distilled into an investigator's notes. Someone faced with that statement has no idea of the context in which it was said. They're getting an investigator's composite summary. In an NCAA investigation, you're just plain stripped of your rights."

After being hired by Illinois to defend Deon, Beckett quickly developed the sense that Deon had, in fact, been stripped of his rights. It seemed, Beckett said, that the 18-year-old was guilty in the eyes of the NCAA simply for having been accused. Frustrated, he decided to take Thomas to a polygraph examiner.

"We were hearing noises about his credibility," Beckett said. "Isn't that interesting that a coach can illegally tape someone and then they worry about the player's credibility, not the coach's. So I asked myself, 'What would make these people see that he is telling the truth?' From my background as a criminal attorney, I know one way to do it is a polygraph. The CIA and the FBI use the polygraph to clear spy cases. It is used in employment screening situations and in employer-employee thefts. Every law enforcement agency I'm aware of has access to and uses a polygraph. Wouldn't it seem logical the NCAA would recognize it, too? I know it is not admissible in court, but why wouldn't it be in the NCAA? They sure don't care about whether tapes are legal or not."

Mike Sheppo, assistant chief of the Illinois State Police Bureau of Forensic Sciences, told the *Champaign-Urbana News-Gazette* at the time that his office routinely uses a polygraph to determine the direction of investigations.

"We call it our 'detection of deception' department," Sheppo said. "We use the exams as investigatory tools. Our examiners are schooled to scientifically read various types of psychological parameters. It is an excellent investigative tool. When our examiner says someone is telling the truth, or not, I feel very confident about the information."

An Illinois assistant state's attorney told Beckett the state used Harry M. Lockhard of Secur-Tech in Champaign. Beckett called and made an appointment.

"I didn't know him and he didn't know me or Deon," Beckett said. "He doesn't even hold basketball tickets. In fact, he knew nothing about the case. He prepared the questions and he's the one who pushed Deon. He got zip on that question and he asked Deon, 'Search your mind. Did you ever get money?' Deon recalled that during midterms, he was feeling like a leper and wanted to get something to eat. He went to Collins's home at 11:00 p.m. and borrowed $10. He paid it back when his grandmother mailed him some money."

The sworn transcript of the polygraph exam showed that the only other monetary benefit Deon received for coming to Illinois was the promise of a $12-per-hour summer job at Illinois Power Company. Lockhard, after the hour-long exam, determined that Deon had been truthful. He signed an affidavit to that effect. The NCAA was unimpressed. Despite the information, the NCAA charged in its Official letter of Inquiry that Thomas had accepted $80,000 and the Chevrolet Blazer for his decision to enroll.

Beckett's submission of polygraph results isn't the first to be rejected by the NCAA. Near the end of its four-year investigation of Louisiana State University, the NCAA interviewed Tiger head basketball coach Dale Brown.

"I told the two investigators when I walked into the athletic director's office that I didn't want to play any games. I said, 'I do not respect the organization that you represent. So let's start out from there, we don't need any niceties.' Secondly, I requested a polygraph exam," Brown said. "I said, 'I request a polygraph exam because I don't have time to play games. For you to ask me a question at 9:00 in the morning and repeat that question at 3:00 in the afternoon to try and trick me is childish and unethical in my opinion.'

"I've watched enough television and know that's how you try to catch people," Brown said. "They told me they didn't think they could do it. I promised them that if the polygraph exam moved one ounce in the wrong direction, I'd resign my position immediately. I was willing to stake my job on the credibility of that test. So, [investigator] Doug Johnson went to the telephone and called the NCAA office and came back and told me that using a polygraph was illegal, it was against the rules. Then I told them I wanted a court reporter there. They told me I couldn't do that. Then I told them I want the whole conversation tape-recorded. They told me they couldn't do that. I said, 'Well, what can you do?' They said, 'Well, we can take notes on what you said and we'll let you see the notes, but you can't have a copy of them.' I asked, 'How do I know what's going to go back in there after you take them away?' They said I had to trust them. You know, to this day [August 1990] I've still never seen the statement they took. They promised it and never delivered. You're going to tell me they really cared about accuracy? If they had, they would have allowed me one of those options. And if they say it's too expensive, that's bull. I offered to pay for the polygraph, for the court reporter or the tape recorder. I just wanted the words to be right. The fact they rejected that told me the whole thing was fake."

Ten years earlier, during the NCAA's investigation of Michigan State football, Spartan assistant coach Charles Butler paid for his own polygraph test, which he hoped would convince the infractions committee that he had not been involved in illegal recruiting. During Michigan State's infractions hearing, "it was immediately pointed out that polygraph evidence was not admissible in many courts of the land," Michigan State's Frederick Williams later told congressional investigators.

"This surely was an ironic invocation of the rules of courts for an organization dedicated to the proposition that it should not follow them," the congressional committee wrote in its final report. "Hearsay, even double and triple hearsay, after all, has routinely enjoyed the infractions committee's blessing."

Like the 12 congressmen who signed the majority report from that 1978 investigation, Beckett can't believe the NCAA doesn't want to employ every means of making its investigations more fair and accurate.

"I'm a trial lawyer, and this is the first time I've been involved in an NCAA investigation," Beckett said. "It is a real shock to me, how totally arbitrary the system is. Everything is stacked against the accused. It is really scary that an organization that operates like this can control so many lives in America, and no one can do anything about it."

Beckett might have been a little less shocked, but likely no less disappointed, by NCAA justice had he stopped in Bob Auler's law office for a chat before taking Deon Thomas on as a client. Auler represented former Illini quarterback Dave Wilson in his eligibility battle with the NCAA in 1980. It was then that he, too, received his first lesson in futility. Auler tells this story about a visit he received from NCAA investigator Charles Smrt:

"He walked in and he said, 'I'd like to speak with you, I'm from the NCAA,'" Auler recalled. "I turned to my office manager and said, 'Andrea, get this gentleman a time and call the court reporter and have her come over.' He said, 'Court reporter?' I said, 'Yeah.' He said, 'What for?' I said that it was so I could have an accurate record of what he asked me and what I told him. He said, 'I'm very sorry. You may not know this, but we have a rule within the NCAA that prevents us from doing things in front of court reporters.' I said, 'Why is that?' And he told me, 'Actually, we take very accurate notes and then we give you a copy of those to look over and you can examine them.'

"I said that I didn't understand why they would have such a rule, but I said a tape recorder would suffice. He said they couldn't speak to a tape recorder either. I said, 'I don't understand that at all.' He said that I had to understand that he took very accurate notes. He repeated the whole thing.

"I told him I wanted to explain something to him. You see, I'm a member of an organization that he may have heard of. It is known as Phi Beta Kappa. Now, I was a poor kid from a family that was all blue collar. My father was an orphan and he valued education and he sent me down here to the university. I certainly knew what the inside of a factory looked like and I did not want to return to the factory on a permanent basis. I thought, and I was taught, that education was my only way out of the situation I grew up in.

"As a result, I attended classes and I wrote down notes as accurately as was possible for me to do. I got dents in the side of my fingers from holding the pencil so hard. I said that even given that kind of a background and the subsequent motivation that developed, I was only able to achieve approximately 96 percent accuracy. Nevertheless, that qualified me for this organization called Phi Beta Kappa, which is made up of a very small percentage of people in any university.

"As hard as I was trying to keep from going back to where I was from, I was still only able to achieve that sort of accuracy rate. I looked at him and said, 'And you ask me to believe that you are more talented and more motivated at taking notes than I was in those days?' I told him that asks a great deal to be believed from a fellow who works for as disreputable an organization as he did. His mouth dropped. He bounced off the floor once and he stuck his hand out and said thanks for my time."

Auler found himself face to face with NCAA investigators again in 1989 when he agreed to represent Illini forward Ervin Small in the fallout from the inquiry begun by the problems of his Simeon High School teammate Deon Thomas. Auler didn't waste his time asking that Small's interview be taped. He knew the rules. Instead, he decided to put that note-taking talent he developed in college to good use.

After first showing up at the wrong office ("This from the folks who are supposed to take accurate notes," Auler quipped), the NCAA investigator began a two-and-a-half hour interview with Small. "I took copious notes, as good as I could take," Auler said. "I was up over 33 full-size legal pages trying to record the nuances and subjectives of the investigator's attempt to ask the same question three or four different ways. During this period of time, the NCAA investigator took exactly three pages of notes and from what I could see of them they looked more like scattered words here and there. Now, how in the world is someone supposed to accurately reconstruct months later the distinctions people make in answering questions?

"That was it. From those three pages will come the NCAA's version of Ervin Small's statement. This is the only institution left in the Western world that doesn't believe in either court reporters or even tape recorders."

During Ervin's interview, NCAA investigator Randy Rueckert produced a hand-drawn map of Aunt Sonya's, a Champaign restaurant where Ervin and Deon went for Sunday brunch during a visit Deon made to his former high school teammate in January 1989. The question was whether assistant coach Collins had come over and talked to the duo after breakfast. If the coach had stopped at their booth, it would be an off-campus recruiting contact and against the rules. The problem was that both Auler and Small wanted to redraw the diagram of the restaurant because several booths separating the players and the coach had been left out.

"So here is this guy with his super-accurate mind and he's

got a diagram that he's obviously going to use at some point in this proof proceeding and the diagram isn't even right," Auler said. "Then during more than a half-hour of questioning about whether Jimmy Collins actually came over and said hello to Deon, the guy took zero notes. At one point, [Illinois investigator Mike] Slive said 'If indeed there is a missing booth here, let the record show . . . .' I cracked up. I said, 'What record? What are you talking about? There's no record here. He isn't even taking any notes. I'm the only one who is writing anything down.' I asked them all, 'Isn't this the pinnacle of stupidity?' No one said a word."

The NCAA interviewed Small on January 11, 1990. More than four months later, on May 20, Rueckert returned to Champaign with his version of Small's statement. Small and Auler were summoned to the Henry Administration Building and shown the statement. Rueckert told Small to write out any corrections, then sign the memo. Although Rueckert made only 3 pages of notes during the interview, his "summary" of the interview was 13 pages long, single spaced. It took Auler and Small three and one-half hours to make changes and corrections.

"We got done with the statement and I wrote out in long-hand, 'This is a gross distortion of what Ervin said, and unless this statement is submitted with all of the changes that we made in margin notes, then it's inaccurate, it's a lie,' " Auler said. "Rueckert came back in the room after I had written this out, Ervin had signed the statement and basically what I was doing was going back over the corrections and trying to write them down. I started trying to scribble down the distortions in a few, maybe no more than five, sentences. There were just gross lies. I couldn't believe the misconceptions. And the things that were left out were as alarming as those that were put in. This is the fallacy in the system. If we had tapes or depositions, we wouldn't have to worry about slanting, false characterizations and omissions. Anyway, Rueckert comes charging into the room and this guy's ready to go. His temples are throbbing and he's just got that choked-off croak in his voice, you know when a guy's going to slug you, and the adrenaline's rushing and the last thing he can do is croak out [an obscenity]—and that's the attitude he had. His face was flushed and he starts, 'You don't be taking things out of my report.' And I said, 'Oh, really? Then how am I supposed to read this little gem?' 'Go to the NCAA office and you can read it like any other member under investigation,' he said. And I said, 'So, I can get in the car with my client, drive to Kansas to read this. Is that right?' He says, 'That's right.' And I reached out and took the completed and signed report, tore it in half and said, 'Stick it up your ass, that's closer than Kansas.'

"I'm telling Rueckert, 'You've distorted these facts and I'm going to report you to the [Illinois] Attorney Registration and Disciplinary Commission if nothing else.' Now this is an interesting angle I've been thinking about. He's the attorney for an organization which Ervin either supports through his athletic sweat or in which he's a derivative member or whatever. There may be an actual legal obligation to Ervin from an attorney working for that organization. At least an obligation of fairness, accuracy, honesty, whatever you want to call it. Might make for a good lawsuit.

"We assume the NCAA enforcement officers are objective, superhuman factfinders, when, in fact, just as my experience in criminal law has been, they're just human beings like you or me. Just like cops are human beings," Auler said. "There are good cops. There are bad cops. Cops have good days. Cops have bad days. Cops sometimes have an ax to grind. NCAA investigators sometimes have an ax to grind. The problem is that the taint they carry in their interview isn't fully disclosed, I don't think, to the infractions committee."

Although the infractions committee did not find Illinois guilty of any major violations alleged in the official inquiry—including those involving Deon Thomas or Ervin Small—it decided in November, 1990 to levy major sanctions against the Illini. Why? "In our *minds* they were true," said Chuck Smrt, a director of enforcement. "We believe the information we collected was sufficient for a finding."

Who needs facts with that logic?

Auler likened his experience with the NCAA to a scene in Mark Harris's book *Bang the Drum Slowly*, where a fictional baseball pitcher constantly barraged by fans decides to take advantage of those who spend so much time admiring him. One by one, the pitcher invites enthusiastic followers to join players on the team for a game of cards. Once the bait is taken, the "fish" is told tonight's game is "TEGWOR." Embarrassed, the fan never asks how to play the game. Each hand ends with someone taking the fan's money, winning on a "superslam" or some other made-up rule. What the fan never figures out is that TEGWOR stands for The Eternal Game WithOut Rules. "That's exactly what we play with the NCAA," he said. "Worse, the rules they do have, rules like this, just can't be explained."

Lonny Rose, a law professor who has represented schools before the NCAA infractions committee, said the rules the NCAA *does* play by—like the decision not to record interviews—are downright confounding to many within higher education, whose life work is teaching the value of accuracy and fairness. "As a teacher, I know my students are writing down what I say," said Rose. "But while they're writing it down they can't be listening to the next sentence. The tape will facilitate the conversation. Later on, if there's any question about what was said, it's there. It doesn't lie, it doesn't shade. There's no interpretation. It simply is the way it is. It would eliminate the defense of the notetaker who says, 'That's not what I heard.' Why do courts take transcripts? They do it because the words that are said are important. That's why every court of record in the country has a court reporter who takes a verbatim transcript so there can be no doubt as to what was said. But that's a formal setting, whereas these interviews are just conversation. Even uncontested divorces are required to be court reported in most states. If it is so important that there be an accurate record of an uncontested divorce, one of the simplest of all legal affairs, shouldn't there be an accurate record, with all that is at stake, of an NCAA investigation?"

With the potential for so many problems lurking in a system that refuses to place a premium on accurate statements, why isn't there a hue and cry from coaches and administrators?

"Well, I didn't know they didn't tape until you just told me," said Georgia Tech basketball coach Bobby Cremins, a 15-year Division I coaching veteran. "I guess I just always thought they did."

"You're right, it doesn't make much sense," said Arizona basketball coach Lute Olson. "But I never knew that was the case. I would guess most of us [coaches] don't know that."

Even the NCAA's president admits there is no rational reason the organization's rules prohibit taping. "It [not taping] is the single biggest defect in our enforcement program," said Al Witte, a law professor at the University of Arkansas and NCAA president from 1989 to 1991. "The costs of adopting that taping proposal are nothing in comparison to the value of the idea and the credibility it would give our investigations. I can't believe anyone would be against that." But Witte said he would listen to NCAA staff and the infractions committee before proposing any changes. That means the NCAA will not be altering its position toward taping any time soon. Both senior staff and the committee have long said things are just fine, thank you very much.

Many investigators, though, believe that the time has come to use tape recordings. Both current and former investigators agree with Witte and many who have been through NCAA investigations: there are problems when an organization wielding the power of the NCAA builds cases using less-than-accurate notes, in this day when a higher standard should be desired. Some investigators say they would prefer to tape interviews, because it would eliminate credibility questions that arise when they claim a person told them something and the school produces a sworn statement from the same person declaring the exact opposite.

"If I had a tape of it, I wouldn't have my integrity called into question," said former investigator Mike Gilleran. "There were times I wondered if anybody would believe that I accurately put down what this kid is telling me. I never got called a liar, but occasionally a school would drop broad hints that maybe I was asleep at the wheel that day and I didn't hear right. Plus, if you had it on tape, it would be tougher for the kid to say he couldn't remember what he said.

"Without a tape, the investigating organization always leaves itself open to questions about how they interpreted what was said," Gilleran said. "I can see how a school that is sincerely interested in learning whether it has a problem could well feel that it could be helpful to know exactly what was said in the interview, rather than having to rely on the process where you've got to have confidence in the investigator's ability to ask a question, hear and understand a response and accurately record the response. I can see a school's good-faith concern about the process."

"It certainly would make our job easier," said former investigator Doug Johnson. "Not having a tape puts the burden of integrity on the investigator."

But the NCAA staff, led by David Berst and Steve Morgan, says no.

"We've had a lot of our investigators who would love to

tape interviews," Morgan said. "They feel like it could help back them up if anyone were to challenge them. We've had a lot of staff discussions about whether we want to lobby the membership to give us the authority to tape. I think the consensus view has been that we're okay with things the way they are."

"We're working by the rules that have been established by the membership," Berst said. "That would be a decision the membership would have to make. Right now, everyone seems to be fine on it."

The consensus, it appears, is only among Morgan and Berst. The two admitted that while many investigators—and a number of schools or individuals that have been investigated—had said the addition of tape recording would better the system, neither of the enforcement supervisors have carried such a recommendation to the NCAA membership. "It has been our judgment that the status quo is working," Morgan said.

As it stands now, NCAA investigators will have to continue the archaic practice of taking notes during the conversation, then dictate a memo outlining the key points.

But even that isn't always the case.

During his deposition in the Tarkanian case, Berst, who is now the top gun in the enforcement department and the man who teaches new employees how to do the job, stated that while he was an investigator he did not always take notes during interviews, opting instead to rely on his memory to recall what was said. Again, let Tarkanian's attorney, Sam Lionel, do the favors.

LIONEL: Did you make notes in all cases?

BERST: No, that's not absolutely the case. When I interviewed individuals that I thought might have some hesitancy to talk to me, it's possible that I would not make notes at that time but would make notes immediately after the conversation.

When asked in 1990 about those comments, Berst said that he still sees nothing wrong with investigators who choose to rely on their memories during hostile interviews. His reasoning: "The memorandums we write are not intended to be verbatim recollections of what was said."

The whole statement-taking exercise can easily be manipulated by a good investigator, since NCAA gumshoes get to sources long before those handling the school's inquiry. University of Washington researcher Elizabeth Loftus has written extensively about the benefit that investigators—whether they be police officers or NCAA employees—gain by being the first to question people about an incident. The concept is called "question formation and eyewitness behavior," and Loftus offers persuasive evidence that the first person to ask questions in a case "clearly has a heavy advantage."

"In the real world, people influence other people sometimes very inadvertently just by the way they ask questions," Loftus said. "An investigator will do the same thing, only it won't be inadvertent. For example, a police officer has a hypothesis about the person who he thinks committed a crime. And he can communicate that hypothesis to an eyewitness by certain verbal expressions—'He didn't have a beard, did he?—or even nonverbal indications like the rolling of eyes that can influence the witness's memory deliberately."

Could the same be said of NCAA investigators? "If their investigator has a hypothesis about what happened and asks leading questions with that hypothesis in mind, the NCAA can shape the testimony of a witness, sure," Loftus said. "I think it is perfectly applicable."

"The first person to interview an eyewitness can affect the way the person remembers the event for everyone that ever asks about it," said Lonny Rose. "Here I am representing the school, coming in a year after an event. The NCAA maybe has a six-month headstart on me and the first person I interview was interviewed that long ago by an NCAA staff member. By the time a school knows what the NCAA is after, NCAA investigators have already determined the school's guilt. That's like spotting them 20 points in a 50-point game. I've got to spend a lot of time getting my 20 points back."

Berst argues that the NCAA has built a safeguard into the system that benefits the school and the people interviewed. An NCAA rule—passed during the congressional investigation in the late 1970s—requires that, "whenever possible," investigators must take their memos back to those interviewed and allow them to read and change words they believe are inaccurate. According to the rule, an investigator must be present when any statement is being revised to ensure the person makes no attempt to copy the NCAA's version. This same rule, you see, prohibits people from keeping a copy of what the NCAA alleges to be their words. Even the supposedly safeguarded system is designed to the NCAA's advantage.

Contract lawyers are the first to admit that they always want the initial draft in any deal. By getting the first shot at writing a contract, for example, they might just build in 50 little clauses that work to the advantage of their client. Even after counsel for the other side begins negotiating out some of those clauses—and law professors will tell you a good lawyer might only catch 50 percent of his opponent's attempts to gain the upper hand—the end result is that the document is more favorable to the position of the original author.

Transfer that analogy to the NCAA's rules on correcting its version of what becomes your statement. If the investigator has filled the statement with his prejudices, you will be lucky to find and change all of those comments to your advantage. Even if you do better than the average contract lawyer, you are left signing a statement that still is loaded with the investigator's biases.

For that reason, some who have been questioned by the NCAA have refused to sign their statements. Nevertheless, those statements are used at infractions hearings. "We would just tell the Committee on Infractions that an individual refused to sign before we introduced it," Steve Morgan said. "That usually was acceptable."

George Davidson, a former part-time NCAA investigator and a retired FBI agent, said he fully understood the decision Cleveland State University officials made in declining to sign statements during his investigation of their basketball program.

"Back when I was with the FBI, I guess this was the late 1960s, we had nine people arrested on a case in Indianapolis," said Davidson. "Eight of them refused to cooperate. But one of them signed a statement, figuring it would help his case, because he thought we would be more lenient in exchange. It ended up the only one we convicted was the guy who signed the statement. I believed before then, but that made me sure of it, that I would never sign a statement admitting to something. I have, though, written a lot of statements for people and talked them into signing them. That was my job.

"We, at the FBI, used to have a setup something like the

NCAA, where you take a statement, then get someone to sign it but not allow them to have a copy of it. But we were told a few years ago to stop that. I think it was Congress that made us stop. They made us start giving copies to people so they had a record of what we had on file. Funny, you couldn't get a copy of your statement at any time with the NCAA. They just don't want people to have them."

Others have reported their efforts at changing statements seemed futile. Marty Kravitz, a Las Vegas attorney, had never experienced justice NCAA style, when he was asked by Lois Tarkanian, wife of UNLV coach Jerry Tarkanian, to accompany her during questioning in a 1990 case.

"Lois didn't say much about it beforehand," Kravitz said. "Just that she didn't think there'd be any problems, but that she'd feel more comfortable if someone were there. But from the beginning there were problems. During the questioning I kept objecting to the ambiguous way in which the investigator, Bob Stroup, asked Lois questions. He would ask two or three questions at the same time, making it difficult to respond to one at a time. I had to ask him to present one question at a time. The advantage of asking questions in such a manner is well known among lawyers because it confuses a witness. The misuse of answers to serially strung out questions also is well known. That's why, when I pointed out to Stroup the importance of asking one question at a time, I was surprised when he told me he had completed law school. I can only come to the conclusion that he knew what he was doing in asking questions in such a manner and was doing so purposely to use the information he obtained to match some pattern he had predetermined.

"Lois told me not to worry," Kravitz continued. "She said the NCAA had a new rule allowing each person interviewed to read their statement and sign it before it was used and that we could make corrections for accuracy at that time. Imagine our shock a few weeks later when we read the so-called statement and found not a question-and-answer summary of what was discussed, but rather an editorialized version where facts were presented inaccurately, out of context and sometimes in a veiled manner which implied actions occurred which, in truth, had not.

"We tried for over two and a half hours to correct that statement, but it was not possible to complete everything. There was just too much that needed to be changed. I suggested she not sign the statement and write on it that it was not accurate. She did and we agreed to come back prepared to make changes later. The next time I brought scissors, scotch tape and a stapler. I took a long yellow legal pad and wrote from my notes what the questions were and Lois's reply and then I cut and added portions of the NCAA's version of the statement as was appropriate. It took about four and a half hours. When we finished NCAA investigators [Dan] Colandro and Stroup said we were not allowed to redo the statement. They would not accept the corrected copy I had put together, so we had to take another of their copies and work from that.

"When we came to parts which were not accurate, we told them so. I'd say, 'This isn't what she said.' Stroup would say, 'That's the way we heard it.' Colandro didn't say much at this point. It got quite heated between myself and Stroup and finally Lois interjected, 'What does it matter what Marty thought I said or what you (looking at Stroup) thought I said. What's important is what's accurate. Aren't we trying to get at the truth?' Stroup then said, 'That's the way we heard it and that's the way it's going to be.' "

"At that point Lois stood up hurriedly, said something like, 'I'm sorry, I have to leave,' started crying and left the room. The Big West commissioner and one of the UNLV people persuaded her to return. She told them she wasn't afraid of any of their questions or of anything she had done, but she was afraid of their misrepresenting what she said. At one point she told them it was no wonder players and others were afraid to speak to NCAA enforcement staff. Here she was with a Ph.D. and over 30 years in education and even she was afraid that this word would be placed wrong or that sentence would be used incorrectly.

"It was one of the most incredible situations in which I've ever been involved. Lois told me later that the most cruel thing about it was that, here she thought the NCAA was working to be more fair and more accurate in collecting information, only to find out that in reality it's worse than before because now they place you in a situation, once you've talked with them, that you sign what is primarily their version of what you said, or they take the statement anyway, unsigned, and make it look as if you haven't cooperated."

Some believe the rule requiring investigators to get signed statements "whenever possible" provides too great a loophole for NCAA enforcement officers. "What if they know that some-one is a bit shaky and might very well change their tune on a second go-round," said one attorney who represented a school in a hearing where two unsigned statements were used. "They might just say finding that person was impossible. They know the infractions committee is going to accept it." Added Sugar Bowl Executive Director Mickey Holmes, a former commissioner of the Missouri Valley Conference, "I think that [whenever-possible clause] leaves it too wide open for abuse. Who makes the judgment that it wasn't possible to get the statement signed? Was it not possible just because they ran out of time? I just have trouble understanding why the NCAA has such a concern about taping. My goodness, I always thought it was the greatest thing I had going for me [in conference investigations]. And I felt for the interviewee that it was the greatest thing he had going for him, because if we ever got into an argument of who said what, or how it was handled, it was right there on that piece of tape. And, besides, taping eliminates the need to take statements back to the interviewee."

"Sometimes people won't see you again," the NCAA's Steve Morgan explained. "You wouldn't want to have a situation where just because you didn't have a second opportunity to get to that person, you couldn't use it."

One might be able to understand the rationale for rejecting polygraphs. One might also be able to see the reasoning behind denying people a copy of their statements, since the NCAA fears those words might end up in the hands of reporters, adding publicity to a case and pressure to others soon to be questioned.

But what could be the logic of turning thumbs down on a good old-fashioned court reporter, or at the very least a tape recorder? NCAA senior staff members say the decision against taping is based on three points.

First, is the previously discussed argument that the presence of a recorder might intimidate some witnesses.

"That's an archaic thought, that it's going to be inhibiting," said former investigator Ron Watson. "You ought to see us as investigators when we sit in front of an athlete or even a booster and have the note pad and pen going 90 miles an hour. First of all, it's hard for the investigator to concentrate, listening to every word that's being said. I wrote every word or tried to. Then it slows down the questioning process, you don't get a spontaneous flow, an exchange. I think by taping you could get the person you're interviewing in a more comfortable mode by just saying, 'Hey, just ignore this thing. You are going to be able to see word for word what you said. I'm going to have this typed, so when I bring it back, the tape is going to tell me exactly what you'll read in that memorandum.' So I think you could do a better job getting the principal person you're interviewing more comfortable if you just simply started in the process taping and didn't act like it was a big deal."

Second, taping interviews would cause a secretarial nightmare since most would have to be transcribed—a process presumably more time consuming than typing investigators' summaries of interviews. "It is a giant hassle to transcribe tapes of interviews," Morgan said, "I think we'd have to expand our secretarial staff substantially if we were going to do that."

"The financial consequences of taping would be enormous," chimed in D. Alan Williams, chairman of the infractions committee.

Huh? An organization that just signed a $1-billion television contract and lives on an $98-million annual budget is crying poor? Besides, many who have requested their interviews be recorded or transcribed by a court reporter have offered to cover the cost in exchange for accuracy.

Third, the NCAA argues taping or transcribing interviews might lead to a loss of confidentiality. During the congressional hearings former NCAA president Neils Thompson said: "The NCAA's justification for its current policy has been to maintain the confidentiality of the individual enforcement proceedings for the purpose of protecting the member institutions and the individuals involved from unjustified and unwarranted public attention." To which the congressional committee responded in its final report: "Since it is in all cases the 'member institutions and the individuals involved' who desire such transcripts in the first place, the policy can only be construed as one designed to protect people from themselves. That kind of arrogance is customarily reserved to totalitarian governments, and it is not unknown to have felled a few."

For most who believe taping would enhance the enforcement program, these excuses don't wash, especially the poor-mouthing. Those are the NCAA's reasons. Now here are three reasons the NCAA should abandon this arcane policy.

First, numerous academic studies conducted over the last 30 years have shown that, during the struggle to take notes, even the best interviewers miss as much as 40 percent of what is being said.

In their book *Listening and Speaking*, researchers Ralph Nichols and Thomas Lewis demonstrate that, in most cases, more than 40 percent of what a person hears is lost in immediate recall and only 25 percent can be recalled after a significant interval. And that is when the subjects were simply listening. Researchers note that when the subjects were taking notes, the loss became even greater.

In addition, the 60 percent NCAA investigators do get can easily be colored by the perspectives they have before they sit down. "You hear what you want to hear, I don't care if you are supposed to be impartial," said former University of Florida basketball coach Norm Sloan, who went through an NCAA investigation while he was head coach at North Carolina State University and who left Florida in 1989 amidst allegations of NCAA violations. "You will write answers in terms of how you are receiving what I am saying," Sloan said in a tape-recorded interview. "You are either with me, you like the posture I have taken, or you don't like the posture I have taken. That will come out in the way you write those answers. They [NCAA investigators] don't want to be that impartial, and there is no question about that."

When the most important thing in a young athlete's life is being threatened, when millions of dollars in NCAA tournament, television and bowl appearance money is on the line, when the careers of coaches and reputations of universities are at stake, is it right to stick with a system that loses 40 percent of what is said in translation? The answer is obvious.

Second, the rapid turnover of NCAA investigators— sometimes so great that one case can be handed off to five, six or even seven people—means that the investigator who may ultimately present the NCAA's case to the infractions committee may be relying on notes from interviews he never conducted. The case may be built on memos written by a half-dozen investigators with a half-dozen different methods of taking notes and a half-dozen different levels of recall or accuracy.

It is reminiscent of that childhood game of "telephone" that begins with one youngster writing down a phrase, then whispering it in the ear of the child sitting next to him. By the time the phrase has made it around a circle, it never ends up as it began. Often, it isn't even close. Even Tom Niland, the athletic director at Le Moyne, and a nine-year member of the infractions committee, concedes that having one investigator read and interpret another's memo "might handicap us a little bit."

Finally, taping interviews would speed an excruciatingly drawn-out process by expediting the investigator's work. "By taping you get things done quicker because you don't have to go back to the office for a whole week to dictate memos," said former investigator Watson, now an associate athletic director at the University of Oklahoma. "I'd have legal pads, those long legal yellow pads, notebooks completely full, several of them to carry back to the NCAA office and dictate exactly what they had said every week. It took a lot of time to get that done. Secretaries had to type it, you had to proof it, then they put it in final form. Today's times, we're in 1990, not back in 1909. I think people would accept taping with no problem. "

Despite the strong arguments his own staff—and many others—have made for fixing this flaw in the NCAA's enforcement program, Berst said he does not see a change forthcoming. "I've heard all the reasons people say we should [tape]," David Berst said. "And I still don't think we need it. Things are just fine right now."

Sure. Just ask Deon Thomas.

3

RULES, RULES, RULES

MARK

Mark Alcorn slipped quietly through the door of Room 74 in the athletic dorm at Louisiana State University during the early morning hours of November 11, 1980. He and a couple of friends on the Tiger basketball team were returning from a Bruce Springsteen concert in the LSU Assembly Center. Alcorn tried hard not to wake his roommate, teammate and best friend, Joe Costello, who had not attended the midweek concert. Then, as he quietly tucked himself under the covers, Alcorn felt a sudden pain in his midsection, worse even than any elbow that usually greets guards his size when they stray too far under the basket.

He tried his best to ignore the pain. But, as he was relaxing into sleep, the unbelievable agony returned. Again and again, as the night wore on, his body would be wrenched in pain just as he was on the edge of sleep.

"I thought it was something I ate," Mark said later. When he told Costello about the ordeal the next morning, the two "weren't really worried about it," Costello recalled. "I was convinced it was because Mark may have had one too many drinks the night before. He didn't drink much, so it didn't take much for him to get sick." But a week later, Costello came back to the dorm room and found Alcorn again doubled over in pain. He called the team doctor, Dr. Marty Broussard, who ordered a mononucleosis spot and a blood test run on Alcorn. Both tests were negative. Based on Mark's comments, Broussard diagnosed the problem as an ulcer. He prescribed medication and Mark dutifully took it, although there seemed to be little relief. "After he started taking the pills, the pain didn't go away," Costello said. "I've known people who've had ulcers and they can stop the pain with the tranquilizers. I had a feeling something else was wrong with Mark, but I didn't know what it was."

Mark and others believed the ulcer was the result of the pressure he was putting on himself to earn playing time on the Tiger basketball team. Nothing had ever been this difficult. He had never seen so much of a game from so deep on the bench.

By all rights, Mark Alcorn shouldn't have been at LSU, shouldn't have been trying for a spot on one of the nation's best college basketball teams. A 6-foot, 140-pound guard when he enrolled at DeSmet High School in St. Louis, Alcorn barely caught the attention of the school's junior varsity coach when he came to the team's tryout. "The first time I ever saw him, he was just a scrawny kid," said Rich Grawer, then DeSmet's head coach who has since become coach at St. Louis University. "I told my B-team coach, 'Take a look at this Alcorn.' The B-team coach frowned. He said he was too little."

Alcorn went on to show Grawer and others that a scrawny kid who handles a basketball like a yo-yo could indeed make it in high school ball. Before he graduated, Alcorn would become DeSmet's third all-time leading scorer and would lead the team to third place in the Missouri state championships. Ranking third on DeSmet's all-time scoring list is a rather impressive accomplishment, since numbers one and two were teammates and former University of Missouri stars Steve Stipanovich and Mark Dressler.

But as Alcorn ended his high school career, he again heard a familiar refrain. "You're too small to make it in Division I college basketball," several coaches told Alcorn. "Try NAIA." Only one Division I school offered him a chance. St. Louis University, where Mark's father Harold starred in the late 1950s, was willing to gamble on him. Alcorn made the most of it.

In only his fifth collegiate game, Mark became the Billikens's starting point guard. During an early-season game against defending national champion Marquette, he played 35 minutes, scoring 6 points and handing out four assists in a heart-wrenching 56-54 loss to the fourth-ranked Warriors in Milwaukee. Alcorn finally proved that a skinny kid with a choirboy face belonged on the court with some of the nation's best players. Later in the season, he had his best game in a 63-61 loss to the high-powered Louisville Cardinals, finishing with 12 points, 10 assists and 3 steals. "I'd never heard of him before," the Cardinal's All-America guard Darrell Griffith said after the game. "But I knew he had to be out there for a reason."

The young Bills, playing the nation's second-toughest schedule according to *Basketball Weekly*, struggled under first-year coach Ron Coleman to a 7-20 record, including 9 losses to Top 20 teams. The Billiken, the mythical god of things as they should be, never smiled on the Bills. Their season ended in the Metro Conference Tournament with a 22-point loss to Memphis State. Alcorn was named to the Metro's All-Freshman and All-Academic teams. Coleman was fired at the end of the year and Alcorn, after starting 22 of 27 games and averaging 8 points and 3.6 assists per game, decided to move on.

It should have come as no surprise that a rail of a young man with a quick first step should idolize the great Pete Maravich. So when Alcorn decided to find a new place to play, he chose the campus where the player he so admired had lighted up scoreboards years earlier. Alcorn received a release from his letter of intent at St. Louis and asked Louisiana State University coach Dale Brown for the opportunity to try his jumpshot in the big time. "Actually, except in special circumstances, I usually don't encourage transferring," said Brown, who had only accepted three other transfers in the six seasons before Alcorn's request. "The grass usually isn't greener on the other side." During his obligatory year on the sidelines, Alcorn worked out with the Tiger team and often seemed awed by the talent around him. "I've never seen so many guys who can do it all," he told one reporter.

Then, in 1979, came the year he had waited for. Although his expectations were high—he told friends he would be the team's sixth man before the season was out—he played in only 10 games. He played a lot the first four games of the year, usually as the first guard off the bench behind starters Ethan Martin and Howard Carter. But his nervousness caused him to make mistakes, throwing the ball away and calling the wrong play on occasion. Then Brown moved Willie Sims to guard, giving him the role Alcorn had so cherished. "I was so nervous," Alcorn told Dave Dorr of the *St. Louis Post-Dispatch* after that season. "And then once the [Southeastern] Conference season started, I was sitting and I wasn't playing at all. I got down—really depressed for a long time. I went into a shell. It bothered me that I came here and wasn't playing. I didn't get a second chance."

It was obvious Alcorn had taken a bigger bite of college basketball's apple than his talents would allow him to swallow. He was confined to the deepest depths of the LSU bench, something his mother and his best friends said ate at him constantly. Unbeknownst to Alcorn, Dale Brown considered allowing him to keep his scholarship while dropping him from the team. But assistant coach Jordy Hultberg talked him out of it. "Jordy told me it would just break Mark's heart to get cut," Brown recalled. "He loved being a part of the team, even if he didn't enjoy his particular position."

Despite his frustration, Alcorn stayed at LSU, determined to prove that his decision to transfer was a wise one. He worked in the off-season erecting scaffolding at a manufacturing plant outside Baton Rouge. The combination of the heavy lifting and the mounds of shrimp and bowls of gumbo that he consumed daily helped him bulk up from 175 to 185 pounds. He was sure that the added strength would finally allow him to battle for playing time.

He had never felt more healthy, never more strong, when the pain began that long night after the Springsteen concert. He asked those close to him to keep news of his dilemma quiet. This was a problem he wanted to handle without telling the coaching staff. But two and a half weeks later, as the team boarded a plane headed for the Great Alaskan Shootout, Mark still had no clue why the ulcer hadn't gone away. On the way to Alaska, Mark called from both the Chicago and Seattle airports to tell his mother he wasn't feeling well. Keeping his worries to himself, Alcorn suited up for LSU's first-round game against Colgate. With the game well in hand, Brown called him from the bench. He played three minutes. It was typical Mark Alcorn. He didn't get into the box score, but played with great emotion.

After the game, though, all Mark could feel was pain. Again, every time he neared sleep, a jolt of agony would remind him that something was wrong. "He was trying to fight it," Costello said. "He didn't want to let anyone know how much it hurt. He didn't want to leave the team or be asked to leave the team. I guess he thought if he told the coaches, they might use this as an excuse to not play him." But finally, when the pain wouldn't let up, Costello went to Coach Brown and pleaded with him to do something for Mark.

"It was one of the days in Alaska where it got pitch dark at 5:00 p.m.," Costello remembered. "And Mark was just trying to make it through dinner so he could go back to the room and try to sleep. When he left for the room, I went to Coach and told him not to play Mark until we could figure out what was wrong with him." Dale Brown went to Alcorn's room and found him coiled up in the fetal position. "He was so sick, his color had changed," Brown recalled. "I told him he wasn't going to play. I didn't let him dress." In street clothes, his stomach hurting and his heart breaking, Mark watched as the team lost to Arkansas 86-76. The next night, he didn't even make it to courtside, watching LSU's 76-67 win over Georgetown on television from the hotel room.

When the Tigers returned from Alaska, Alcorn went straight to Our Lady of the Lake Hospital in Baton Rouge. He checked in and out as doctors tried to diagnose his problem. The first set of tests came back inconclusive; more tests were ordered. He tried to practice and couldn't understand the reason for his sluggishness. He had no idea it was because he was playing with a tumor the size of his fist knuckling into his spleen, another the size of a golf ball hidden beneath his neck and a third growing under his arm. "I look back on it, and I can't believe I practiced," Alcorn would say later. "I knew I had a lump on my neck. But, you know, I didn't want to pay any attention to it."

On December 5, Alcorn became so sick that he got Stan Harris, the team's trainer, to drive him to the emergency room at Earl K. Long Hospital. There, doctors tried a new set of tests. As he lay in the emergency room, Dr. James Osterberger came in with the worst of news: Mark had cancer of the body tissue.

Harris called Coach Brown. Brown hung up and made "the most difficult call of my life." On the other end was Harold Alcorn, the successful owner of Alcorn Equipment Company in St. Louis. Harold Alcorn couldn't believe what he was hearing.

He asked Brown to repeat the words, a little more slowly this time. They came out just as before. The drive from Harold Alcorn's office to his home is seven miles. During that drive, Alcorn said he twice felt himself slip into a black vertigo and, out of anger and pain, tried to punish himself. "I hit myself in the mouth," he later told reporters when describing his reaction.

Harold and Sheila Alcorn caught the first flight to Baton Rouge. The next day, when Dr. Osterberger came for the morning checkup, Harold Alcorn wasted no time getting to the point. "I said to him, 'Doc, I want to know what the problem is,' " the elder Alcorn recalled. "He was blunt. He said 'Mark, the slides show you have embryonal carcinoma, a rare cancer, one that strikes only one-tenth of one percent of the population.' "

Embryonal cancer mostly strikes men in their early 20s. According to the National Cancer Institute in Bethesda, Maryland, the disease claims 8 of every 100,000 people. "It's always hard to tell somebody they have cancer," Osterberger told the *Shreveport Times*. "But it was especially difficult to tell Mark, who was healthy and young and who had so much to look forward to." The Alcorns were horrified. The cancer was inoperable. Mark had 90 days to live . . . maybe. "Until then, I think Mark thought it was a fuzzy dream," his father said. "But I looked at his face and the tears were streaming down his cheeks." The clock showed 11:15 a.m., but for the Alcorns, it felt like midnight. At 21 years of age, Mark Alcorn was told the best years of his life had passed.

Fifteen minutes later, Mark's three best friends, Costello, J. Brian Bergeron and Andy Campbell rounded the corner of Mark's room. "I could tell just by looking at his mom and dad," Costello said. "Then I saw Mark. All he said was, 'They say the tumor is malignant.' I lowered my head. Then I looked at Andy. We couldn't talk. We couldn't say a word."

The Alcorns thought it best for the family to catch the late afternoon flight to St. Louis. Mark checked out of the hospital and decided he wanted to share pregame lunch with his teammates before he left. The Bayou Bengals were set to play Tulane that night in the first home game of the season. There wasn't any speech, but Mark said good-bye to his teammates. They decided to have a prayer meeting and ask God to take Mark's care into His hands. That done, Mark, J. Brian, Joe, Andy and trainer Harris went back to Mark's dorm room to begin loading Mark's college life into cardboard boxes. As the Alcorns drove away from the red-brick dorm, every member of the team stood outside and cried. They stayed there for an hour, no one knowing exactly what to do or say.

About the same time Mark's plane left the ground at Baton Rouge Municipal Airport, Dale Brown brought the team into the locker room at the Assembly Center. "Let's play this game for Mark Alcorn," the coach said. Nothing else was said. Nothing more was necessary. The team's star, Durand (Rudy) Macklin, took two pieces of black tape and fashioned the number 11—Alcorn's jersey number—inside the zero on his No. 40 jersey. The Tigers blew rival Tulane out of the gym, winning by 38 points, 119-81. The first thing Mark did when he got to St. Louis was check the score. The first thing his teammates did when the game was over was autograph the game ball and send it and a Bible to him. The Tigers dedicated their season to Mark and he promised them he'd give it his best fight. Each day became a bonus.

Thirty-eight days after he left campus, Mark returned to Baton Rouge for the first time to watch LSU's crucial Southeastern Conference game against Kentucky. Brown took him to half court before the game, presented Mark with his LSU jersey, and introduced him to the crowd that had been flooding his parents' home with cards and letters. As Mark moved to the microphone, the largest home crowd in LSU history—15,192 strong—silently rose to their feet. He told the fans that he appreciated all they had done for him. "I'm going to keep on fighting," he said, as many in the crowd wept openly. "I'm not going to let this thing beat me." The fifth-ranked Tigers, with Alcorn sitting on the bench, then hammered No. 6 Kentucky 81-67 to take first place in the SEC race.

A few days later, Coach Brown received a call from Rich Grawer, Alcorn's high school coach in St. Louis. Grawer had decided to host a dinner in Mark's honor to help his family offset some of the costs of his expensive chemotherapy treatment. Grawer was ecstatic. He had lined up sports announcer Bob Costas, who began his career in St. Louis and had covered Alcorn while he played for St. Louis University, to be the master of ceremonies. University of Missouri coach Norm Stewart had agreed to come and to bring with him Stipanovich and Dressler, Mark's high school teammates. Marquette coach Hank Raymonds, whose team had nearly lost to the Alcorn-led Billikens two years earlier, also promised to be there.

"He [Grawer] asked if I could make it and I told him I wouldn't miss it," Brown said. "Then a couple of days after that, I got a call from Mark's mom. She said 'We know he's at the end of his rope, so we asked Mark if there was anything that we could do that he'd like, one wish that we could grant him.' And he said 'Yes, mom, I'd love to see my three good friends.' His three good friends were three of the last guys on the team, Joe Costello, Andy Campbell and J. Brian Bergeron. And she said, 'I'm embarrassed to inform you that we just don't have any money.' She said they just didn't have anything, they had mortgaged their home a second time to pay for Mark's treatments and they wanted to know if there was any way that I could get the players to come. I told her it was as good as done."

Sheila Alcorn, like her son, is a proud person. She said asking Brown to pay airfare for the players—all of whom spent most of their time sitting with Mark at the end of the bench, and whose combined average was 3.1 points per game—was no easy request. "I'm not much good at asking for things like that," she said.

It didn't take long for news of Mark's February 8 benefit to hit the Baton Rouge papers. When it did, Brown got another call, this time from Governor Dave Treen, who wanted to send Brown and the players to St. Louis on the state airplane. He also wanted Brown to present Alcorn with a special state commendation for courage.

"This was all so clean cut," Brown said. "The governor had offered his plane, so it wasn't going to cost the university a nickel. But then we got to talking about the trip in a staff meeting. I don't even know how I brought it up, but I said something to the extent of, 'Well, with the NCAA's goofy rules, they'll probably call—and I literally said—'almost going to Mark's funeral free entertainment off campus.' I was just being facetious about the stupid rules. After the meeting, I got to thinking. As verbal as I am in my criticism of the NCAA, I'd better be careful, I'd better call.

"So, I called the NCAA and the SEC office and I explained all the circumstances—that he was dying, his mother made a request—and then I asked is there any possible way that I could take these kids. I told them that the high school was trying to raise money so Mark could go back to get his cancer treated, and this is kind of a last wish he gave his mother. The SEC was really apologetic, they said, well, according to the rules, you can't. But you can call the NCAA and see.

"I called the NCAA and I might as well have talked to that Romanian ruler that just got kicked out—Ceausescu—yeah, I might as well have talked to him. I thought I had dialed the wrong number. I thought I had dialed the Kremlin. Who was I talking to, Molotov or Stalin, or Krushchev? The answer from the guy on the phone was, 'Absolutely not.' He said I could not transport them to a function off campus. That was illegal entertainment by NCAA rules. So I said to the guy, really upset, 'You watch, they'll be there.' Oh, he got real defensive. He asked me, 'Are you turning yourself in?' I said, 'Just forget about it,' and hung up. I couldn't believe that something this simple had become such a problem," Brown said.

The night before the benefit, LSU defeated Mississippi State, 94-89, for their 20th consecutive win since Alcorn left the team. Costello said Brown called him, Bergeron and Campbell to his office before the game. He told them that after the game, they would get a call with flight information and to be ready to go. "We all went back and packed our bags," said Costello. "He told us that five or six businessmen were going up with him in the governor's plane and that there were seats on the plane for us, but the NCAA wouldn't let us go that way."

One by one, Dale Brown took the players into his office and gave them the money to pay their round-trip airfare. "I felt like I had to take a shower or something," Brown said. "I put it in a brown envelope, $300 each. It was enough to cover the cheapest red-eye flight, meals at McDonald's and a shared motel room. I pulled the blinds in my office, and I called each kid in individually and it was just like I was being filmed or something. I mean here I was doing this nice act by giving them the money, but I felt almost like there were cameras peering down on me."

"We basically knew it was a violation," Costello said. "But we wanted more than anything to be there for Mark."

When the three players finally arrived in St. Louis, they rented a compact car and, with the 7-foot Campbell crammed in the back seat, began looking for DeSmet High. They became lost; the 20-minute ride took nearly an hour and a half. By the time they finally found the school, more than 600 well-wishers who paid $25 apiece had packed the gymnasium, which would later be named the Mark Alcorn Gym. They watched on big-screen televisions as UCLA beat Notre Dame 51-50. Then they listened to Bob Costas and the three college coaches talk about courage, a word Mark Alcorn had come to embody. "A lot of kids at that age try to take on some kind of attitude or put on a facade that they think is hip," Costas, now an announcer with NBC, said in 1990 when asked about the Alcorn dinner. "But Mark was so well-grounded, so unassuming. He came to that dinner looking very thin and wearing a wig, because his hair was falling out from the chemotherapy. But he was there with a smile on his face and nothing but good things to say about the future. Sometimes out of sympathy, people say of a person that dies at an early age that they were courageous. That's not always true. It was true here."

When Costas finished speaking, he handed the microphone to Dale Brown, who spoke so emotionally about Mark that many in the audience were left in tears. "As soon as Coach was done, he was so caught up in the moment that he came to us and told us to stay in St. Louis as long as was necessary," Costello said. "I'll never forget it. He said, 'Just make this boy happy.'" The dinner was on Sunday afternoon. Costello, Campbell and Bergeron went to the Alcorns' home that night and stayed up late talking with Mark. They remained in St. Louis until Tuesday, when they hopped a late flight back to Baton Rouge.

Less than a month after the benefit in St. Louis, a group of Baton Rouge leaders decided to host "Mark Alcorn Day," which included another fundraising dinner in Louisiana's capital. Alcorn's parents, still financially strapped despite the $24,000 raised at DeSmet, were hoping to schedule Mark for special treatment at the M. D. Anderson Hospital in Houston and the Simington Clinic in Fort Worth, two of the nation's preeminent cancer clinics. The Baton Rouge dinner raised $43,000, but, according to his father, Mark almost didn't attend.

"I couldn't figure out why he didn't want to go," the elder Alcorn told the *St. Louis Post-Dispatch*. "Then he told me, 'I'll have to speak and they'll all be clapping.' He wasn't into that. I said they probably will, but I said let's reverse the situation. Let's assume you are giving, not taking. You can go down there and you may be able to touch somebody and maybe this is God's way of letting you spread the gospel." Mark went to his room and started packing.

Then, as can happen in the emotional game of basketball, a little-used guard became the rallying point for an immensely talented team. LSU continued on its roll and received an invitation to the NCAA tournament. The Tigers knocked off Lamar, then drubbed Arkansas—the team that beat them in Alaska the day Mark became too ill to dress—before beating Wichita State for a berth in the Final Four.

Mark was on the bench during the regional final win over the Shockers, having been invited there by the team. To be there, Alcorn asked his St. Louis physician, Dr. Shabbir H. Sadfar, to postpone surgery for the removal of two tumors behind his sternum. By that time, Alcorn had undergone four chemotherapy treatments in three months. Sadfar told reporters that progress had been "remarkable" and that some of the cancer had been eradicated. He said the delay in surgery was possible because the powerful doses of chemicals Mark took had reduced the two tumors on his sternum from the size of a man's fist to the size of a silver dollar.

After the Wichita State game, a pale, weakened Alcorn mustered the strength to climb a ladder, reach high and clip the final cord of net in the Superdome. "That was great. That's the greatest moment of my life," he said, stepping down from the ladder as 34,036 fans cheered. "That's the best feeling I've ever had."

When the Tigers won the regional and headed to the Final Four to face Indiana, the team asked Alcorn once again to join them on their bench. Sadfar agreed to postpone the surgery once more and Alcorn's battle became part of Final Four lore. The United States Basketball Writers Association presented him with its annual Most Courageous Athlete Award. "Here's a man who walks on earth like a man," Dale Brown said as he introduced Mark to the awards luncheon crowd. But for Alcorn, the award was bittersweet. The Tigers were dumped 67-49 by the Hoosiers and went on to lose to Virginia in the consolation game. "All year long, I felt like if they could win their battle and I could win mine, it would be a perfect season," Alcorn told the sportswriters group.

Neither was meant to be. In the quiet of a September Sunday evening, not long before he went to the M. D. Anderson Hospital for his final all-out assault on the malignant cells that were rapidly multiplying in his body, Mark scribbled a four-page letter to God. The letter expressed faith, hope and trust. He asked for wisdom and he asked that God be with his parents and sisters.

He ended the barely legible letter: "I know You love me. Lord, I am a strong person. You made me that way. I won't quit because I know You won't quit."

Mark Alcorn didn't quit. Just three days after telling his mother he believed he was going to win his fight, he died peacefully in his sleep at home. His father was holding his hand. On the shelf above him was the basketball from LSU's blowout of Tulane and the net from the regional finals.

Given 90 days to live, Mark Alcorn had fought for nearly 14 months. He was 23 years old.

Costello still hasn't forgiven the NCAA for its callous response to a dying athlete's desires. "I had a hard time understanding their position," he said a decade later. "This was a guy that people should want their kids to grow up to be like. And when he needed friends, they made us break rules to be there. That's wrong."

Others involved in the fundraiser still harbor strong resentment about the NCAA's interpretation of its rule. "Whoever said no when Dale called the NCAA is a horse's ass," said Bob Costas, who has become one of the nation's hottest sportscasters. "I find that decision unfathomable. It is the emphasis on those ticky-tacky rules that destroys the NCAA's credibility. There are things that happen in the real world that require an organization like the NCAA to show some flexibility. To not do so is disgusting."

And Dale Brown, long a critic of college sport's governing body, made the Mark Alcorn story his rallying cry against NCAA rules. "That turned me so off to the whole organization, that you can't even implement human dignity in death, " he said. "They didn't punish us, but they made us 'cheat'—and I put that word in quotes—to do something that was good and decent. What we did isn't cheating in anyone's eyes but theirs."

NCAA staff, while admitting its decision appears callous, hid behind its standard "we-don't-make-the-rules-we-just-implement-them" defense.

"It may be perceived by the people who are aware of the situation to be a lack of compassion," NCAA Associate Executive Director Steve Morgan explained when asked about the Alcorn case by television reporter John Camp. "There are all kinds of emotional situations and this one obviously is one that would evoke compassion from anybody in the hearing of the story that you have this terminally ill student who needs help and wants his buddies to come help him. And then the public sees—they see this terminally ill kid and ask what kind of heartless people are involved in the NCAA. That's the general perception of it. And unfortunately, those of us on the staff who have the responsibility of trying to answer these questions as to how the rules apply to given situations and providing advice, unfortunately a part of our job is to provide the hard answers to those questions."

"Someday, their interpretation of rules like that is going to come back to haunt them," Costas said. "Someday it will."

THE NCAA: JUST SAY NO

Missy Conboy pulled into a service station about two miles from the Notre Dame campus during the summer of 1988, and noticed a Fighting Irish basketball player standing in the rain. His car had been towed in for service. Conboy, a former NCAA investigator who is now assistant athletic director at Notre Dame, considered offering the young man a ride. Then she decided not to. It wasn't that she lacked compassion. She just knew it was against NCAA rules. "I would have done that for any other student I know," she said. "But I had to drive on by."

Such is life in the NCAA, where the same rules that say you can't buy a kid a car also say you can't offer him a ride to campus from the gas station. A quick glance through the 400-page *NCAA Manual* provides ample evidence that this is an organization with more rules than Robert. Lots of rules—numerous, byzantine and often just plain silly rules. They cover the gamut from player bribery to the number of colors a school can use in its recruiting brochures. "If it sounds good and it's probably going to benefit a student-athlete, 99 percent of the time it's illegal," said former NCAA investigator Ron Watson, who is now assistant athletic director at the University of Oklahoma.

Who's to blame for the frivolous rules? NCAA members themselves. The rules are proposed, voted on and passed by NCAA member schools in an effort to create a "level playing field" among a diverse group of colleges and universities that often shouldn't even be in the same stadium.

The motive behind the rules is often mistrust or jealousy of competitors. "The problem is that the membership has philosophically wanted everybody to be playing by the same criteria," said former NCAA president Wilford Bailey of Auburn University. "You'll never have a flat playing field. You just keep putting in more and more rules. As [NCAA Executive Director] Dick Shultz has said, there has to be more trust among ourselves and a commitment to be fair and honest without having to be forced into that."

As it is, coaches and others in athletic departments face a vast array of frustrating situations. For example:

■   The University of Oklahoma displays only one copy of *Sooner Illustrated* in the lobby of its football offices. That copy is marked "office copy" in large, black letters. Other copies are hidden, the receptionist says, because they might fall into the hands of a football recruit, an accident that would be an NCAA violation.

■   Another time, Notre Dame's Conboy offered a ride to an athlete's parent, not realizing she was driving the parent to an event the athlete would participate in. That is an NCAA violation. "It hit me as soon as it happened," she said. "I turned myself in." She received a letter of reprimand from the NCAA for the incident. "When you're out here in the real world, you see a lot more of the impractical aspects of the rules," the former investigator said.

■   University of Georgia Athletic Director Vince Dooley, who also was the Bulldogs' football coach until 1989, was told he could not go watch his son in a high school all-star game because the game was being played during a period when coaches are not permitted to have contact with prospective student-athletes. NCAA rules provide for no exceptions. "I don't think anybody that voted on that rule would have said it was intended to keep a father from watching his son play in an all-star game," said

Dooley, who had to watch the game on television from an Atlanta hotel.

"The problem with the NCAA is the rules and regulations are drawn up in the legislative process," said Eamon Kelly, Tulane University president. "You have the same problems that you have in Congress. No one seems to acknowledge that someone always will get away with something. Accepting that is the cost of doing business. In attempting to draw rules and regulations through that process, some foolishness gets built in."

The conventions themselves can seem pretty foolish. Read what respected *Atlanta Journal-Constitution* columnist Furman Bisher had to say after attending the NCAA's 1990 convention: "I have just come from the second most frightening experience of this decade, and the last one, too. The San Francisco earthquake was first. I've been in Dallas watching the legislators of college athletics doing their legislation. It's like watching palsy take effect. It's a wonder, my fellow Americans, that any college team ever gets to the field, considering the plodding of their leaders. Those that do get to the field need an interpreter to keep them legal and the rules translated. They preach and moan about cost reduction. Then they send six or seven delegates here to do what two, three tops, could handle. Some are sent here who mainly stand around, it seems.

"You can expect a state legislature to foul up parliamentarian stuff, for a lot of them never saw the inside of a classroom," Bisher wrote. "They have to leave the filling station or the lumber mill or the cotton gin to go to the state capitol and legislate. But here are guys who read Shakespeare and go to concerts. Well, there was this proposal, No. 38, allowing certain academically borderline athletes, nonqualifiers they are called, to work in a fourth year of eligibility through a loophole slyly introduced by the Big West Conference. If passed, it would in effect undo Prop 48, that embattled legislation from 1983 in San Diego that upgraded academic standards. Darned if it didn't pass.

"Nobody caught it until about an hour later when a delegate from Washington State called for reconsideration. Great howls of grief and surprise arose, for truly, several delegates had been napping or not paying attention. Frankly, they weren't sure what they'd voted for. 'This is sending a disastrous message to high school athletes,' Thomas Hearn, Wake Forest's president, cried.

'Since Prop 48 came in, grade averages of our recruits have gone up markedly,' Penn State football coach Joe Paterno said. They voted again. No. 38 bit the dust. There was a swing of 126 votes. It might have been laughable if it hadn't come so close to slipping through a crack."

Despite constant haranguing from NCAA members about the organization's overabundance of rules, they come to conventions every year willing to pass additional restrictions within which they cannot live. The last three conventions of the 1980s saw NCAA members debate an average of 146 new rules a year. The result: an *NCAA Manual* that was a mere 25-page brochure in 1952 now fills 400 8-1/2-by-11-inch pages. And it's still growing.

Debate on all those rules can, and often does, become tedious. Reporters at the 1989 convention amused themselves by counting the number of times University of Arkansas Athletic Director Frank Broyles dozed off to sleep. When the count had reached six, the legendary coach was roused for good by a thunderous applause. The reason for the applause? Someone asked that debate on an issue be limited.

In this convention setting—a room filled with two thousand bored, mostly graying, middle-class, white males—rules are passed that affect the lives of student-athletes—a group of young and, in the case of the "money sports," mostly black males. "No wonder the rules read as they do," former Marquette basketball coach Al McGuire said. Every NCAA meeting, McGuire once said, "should be held in a fourth floor tenement house in Brooklyn." Even NCAA insiders question the ability of such a diverse and diverted group to provide intelligent leadership in the tumultuous world of intercollegiate athletics. "I'm concerned that our membership comes [to the convention] not as informed as it could be or should be, that we don't take a serious look at elements of legislation that have far-ranging effects," said Southeastern Conference Commissioner Roy Kramer, a member of the powerful Committee on Infractions.

Duquesne University Athletic Director Brian Colleary said the doldrums of NCAA business is often the reason the organization "passes so many bad rules. The truth is, a lot of these rules have gotten through because you get a thousand guys in a hot room listening to boring debate. Then they call for a vote and the guy next to you holds up his [voting] paddle, so you hold up yours. You don't have any idea what it means."

The situation is even more confusing once the convention is over. That's when it becomes the responsibility of NCAA staff to begin interpreting the meaning of the new rules. That's also when the unelected staff exerts great influence over the organization's membership.

"You want to buy a kid a Christmas present, a kid you know well on a personal basis," said Lonny Rose, a University of Miami sports law professor. "You can't because that's a violation. Now, who makes that rule? The schools vote on that rule, but how that rule is interpreted is a legislative services or enforcement decision. What the schools actually voted on were no extra benefits. It was the staff that decided that a Christmas gift was an extra benefit. It is an interpretation of the rule. Those are decisions made administratively. I think the NCAA should be like the federal government. Whenever it decides it is going to issue a regulation which interprets a law passed by Congress, it should put it out for public comment for 60 days. Say this is the rule and this is how we're going to enforce it. Who is going to be in a better position to comment on how things will be practically received than the people who are being asked to comply?"

"You want to talk about unbridled authority?" asked former NCAA investigator J. Brent Clark. "You've got a kid fresh from law school who's got an *NCAA Manual* and 48 hours later, he's giving interpretations." That authority grew immensely in 1989. The NCAA Council, in a decision that still is unknown to many members, agreed that the extra-benefits rule—which prohibits giving anything to a student-athlete that is not given to the entire student body—can now be extended for the life of the athlete. "Cradle to grave enforcement," a member of the Council called the ruling, which states that if a coach or booster gives a former student-athlete anything he wouldn't give anyone off the street, it will now be an NCAA violation.

"We probably have 15,000 former student-athletes around the country," said University of Nevada–Las Vegas Assistant Athletic Director Mark Warkentein. "And now we have to worry about any of them getting anything that might in any way be construed to have been given to them because they were a student-athlete. That's impossible to control. How can the NCAA realistically expect that?"

UNLV officials didn't learn of the NCAA's new authority

until it asked whether a member of the school's athletic staff could help a former basketball recruit, who had gone on to play in the Continental Basketball Association and thus had no college eligibility left, pay for dental expenses. No, the NCAA said. "Bylaw 16.12.2.2.1 precludes an athletics department staff member from providing student-athletes with professional services without charge or at a reduced cost," NCAA Legislative Analyst Richard Perko wrote in a letter. He added, "Please note the NCAA Council recently confirmed that the extra-benefit rule applies to those individuals who have exhausted intercollegiate athletics eligibility, as well as to current student-athletes."

Rick Evrard, NCAA director of legislative services, admits this opens a whole new can of potential worms for the NCAA to investigate. If the NCAA can prove that former football player A got a good deal from booster/auto dealer B even 20 years after player A graduated, it could be an NCAA violation. "Difficult to prove—well, yeah, I think that's correct," Evrard said. "The standard is a tough standard, there's no question about it. The principle of the NCAA and the membership that has voted on these rules is that they don't want inducements given to prospective student-athletes, nor do they want extra benefits to be conferred upon student-athletes. And that does extend beyond the point that the student is enrolled in the institution. The primary reason is there's no real difference between the day I graduate from college and two days after I graduate from college. And if I'm permitted to give a car and expenses and whatever I want three days after graduation—or three years after graduation— is that the same as three days before, when they're still a student-athlete? The ruling is that it is."

Some argue the real problem with the rules is that the NCAA's interpretation of them is always changing. "Call up there sometime," said former University of Florida basketball coach Norm Sloan. "I have done it numerous times. Get one of the interpreters on the legislative side. Call back the next day, and get somebody else. You will get an entirely different response. Same question, same group, entirely different response. I have done that time and time again."

Others say the problem with the rules is that the rules themselves are always changing. Penn State football coach Joe Paterno, one of the shining examples used in the argument that winning does not require cheating, tells an amusing story about a 1988 College Football Association meeting he attended. During the convention, the leaders of 64 major college football programs were debating what position the group should take on recruiting rules at the next NCAA convention. "I spoke up and said we should go from six visits at the high school to three," Paterno told the *Orlando Sentinel*. "It got real quiet. Then someone says, 'Joe, we just got it back to three.' "

That "contact" rule that confused Paterno, in fact, had changed in each of the four previous NCAA conventions. "I've nearly been in a jam with the rules a few times," Paterno said. "From our end, we change the rules so much, we don't give people a chance to adjust. Maybe instead of those 30-second TV spots they do on each college [during televised football and basketball games] saying how great we are, they could have a spot on the rules."

The NCAA's Evrard dismissed complaints that rules change too often as "a copout." Paterno took issue: "It's not a copout; it's absolute fact," he said. "I think people have a legitimate gripe."

Whether it is the rules or the interpretation of those rules that is changing, there is little doubt most remain confused by the NCAA's guidelines. A 1986 Associated Press quiz given to the football coaches of the Top 20 teams in the nation underscored the scope of that confusion. The 10-question quiz, AP noted, came straight out of the NCAA rule book. Coaches from 18 of the top 20 teams participated. None scored 100 percent. Most missed three or four questions. Two missed five. One missed six. Basketball coaches aren't much more well-versed. "If you want to read and understand their rule book, you can't just be any lawyer," said Abe Lemons, the colorful former coach of the University of Texas and Oklahoma City University. "You've got to be a lawyer at the top of your class. Hell no, I wouldn't say I knew all the rules." Added Virginia Commonwealth basketball coach Sonny Smith, "No one can follow the book. It is just too complicated."

The coaches most affected by NCAA rules don't know them. The athletes who stand to lose their eligibility if they stray from those rules don't know them, either. In 1989, the *Orlando Sentinel* conducted a 23-question quiz on NCAA rules with the nation's top 100 high school football and basketball players. The average score was 62.5 percent, an F in most college courses. There wasn't one of the questions that all 100 athletes got correct.

Some of the more inexplicable rules are proposed by smaller schools, trying to curb the financial advantages held by their larger counterparts. Others are directed at specific incidents that one or more schools found unfair. D. Alan Williams, chairman of the NCAA Committee on Infractions and a history professor at the University of Virginia, recalls one such situation. Shortly after Ralph Sampson began playing basketball at Virginia, stand-ups, or life-sized photographs, of players became popular, he said. "The next thing you know, we've got a seven-foot brochure with Ralph Sampson," Williams said. "Then Clemson comes up with a thing of the Fridge [football player William Perry]. What happens next is every recruit comes in and there on the wall is Number 89 in all his glory. First thing you know, every recruit wants his own poster and it's costing you $180,000."

Afraid that some schools would begin featuring their players in promotional posters as a recruiting inducement, others promoted legislation. NCAA rules now limit the types of printed materials recruits can receive, allowing only one color printing inside brochures and press guides. "There are a lot of rules that get in because one conference or one small segment can't handle it, so we end up with a national rule," Williams said.

"Many of the rules are written for a specific incident rather than a national problem," said former investigator Doug Johnson, now associate athletic director at the University of Miami. "The poster rule is a good example. Little schools didn't like the fact that big schools had great four-color posters that they could use in recruiting. So they made a rule."

"I personally would like to get a lot of that stuff out altogether," Williams said. "They're silly, and they're in there because coaches don't trust each other. I remember another example of a UVA coach saying another school got his recruit because they had a soft ice cream machine in the dorm. Our coach wanted a rule against ice cream machines."

Still other concerns generate more rules. "A college can't advertise in a high school program or even in a high school all-star program," Williams said. "Why? Because [high] schools were blackmailing—charging high rates and demanding advertising in exchange for access to recruits."

"We in the NCAA believe that every problem has a solution," said Tulane's President Kelly. "And when you've got a problem, you pass a law to correct that problem. The fact of the matter is, certain infractions and mistakes are small enough that it is not worth passing a law to correct them."

In the end, the goal of creating a level playing field can never be achieved, said Thomas J. Niland, Jr., Le Moyne College athletic director and a member of the infractions committee for nine years. "It is one of the basic premises of life that you can't legislate equality," he said. "You can legislate fairness, but not equality. Because no matter what rule you change, some people will be given an advantage. There is some difficulty in trying to make legislation which affects so many people who are unalike."

The only group that benefits from this plethora of rules is the NCAA's enforcement staff. Because the rules are so pervasive and touch nearly every facet of campus life, they ensure that an investigator can find at least a little dirt under any school's rug. "Give me six weeks, and I can get any college in the nation on probation," former investigator Clark said. This provides the NCAA with the "Al Capone" enforcement advantage, he said, referring to the federal government's decision to prosecute the famed gangster on tax evasion despite its knowledge that he was guilty of greater sins. "Everyone is guilty—there are only varying degrees of guilt," Clark said. "So if you can't get a school for a major violation, you just get them for a bunch of minor ones and say that shows the school is out of control."

"Every institution has probably violated some rule," agreed former investigator Mike Garnes, who left the NCAA in 1987 and now helps schools create programs to avoid major rules violations. "In most cases, though, it was unintentional violations."

But knowingly breaking rules is a problem that feeds on itself, said Oklahoma's Watson, a former NCAA investigator. "The problem is, we have allowed television revenues and we've allowed bowl money to escalate at such a rapid pace that, all of the sudden, the importance of these rules fades," Watson said. "Too much emphasis is on the almighty dollar. We've let the win-loss record, the going to bowls, the number of times you're on TV become more important than being ethical. Once you break one [rule] and you don't feel too bad about that, you go a little further."

Former Sooners coach Barry Switzer differentiates between improper benefits offered by coaching staffs and those provided by boosters without the staff's knowledge. He said the latter violation may happen more frequently, but is harder to control. "When I played, and I needed new tires for my car, I went to the guy who would sell it to me at cost because he liked the program," Switzer said. "It happens in every city in the U.S. where football is king. There are those places where football players know where to go and get done what they need to do."

"I think there are a lot of places that operate under the 'What you don't know, won't hurt you,' what I call the 'blinders attitude,'" said Butch Worley, a former NCAA investigator who is now assistant to the athletic director at the University of Texas.

Others suggest looking for crafty ways around the rules. One Southern Methodist University supporter, Galveston attorney David McCormack, suggested that SMU could have used a loophole approach to avoid the "death penalty" its football program received for paying players. Created during a 1985 special convention, the death penalty rule allows the NCAA to terminate a sports program if a school is found in violation of NCAA rules twice in five years.

The key to McCormack's theory is an NCAA rule that allows a student to be a professional in one sport and an amateur in another. For example, Deion Sanders earned $60,000 playing professional baseball for the New York Yankees in 1988, then returned to Florida State University to play "amateur" college football. "The NCAA is an association who has promulgated these rules to maximize their profit," said McCormack.

"The SMU football team could have been made into a pro soccer team during the summer," providing a legal avenue for the players to receive money, McCormack said. "There are certainly legitimate ways of circumventing the guidelines. To me, that [rule] exposes the whole illogical nature of their system."

WINNERS AND LOSERS

From behind the half-court line, Mike O'Hara let sail with the last shot. The buzzer sounded just as the ball left his hands. The small crowd at Chicago's Rosemont Horizon watched, as 53 feet away, O'Hara's shot ripped nothing but net. The crowd roared its approval. O'Hara thrust his fist in the air. Victory.

What a story. A 19-year-old kid who once was cut from his high school freshman basketball team is one of three fans picked from the crowd at a college basketball game six years later. He makes five shots—a layup, a free throw, a 20-footer from the top of the key and half-court shots of 47 and 53 feet—in a 45-second halftime contest. His bounty: a case of Pepsi, a Loyola University sweatshirt, a pizza, two airline tickets and a little ol' $20,000 car. A red convertible Ford Mustang GT, to be precise. Stop the presses. This is the kind of stuff America loves to read.

"You have to admit, it was pretty incredible," O'Hara said. And you have to admit that what happened later was incredibly stupid. O'Hara, you see, wasn't just an ordinary fan sitting in the stands that night dressed in street clothes. He happened to be one of the 250,000 college athletes who live each year under NCAA rules. Now he wasn't a basketball player, mind you. He wasn't even a student at Loyola. He was just, as his father said, an "average runner" on the Marquette University track team who decided to attend a basketball game with his brother while he was home for Christmas vacation in January 1990.

O'Hara's euphoria didn't last long. "I got home that night and I told my father about it," the Marquette sophomore said. "He sensed that something bad was going to happen. He said people that win the lottery and stuff, they always end up, like, being miserable. He told me not to get too caught up in it. He was right."

The next morning, the phone rang at the O'Hara residence in Lombard, Illinois, a Chicago suburb. It was answered by Mike's father, Tom O'Hara, an Olympic star who held the world indoor mile record in 1963. It was Tat Shiely, Marquette's women's athletic coordinator and the school's compliance officer for NCAA rules. Shiely had read about Mike's haul in the Milwaukee morning papers. There was a little problem. By winning the contest, Mike had just violated NCAA rules and was now ineligible to run at Marquette. Not a good way to start your morning.

"I asked if there was anything I could do and was told that if I gave it all back, everything would probably be all right," Mike said. Talk about a tough choice. Mike, who was only on a partial scholarship at Marquette, had to pick between a $20,000 sports car and three more years of long practices, little fanfare and hard work. He chose the latter. "I love to run," O'Hara said. "I know it sounds crazy. But it's pretty simple."

What wasn't simple was understanding why the NCAA would care if a guy who runs the mile in 4:15 might be so lucky ("That's all it was, luck," he said) that he would hit five shots in 45 seconds. The contest was so difficult and the odds so astronomical that auto dealer Jerry Gleason, who sponsored the contest at all Loyola home games, was almost sure he'd never have to pay up. "We have insurance, Lloyd's and hole-in-one type of insurance," Gleason told the *Chicago Tribune*. "But that isn't supposed to happen."

Buried in the *NCAA Manual* —page 66, to be precise—is a rule that states that "the receipt of a prize in a promotional contest held in conjunction with a member institution's intercollegiate competition by a prospective or enrolled student-athlete" is prohibited, unless "in the case of a Division I or Division II student-athlete, no athletic ability" is required. But O'Hara was a runner at Marquette and the contest was sponsored by Loyola. Why would that be a violation? Because having won the contest, O'Hara might now transfer to Loyola, making him a "prospective" Loyola athlete, NCAA officials said.

"I understand they don't want a basketball player going to half court and winning a car," O'Hara said. "But I didn't even make my freshman team in high school. I've never played basketball on a team. I understand, but I think it's stupid. They say the rules are to keep us [athletes] from getting things that other students can't get. Anybody in that arena could have been chosen. I don't know what my athletic ability had to do with it. Like I said, I was just lucky. I was, really, penalized for being a student-athlete."

As promised, O'Hara showed up at Loyola the next day and handed over the keys to the car, the airline tickets, the sweatshirt and the pizza coupon. He had a little problem with the case of pop. After the game, he and a few friends polished off half the case. But he gave back what was left. Marquette still was forced to rule him ineligible. The rules say he was in violation simply for having participated in the contest. That penalty lasted only a week, though, before he could begin running again.

"I can see where they need rules in college sports," O'Hara said. "But this didn't make much sense."

Funny, Steve Hollar said almost the exact same thing three years earlier. Hollar was a guard for the Division III DePauw Tigers basketball team when he learned the price of fame. For him, it was $632 and a week's worth of headlines and headaches. Hollar, a starting guard for Warsaw High School's Indiana state championship team, accepted an offer to play for the Tigers, despite the fact that Division III schools offer no athletic scholarships.

But before his freshman year began, he heard Hollywood's call. Hollar, along with DePauw teammate Griff Mills, read that casting directors had come to Indiana seeking bit players for the movie *Hoosiers*. The two tried out, as did dozens of other starstruck hopefuls. Hollar, a solid player and a clean-cut kid, wowed the moviemakers. He landed a major role as Rade Butcher of Hickory High School. Mills was fortunate, but a little less so. He was hired—at minimum wage for an afternoon's work—as an extra, appearing in the movie for about three seconds.

Everything was just fine until the box-office hit was previewed in Greencastle, Indiana, the quaint little college town where DePauw is located. Promotional advertisements encouraged the town to show up and see one of its own on the big screen. Then, like Big Brother, came the call from the NCAA. Go ahead and enjoy the popcorn, the NCAA said, because the movie is going to give you heartburn. An NCAA rule, DePauw officials were told, says that any student-athlete who "has directly or indirectly used athletic skill for pay in that sport" must immediately be declared ineligible.

That left DePauw to prepare for the next night's Anderson College Invitational without Hollar and Mills. Further screening of the movie by the NCAA showed that Jim Rayl, an Indiana University–Purdue University at Fort Wayne freshman, Mike Ricks of Wabash (Indiana) College and Greg Eckstein, a Rollins (Florida) College player, also had flashed across the screen for a few moments. Ban them all, came the edict from the NCAA. Unless, of course, they want to return their paychecks.

For Mills, Ricks, Rayl and Eckstein, that wasn't so bad. Each earned less than $100. Hollar, on the other hand, had a little more at stake. As a "star" in the movie, Hollar had been paid in excess of $15,000. Either give it back, the NCAA told Hollar, or forget that nonscholarship spot you have on the basketball team. Hollar, and many others, were outraged. "I think it's a ridiculous ruling," DePauw coach Mike Steele told the *Indianapolis Star*. "I told 'em [the NCAA] we've got a Logic 101 class here that some of their people should be taking. I just don't think the NCAA is using common sense. I don't condone breaking rules. But in this instance, there was nothing malicious done on the part of the kids. In Steve's case, it was a great opportunity to appear in a major motion picture. All Griff was doing was killing time one afternoon."

Mills and the other bit players, after handing over their paychecks and sitting out a three-game suspension for their violative behavior, had their eligibility restored. But Hollar and his attorney, Thomas Lemon of Warsaw, argued that $15,000 was an awful steep price to pay. For more than a month, the NCAA left Hollar in limbo. Meanwhile, newspapers throughout the Midwest were lampooning the NCAA for its senseless handling of the case. Finally, an NCAA committee agreed that 95 percent of Hollar's time on the screen was as an actor and 5 percent was as a basketball player. Hence, the committee ordered Hollar to repay 5 percent of his actor's fee—$632. "We still don't consider Steve's action in violation of the spirit of the rule," Pat Aikman, DePauw's spokesman, said after Hollar agreed to the settlement. "But the NCAA felt otherwise."

"I guess you could say I'm pretty bummed right now," Hollar told the *Star*. "I'm just very disappointed. In my eyes, I did nothing wrong. Everything had been so neat until now. But this leaves a sour taste in my mouth."

Funny. Tracy Graham said almost the same thing a year

later. You couldn't find a better model for a student-athlete than Graham. She had led the Lancers of North Scott High in Eldridge, Iowa, to a state volleyball championship and two state championship runners-up in her three years. She was a third-team All-State basketball player and was a shot putter in track. Most importantly, she carried a 3.23 grade-point average through high school and scored a 25 when she took her ACT college entrance exam.

But it was that ACT test that got her in trouble. Not that anyone questioned her score, which was significantly higher than the NCAA-mandated 15 at the time. It was the fact she didn't take the test on an NCAA-mandated date. Graham, who had accepted a scholarship to play for Iowa State's volleyball team in the fall of 1987, was supposed to have taken her college boards in April. But North Scott High had a track meet that day, so she waited until July 20 to take the test. Big deal, she thought.

It was. Ignoring her other credentials, the NCAA decided to penalize Graham for her wanton disregard for its rules. Because she took the test on the wrong date, the NCAA ruled that Graham would be ineligible for her freshman year of volleyball. A whole year. They further demanded that she be prohibited from practicing or playing with a noncollegiate club team. The NCAA defended its position, arguing the rules required student-athletes to take the test on certain dates so it can "better monitor the results." The organization's Academic Requirements Committee had steadfastly denied appeals from others with similar sob stories. Graham would be no exception, the committee said. A letter from the NCAA Council informed her that the Council "has consistently refused to grant waivers for students taking the tests on other than [NCAA recognized] national testing dates." Two other NCAA committees, to which Graham pleaded her case, shot down her appeals as well.

The decision shocked even the most hardened NCAA cynic. Simply because Tracy Graham decided to participate in a high school track meet and delay taking her college entrance exam, she should be dropped from her college roster? "The fact this happened inadvertently, and the purpose of the [NCAA] Council is to help student-athletes, why in the world, if they have looked at the facts in this matter, would they not make a decision to make a waiver?" Iowa State Athletic Director Max Urick asked rhetorically. "It certainly doesn't take a bunch of experts to look at her records to see she is qualified. The integrity of the testing process is not being violated."

"It would seem easy for the NCAA to look at this case and see that a truly qualified student is being cheated of the chance to compete for an athletic team," Bill MacLachlan, women's volleyball coach at competing Drake University wrote in criticism of the NCAA. "I guess you have to get bailed out of jail by your coach, accept money from agents, or take illegal loans from coaches in order to be able to get your eligibility back."

MacLachlan's reference was to a string of NCAA decisions that had occurred in the months prior to Graham's loss of her eligibility. When Pitt football defensive back Teryl Austin admitted accepting $2,500 from agent Norby Walters, he was given a two-game suspension. Minnesota quarterback Rickey Foggie, who was loaned money for an airplane ticket to his grandmother's funeral from assistant coach Larry Beckish, received the same penalty. And Auburn quarterback Jeff Burger, who was bailed out of jail by assistant coach Pat Sullivan and later took a duck-hunting trip on a booster's airplane, avoided any penalty when he appealed his suspension to the NCAA Council. And Tracy Graham lost a year of eligibility?

It was such an embarrassment for the NCAA that Executive Director Dick Schultz—after initially pointing fingers at Graham's high school counselors for giving her bum advice—was forced to admit it was wrong. "On the one hand, we have a football player who takes money from an agent, but because he pays it back and sits out a game or two, he is allowed to play again," Schultz said in his address to the 1988 NCAA convention. "And on the other hand we have an honor student who isn't allowed to play. That doesn't make sense."

At that convention, delegates passed another rule, this one empowering the NCAA Council to make exceptions in eligibility cases where an athlete's superior academic record warrants such action. They called it the "Tracy Graham Rule." When the Council met to hear Graham's case, it agreed to restore her lost year of eligibility. But the season was already over.

"We're just sick about this," Julie Graham, an instructor at Marycrest College, said of her daughter's predicament.

Graham isn't the only student-athlete to have an NCAA rule named for her. Former Indiana University basketball star Steve Alford was trapped in an infamous NCAA snafu at a most critical time. Alford, when asked by two members of an IU sorority to pose for a charity calendar, agreed to be Mr. February. "This is strictly a charitable thing," Alford quoted the girls as saying in his book, *Playing for Knight*. "All the money goes to a specialized camp for handicapped girls."

"I gave it a few seconds' thought," Alford wrote in the book. "Charity? Handicapped girls? Sure, why not? It's not against the rules, is it?"

Not specifically.

NCAA rules do prohibit athletes from posing for any picture or film that would be used for commercial purposes. No endorsements, in other words. But that rule had been interpreted by the NCAA to extend to charity work, as well. Ignorant of that interpretation, Alford fulfilled his promise to pose for the calendar. The calendar went on sale the next fall and, as the Hoosiers were preparing for a nationally televised showdown with archrival Kentucky, the error of Alford's ways became known. The NCAA suspended Alford for one game—the Kentucky contest—sparking letters of protest from Bloomington, Indiana, to Bloomington, Minnesota. How could they suspend a kid like Steve Alford for helping handicapped girls?

"The NCAA in some instances, and this is one, absolutely amazes me," IU coach Bobby Knight said after his team, sans Alford, lost to Kentucky, 63-58. "They worry about their image, and they're concerned about how people fail to understand what the NCAA responsibility is; and yet they have absolutely no machinery to look into what was the intent of the violation of the rule. There was a mix-up in communication that led to a violation of the rule. My fault with the NCAA is with their not being able to look at this and say, 'Here's a mistake that nobody intended to make, that in no way benefited anyone except some kids who were in need of something in the summer,' and leave it go at that. That just absolutely amazes me. Apparently the Eligibility Committee of the NCAA looked at this and decided in their infinite wisdom that Alford had not taken sufficient steps to prevent this from happening. Yet this same NCAA had asked Steve to appear in a drug-abuse ad for them, again taking his own time to do that."

The next year, at the NCAA convention, outraged members passed the "Alford Rule," which allows student-athletes to be pictured in charitable money-makers like calendars. The same anger led to the passage of a rule explicitly permitting universities to pay for student-athletes to attend the funeral of a teammate. That rule grew out of an NCAA interpretation claiming the University of Alabama had broken the "entertainment off campus" rule by rerouting its charter team flight from an away football game so that the team could pay respects to the Tide's Willie Ryles. "How could the NCAA even think of looking for a violation in Alabama's actions?" *Sports Illustrated* asked. "'Transportation to a funeral is not one of the permissible expenses an institution can provide a student-athlete,' explained an NCAA source."

The entire North Carolina State basketball team, after winning the 1983 national championship, learned how unyielding NCAA rules could be. The day after the underdog Wolfpack defeated Houston's Cougars, President Reagan invited the entire squad to the White House. Coach Jim Valvano accepted. Hold on a minute, unpack your bags, the NCAA told Valvano's players. That trip to the White House would be excessive transportation since an NCAA rule prohibited an institution from paying for its student-athletes to travel more than 100 miles from campus. Never mind that college athletics is supposed to be about education and there aren't many times in an educational experience that a student gets to meet the leader of the free world. NC State appealed. The NCAA said no again.

The rejection prompted Capitol Broadcasting Corporation, owner of a Raleigh television station, to offer its help in paying for the $118-per-player roundtrip tickets. If NC State can't pay for the players to go, who's to stop a private company from donating the airline tickets to the school? The NCAA, that's who. The offer had to be turned down, the NCAA said, because it would be a violation no matter who picked up the tab. All remedies gone, NC State settled for a television satellite hookup where Reagan spoke to the team. The 10-minute satellite feed, which was donated by Capitol Broadcasting within the rules, cost $6,000— about $4,300 more than it would have cost to fly the 14-member team to Washington. North Carolina State Chancellor Bruce Poulton, who said he was "truly disappointed" with the NCAA's handling of the matter, led a floor vote at the 1984 convention changing the rule for future champions.

Nightmarish tales like these could fill volumes. Some have caught the public's attention and raised a few eyebrows. Many have not. But each time a ludicrous application of NCAA rules makes the news, it leaves a lot of people asking a lot of questions. Doesn't the NCAA have anything better to do? Doesn't it have any means of rationally weighing the special circumstances surrounding certain violations of a rule book most cannot understand? Why should it take media coverage and public pressure to get the NCAA to step down from on high and rescind some of these rulings? How can the NCAA, in good conscience, make these kinds of judgments? Were these really the results the NCAA members wanted when they passed these rules? If so, all hope truly is lost. If not, students must hope more reasonable interpretations are on the way.

STUDENT-ATHLETES: WHO'S CHEATING WHOM?

The only group without a voice in college athletics is the group that makes it all possible—the student-athletes. This group, the arms and legs and beating hearts of the big business of college sports, must live by the NCAA's incongruous rules, yet has no say in their passage. Students are caught in the middle, some say exploited, by a system they can only watch.

That exploitation is best exemplified by the NCAA's continuous defense of the notion that student-athletes are amateurs participating in amateur sports and thus should live within rules restricting their employment and even the value of gifts they can receive from nonfamily members. At the same time, the organization signed a $1-billion network television contract for broadcast rights to its basketball tournament.

"The NCAA is thought of by the public as an organization doing everything it can for the athlete," said Dick DeVenzio, a former Duke All-America basketball player who now is trying to organize athletes and gain a voice in the NCAA. "Nothing can be further from the truth. The NCAA is there to maximize profits."

Those profits have enriched coaches, university athletic departments and even those connected with the NCAA, which grossed more than $98 million in revenues in 1989-90, according to its financial statements. *$98 million*. Those revenues allow the NCAA to offer its top executives a benefit package that includes no-cost rented cars and no-interest or low-interest home mortgages. The NCAA began leasing autos in the early 1980s, Chevrolet Caprice Classics at one point, for the executive director, four associate executive directors and eight assistant executive directors. The benefits package for NCAA staff also includes free legal advice, the cost of which is built into the organization's $1-million-plus annual legal tab. And they get free entrance to NCAA championship events, which at times can be the hottest tickets in America. NCAA committee members fly first class to meetings, stay in the very best hotels and are sometimes treated to free entertainment provided by sports-related interests trying to woo their business, according to Louis J. Spry, NCAA controller and associate executive director. If a committee member elects to fly coach, the NCAA pays him $100 in extra travel expenses to supplement the $30-per-day annual meeting expenses. Of course, that expense money doesn't include lodging at meeting places in San Francisco, San Diego, Dallas, Chicago, Kansas City, Hyannis, Massachusetts, or Monterey, California, among others. The NCAA picked up the lodging tab for those committee events. The organization spent almost $1.3 million to hold committee meetings across the country in its 1989 fiscal year.

NCAA executives are taken care of at home, as well, paying far less for mortgages than their neighbors. Former Executive Director Walter Byers's use of the no-interest loan program sparked quite a controversy when it became public knowledge in 1985. But Byers was outdone—or, rather, outspent—by his successor. According to public records, Dick Schultz and his wife, Jacquelyn, borrowed $260,000 from the NCAA when Schultz became executive director in 1987 to buy a home in Overland Park, Kansas. The interest rate: 6 percent, considerably lower than the typical mortgage rates at the time, which were between 10 and 11 percent. How big a deal is that? Consider: If it weren't for the fact the NCAA is so wealthy, Schultz would be paying the same as everyone else and his 10 percent mortgage would cost him $2,281.69 a month. But because of this sweetheart deal, Schultz's payments are $1,558.83 per month, mortgage lenders who reviewed the arrangement said.

After handing Schultz control of the organization he ran for 36 years, Byers began benefiting from another small-print clause in his contract—a noncompete deal that pays him $8,600 every year, as long as he doesn't accept another sports job. Byers had borrowed $80,000 against that contract in 1989, little more than two years after he retired, records show.

A $260,000 low-interest mortgage and first class flights apparently weren't enough for Schultz. In his first year as executive director, the NCAA took a $1.75-million loan to buy a jet, which was then sold to a private company and leased back to the association. Schultz gained approval for the transaction from the NCAA executive committee by contending that time and money would be saved over commercial air transportation by having his own jet. Subsequently, the NCAA employed a director of aviation—imagine, the NCAA with its own director of aviation—and budgeted more than a quarter of a million dollars for aircraft maintenance.

The NCAA's pilot? Schultz, who holds a commercial pilot's license. The jet's $1.7-million pricetag, some smaller college athletic directors noted very quietly during the 1990 NCAA convention, is four times larger than the entire athletic department budget of some Division I schools.

The NCAA doesn't merely use its financial largesse to please Schultz and his staff, it also uses its money to sway—and if that fails, to fight—its adversaries. In 1989, for example, the NCAA spent more than half a million dollars on "governmental affairs." With Congress considering (and eventually passing) a measure aimed at improving and making public the graduation rates of student-athletes, the NCAA hired lobbyists and went to Washington to make sure that the bill didn't include any diminution of its authority to regulate college sports. Then, as a continuation of that lobbying effort, they decided to bring Washington to the NCAA, providing an elegant Final Four buffet reception for those members of Congress who had accepted the NCAA's invitation to the basketball extravaganza in Seattle.

With all that money, it would seem inevitable the organization that polices college sports would eventually find itself under the microscope. The NCAA may now be facing its toughest opponent—the Internal Revenue Service. The U.S. Tax Court ruled in 1989 that the NCAA should have paid taxes on income from program advertising in 1982—a case that, of course, the NCAA has appealed to the U.S. Circuit Court of Appeals. Meanwhile, the IRS is auditing the NCAA's books for 1986, 1987 and 1988. While the NCAA continues to bask, for the moment, in its not-for-profit status, it parents two for-profit subsidiaries, the National Collegiate Realty Corporation and the NCAA Marketing Corporation. The realty arm held more than $7.4 million in land and property at the end of 1989.

And the organization devoted to ensuring that college athletes have not a donated dollar in their pockets or an illicitly provided shirt on their backs had more than $21 million in the bank, ready to spend, at the end of its fiscal year in August 1989. A private jet, first class travel, low-interest mortgage loans, noncompete contracts, leased automobiles—all are perks that might be expected for employees at private corporations. But these are benefits being enjoyed by employees of the NCAA—a not-for-profit organization formed to govern college sports. All while the rules say student-athletes must be limited to room, board, tuition, fees and books.

"The NCAA is looking out after the interest of athletic departments and their budgets," said Nebraska Senator Ernie Chambers, who has proposed several bills benefiting students in his state. "There's not one single rule that the NCAA has which is designed to benefit the athletes. There's only one that people can mention, and it's the one that says that a scholarship, as they call it, cannot be withdrawn for the school year for which it was granted, even if the athlete quits the team. That seems on the surface to be for the players, but it's not, because if the university were to lift a scholarship for any reason, it would then be considered income. It would be tied to performance and the ramification of that would be awesome to the NCAA. If the scholarship under those circumstances is income, then it must be paid and the relationship between the athlete and the school then is that of employer and employee, and you have a whole new set of problems with workers compensation and all the other things that tailgate on that. So rather than face that, the NCAA adopted a rule that sounds good for public relations. And, as a result, the scholarship will not be deemed by the IRS to be income. The whole assertion that an athlete should be treated like any other student is ridiculous. Think about it. Players are the only students that generate revenue rather than consume it. They are the only ones who are required to spend more time outside the classroom than in it on nonacademic subjects. They can be publicly humiliated by a coach, which would happen to no other student in a classroom. You have to draw the conclusion that every NCAA rule related to the players either places a burden on them that is not placed on other students, or takes away from them a right that other students have."

Added a more succinct Stanford University President Donald Kennedy, "The system, to be brief and blunt about it, reeks of exploitation."

NCAA Executive Director Schultz admits that the system created by the NCAA may not be best for college athletes. "I don't think there is any question that many times athletes are actually discriminated against," he said. "Most of the rules are put there to try to put the athlete in the same situation as the average student. But also, the rule sometimes becomes discriminatory because the athlete ends up not being treated the same way that a regular student would. I made this statement when I was a coach: You can't do for the athlete what you can do for the neighbor's kid next door. If I was driving from [the University of] Virginia to Richmond and there was a UVA student out there hitchhiking, I could pick that student up and give him a ride to Richmond, no sweat. But if I recognize an athlete hitchhiking to Richmond and it was purely legitimate and I stopped and picked that athlete up, I've provided illegal transportation. In a way that's silly."

In hopes of ridding the NCAA of some silly rules, Schultz proposed a Student-Athlete Advisory Committee to offer input on issues affecting players. "My concern was that many times, when the membership passed a rule that it believed was for the benefit of the student-athlete, it may not benefit the student-athlete at all and we should know how they feel about a number of these issues," Schultz said. "There are a lot of situations that come up, for example freshmen eligibility, length of the playing season, practice times. A lot of times the decision is made that if we do this, this will happen. It will give students more time. Well, maybe they don't want more time, maybe they do. It would be nice to know what their thoughts are. Do they think spring football is valuable or is it just a pain in the neck?"

But even Schultz's altruistic effort blew up in his face. The Student-Athlete Advisory Committee received its first invitation to the NCAA's convention in 1990. When debate turned to shortening the playing and practice seasons, the students decided it was time to offer input—which was, they were told, the reason they were invited. They chose Julie Zuraw, a women's basketball player at Division III Bryn Mawr College outside Philadelphia, to do their talking. But when Zuraw stepped to one of the 12 microphones situated in the Loews Anatole Hotel's massive ballroom, she wasn't recognized to speak. Moments later, an NCAA staffer asked her to sit down. Seems only credentialed delegates can get a word in and the students weren't delegates. "We were given a lot of encouragement in advance of the convention to speak out," Zuraw said. "Guess they just didn't want us to speak out when everybody was there together." So much for a student voice.

Inviting students to the convention, though, did provide an eye-opening experience of another sort. "This is a pretty expensive place," said Forrest Barnes, a basketball player from Division II Cal State–Pomona, as he surveyed the gold-plated landscape at the Loews Anatole. "It can't be cheap to bring all these people here." It wasn't. It wasn't cheap to run any previous NCAA convention either, all of which were held at expensive hotels. Here's the convention rundown from the 1980s:

1990	Loews Anatole, Dallas
1989	Downtown Hilton, San Francisco
1988	Opryland Hotel, Nashville
1987	Town & Country Resort, San Diego
1986	New Orleans Hilton, New Orleans
1985	Opryland Hotel, Nashville
1984	Loews Anatole, Dallas
1983	Town & Country Resort, San Diego
1982	Hyatt Regency, Houston
1981	Stouffers Riverfront, St. Louis (special convention)
1981	Fountainbleau Hilton, Miami Beach
1980	Fairmont, New Orleans

By questioning the great expense of making convention delegates comfortable, Barnes hit on at least one criticism often made by those who believe students should share in the wealth of college athletics. Athletic departments, coaches and the NCAA never seem to run out of money until the topic of giving students a piece of the pie comes up. And there is no way students will get a bite from that pie if they don't have any say in how it's cut, Dick DeVenzio and others say. "As blacks will tell you, whenever you're left out of the political process, you get screwed," DeVenzio said. "Major college revenue-producing athletes are exploited because they are too transient. They are too busy, too unorganized to do anything about their plight."

If the NCAA doesn't give students a say in college sports, it could be faced with renegade tactics such as those espoused by DeVenzio. Each year he writes players in an attempt to form an association similar to those representing the interests of coaches and athletic directors. He has repeatedly attempted to get players at major bowl or televised games to delay coming onto the field as a sign of unity. To date, his efforts have failed. But his work is starting to make headway as more and more big-name players are jumping on his bandwagon. "His message is in the crusade stages right now," Auburn wide receiver Lawyer Tillman said in 1987. "And a lot of us have been listening. If guys could hold up a nationally televised game for 10 minutes, just think what kind of effect that would have." Tillman hosted a meeting that year where he introduced DeVenzio to "40 or 50" other players. Others are starting to ask "the common sense questions," DeVenzio said. "There was a player at USC that I know who, when they went to the Rose Bowl, asked if he could stay at his apartment there in Los Angeles rather than at the Beverly Hilton Hotel, where the school was paying $240 a night for them to stay just a few miles away. He wanted the school to send his $240 a night to his mother, who was on welfare. The NCAA said that would be preposterous and against the rules."

Some believe the fact that many of the top athletes in football and basketball come from poverty-level backgrounds has allowed the NCAA to continue passing rules exploiting their talents. Those athletes haven't yet learned how to stand up for themselves. But that, too, could soon change. "I think one of our problems is we take so many student-athletes out of some difficult socioeconomic conditions and we put them in an atmosphere where they're living around and spending a lot of time around people who have the means to have the luxuries," said

Kansas Athletic Director Bob Frederick. "But all we do is provide them a place to live and meals, and they don't have anything else. The athletes are becoming more and more aware of that and are asking questions."

NCAA rules prohibit athletes from working when school is in session, from accepting work-study jobs available to other students and from accepting any kind of financial assistance not available to other students. NCAA rules even prohibit athletes from accepting part-time jobs even if they reject an athletic scholarship.

For example, in 1986 journalism major Terry Rodgers, son of legendary Nebraska Heisman Trophy winner Johnny Rodgers, considered turning down an athletic scholarship at Nebraska. The younger Rodgers planned to write a weekly column on Cornhusker football for United Press International, where he held an internship during the summer. UPI offered to pay him enough for the column that he wouldn't need to take a scholarship. So although he was recruited to Nebraska, he wanted to walk on and reject the scholarship offer.

But the NCAA told Rodgers he would be ineligible for the team if he accepted the UPI job and earned more than the $5,700 that an athletic scholarship was worth, Nebraska officials say. Rodgers turned down the job and took the athletic scholarship.

"He didn't want their money and was willing to let them give that scholarship to someone else," DeVenzio said. "But the NCAA said that by virtue of the fact he was 'recruited,' he couldn't make more than the cost of the scholarship. Their definition of 'recruited' means that he was contacted by a university. All he wanted to do was to go school on his own. What's the difference between him and Brooke Shields? She had made her million dollars and didn't need financial aid. He wasn't going to make a million dollars, but he would have made more than $5,700. And the NCAA told Terry Rodgers, 'If you want to play in our games, you've got to play by our rules.' That's absurd. Why should the NCAA have any policing function whatsoever regarding a player's economic opportunity? I don't know that they've ever been empowered to do that. I think it's a crime to limit someone's opportunity. The coaches haven't been limited. Shoot, the coaches get money for making a player wear a certain shoe."

Indeed, players see money all around them. From the coach

who earns $200,000 on a shoe contract (as Georgetown's John Thompson does from Nike), to the bowl game selection committees that spend $86,000 traveling the country to invite one team to one game (as the Orange Bowl did in 1988, the most recent year its tax returns were available); from the boosters who are spending hundreds of thousands of dollars to buy out coaches' contracts (as North Carolina did for football coach Dick Crum), to the universities that have begun selling corporate sponsorships of their home football games (as Georgia Tech does); from schools that have established their own television contracts (as Notre Dame did for some $30 million), to schools that are discussing the creation of megamarket superconferences in hopes of earning even more from football on television (as everyone was doing in 1990).

Is this big business or amateur sport? Consider what John Merwin wrote in a 1985 article for *Forbes Magazine*: "What would you nominate as the most profitable, but still legitimate, business in the U.S. these days? Round up the usual suspects—broadcasters, cosmetics producers, cigarette companies and maybe a hot technology venture—and you would be hard put to find a business pocketing more than 15 cents of every sales dollar after taxes. What if we could show you a business likely to bring 75 cents of every revenue dollar to the bottom line this year? Interested? Our candidate, it is true, doesn't pay taxes. But even if it did, at the full 46 percent corporate tax rate it still would net 40 cents on the dollar, putting IBM to shame. Our nominee: big-time college basketball."

And still, student-athletes are told there is not enough in the pot to provide them with money for a pizza and a movie.

"We coaches also have to examine our conscience," said LSU's Dale Brown. "I sometimes wonder if we're not more concerned with our summer camps, our shoe contracts, our television appearances, our salaries, our paneled offices, our leased cars we get free, our free country club memberships, than we are with the kids, whose sweat fuels this machine we're driving. We somehow have forgotten where we came from. Our lifestyle is directly related to poverty-stricken kids, most of them, who haven't got anything. And a Top 10 coach can make anywhere from $500,000 a year up. Why should I, Dale Brown, be able to tell players that they have to wear a certain brand of shoe and then take $150,000 for doing nothing?

"They get nothing for wearing the shoe I force them to wear. How can that be right? How can there be nothing wrong with that? Imagine this: I was with Converse [in 1989-90] when Chris Jackson, our star, was on the cover of *Sports Illustrated*, and he was walking through campus wearing Nikes. Roger Morningstar from Converse called [LSU athletic director] Joe Dean to complain. Can you believe that? I don't believe we, as coaches, should force the kids to wear any particular shoe. But our shoe contract said my players had to wear Converse during games and photo sessions. All of the shoe companies demand that, not just Converse. I also don't think we do enough for our athletes. There's a false concept that these kids are on full scholarship. They're not. That's the greatest legal con in America. Their basic needs are not taken care of. The dorm is closed, there's no breakfast there on the weekend. There's times at night they've got to eat. Do you cut yourself off at 6 o'clock at night? But we can't, even though our arenas are full, give them some figure each month so they can go get a burger if the food service line is closed."

Such prohibitions on athletes, the NCAA claims, are made in the name of amateurism. The NCAA, after all, was founded to "retain a clear line of demarcation between collegiate athletics and professional sports." But, truth be known, amateurism went out the window when schools began offering athletic scholarships. That was the beginning of accepted pay-for-play college sports. Notre Dame basketball coach Digger Phelps puts it bluntly: "I don't care what you call it. We are professionals. As soon as we get room and board and tuition, we are professionals. Let's grow up to the fact it's big-time business. We're a part of it, but let's regulate it and control it versus looking as bad as we do because all these things do go on. Give a kid a stipend that covers his spending money while he's there at school, and we're on target. Then, if he breaks the rule, you take away his eligibility, which takes away his exposure to pro contract."

The idea of a monthly stipend for athletes is gaining supporters, including Phelps, Frederick and others. "It's ridiculous to take a kid out of the ghetto, send him 100 miles from his home and give him books, tuition, and board and not give him spending money," said Marshall Criser, former University of Florida president. "Frankly, some of these kids don't have simple spending money. They aren't even able to afford to take a date to the movies. For a kid to have to go through four years of financial chastity while waiting to see if he can make it in the pros is not reasonable."

Nebraska football coach Tom Osborne told a meeting of the College Football Association in Dallas that if students aren't paid some sort of stipend, they might rebel. "We're going to see the day where the athlete is either going to have to be recognized for what he contributes financially and in other ways, or we're going to pay a certain price that we may not want to pay," he said.

Added Dean Smith, basketball coach at the University of North Carolina, "Legislatively, we are too large an organization. And eventually, the victim of the NCAA's lethargy in terms of reform is the student-athlete. The NCAA takes considerable amounts of revenue generated from basketball, then uses it for travel, committee meetings, nonrevenue sports. . . . but notice how well those administrators live when they take those trips for meetings; the meetings are always in some fairly exotic place. And then there's the student-athlete, who doesn't have the spare change for a hamburger, trying to scrape living expenses together. The sad thing is, we have the money in Division I basketball and football to help these young men, but the college administrations keep getting in the way. If this sad set of priorities stays intact, then the exploitation of student-athletes will be as difficult as ever to curtail."

"This kid gets to school, he's got no money, he can't afford to buy clothing, toothpaste, soap," said George Bisacca, a Connecticut attorney who represents schools under investigation by the NCAA. "He can't go to the movies. He can't just live like a human being. Meanwhile, all these rich kids that he's with have cars, a different outfit every day. He's denied all that. I think he should not be. He should be given a reasonable sum that will give him the opportunity to take care of his basic needs. If you give a kid a scholarship based on need, how can you cut it off at room, board, tuition and books? That's not everything it takes to go to college."

NCAA Executive Director Schultz acknowledged the time may have come for a change in the no-compensation rule, particularly for impoverished student-athletes. "If the members are interested, I would certainly support something that would provide the needy athletes with additional funds," Schultz said in 1989. "In some cases, it may be $300 to $400 a month."

Already in the works are plans that would provide minimal spending money for athletes in revenue-producing sports. Tom Osborne told College Football Association athletic directors gathered in Dallas that if the group set aside 10 percent of the $75 million that was paid out in 18 bowl games last year, it could have provided every Division I-A football player $75 per month. As one Dallas columnist noted "This would cover normal expenses incurred by college students such as laundry, theme paper and Rolling Stones concert tickets. It would not, however, cover extravagances as, say, staying the night at the Anatole Hotel, site of the NCAA's convention, where the regular rate for a single room is $130, plus tax."

"I don't think we need to do it out of fear or threat. I think we need to do it out of a sense of rightness," Osborne said as he explained his $75-a-month idea. "It just seems to me a matter of right and wrong. Generally speaking, in our country, there has been a sense that those people who generate wealth should share it in some degree. About one-third of college athletes, probably more, today get no help from home. Their parents exist at the poverty level. Paradoxically, a very high percentage of those same athletes have to stay in summer school at least part of the time [to stay eligible]. As a result, they can't make money in the summer, and they're the ones who need it the most."

Similar ideas have sprung from an NCAA committee's debate over how the organization should divide the $143-million-a-year windfall it will earn from the new basketball television contract. Dick DeVenzio is quick to point out that was one committee the NCAA didn't invite a student to join.

Those who prefer the status quo argue that a stipend might be fine for football and basketball, but how does a school deal with all those other student-athletes when most schools are losing money as it is? Former NCAA president John Davis, expressing that sentiment, asked, "But what about the wrestlers? They'll want money too. And how are the wrestling coaches going to like that? All of their wrestlers will be going out for football."

The answer is almost as simple as the question, DeVenzio says. When the sports those students play become revenue positive, those athletes can share in the profits, too. "What realistic hope is there for change within the system when the leaders are making inane comments like that," DeVenzio asked rhetorically after hearing Davis's words. "What about the wrestlers? Really. And what about the band, the rugby club and the Little Sisters of the Poor? What about Biafra, Ethiopia and Outer Mongolia? What possible reason could there be for giving the producers of millions of dollars of revenue some return—as long as there is poverty in the world? Is that Mr. Davis's question?"

Tulane President Eamon Kelly said that, at the very least, athletes should be eligible for work-study programs available to other students. "Let them work 12 hours on campus each week to give them some spending money," Kelley said. "Let the student athletes get the allowed $1,400 a year for student work programs. The student-athlete needs spending money of some kind."

The NCAA's influence on student-athletes extends beyond the financial realm. Ask Chicago Bears's defensive tackle Trace Armstrong, formerly of the University of Florida. Armstrong began his college career at Arizona State University in 1984. But shortly after enrolling at ASU, it was discovered that his high school grade point average had been miscalculated. Instead of a 2.03, his high school GPA was 1.98, which was below the NCAA's required 2.0.

The NCAA determined ASU was at fault for miscalculating his GPA, but they ruled Armstrong ineligible in 1984 because he was allowed to practice at ASU while his GPA was being debated. Communicating through Arizona State's athletic department, the NCAA then reinstated Armstrong in 1985, giving him three years of eligibility, with the option of appealing for a fourth year. Armstrong played three years at ASU, appealed the NCAA ruling, but received word his appeal had failed in December 1987, leaving him no choice but to transfer in order to play a fourth year.

"I thought, any idiot that sits down and looks at this thing rationally, will see that I had nothing to do with what happened and I should be reinstated," said Armstrong. "It would be ridiculous for me to be penalized credit hours and have to pick up and move 3,000 miles for one year of college football, when I didn't do anything wrong. But that wasn't the case."

Florida was attractive to Armstrong because he would have a chance to start and because one of his former coaches, Rex Norris, was hired as the Gator's defensive line coach. He transferred to Florida in December 1987, losing some credit hours in the process. He played his final year of college football in Gainesville, and remains outraged at the system that forced him to leave ASU. "This thing dragged out for five years and I never talked to anybody from the NCAA," Armstrong said. "They never sent a letter to me. I think that's wrong. This is my future and they're not consulting with me on anything. That's ridiculous. They've really lost sight of the individual, the athlete."

Trace Armstrong believes it's time for the NCAA to change its own ways, if the organization wants to remain true to its mission. "If they want to return it to true amateur athletics, they're going to have to make some concessions," he said. "They can't have their revenue and expect these things out of the kids because they just don't follow each other. The original intent of this system was good—to protect the integrity of college athletics and the student-athlete. But somewhere along the line, they lost sight of that purpose. Sometime, somewhere, somebody has to call attention to that fact."

Chambers, the flamboyant senator from Nebraska, has made an annual ritual of filing bills that call attention to problems with NCAA rules. He believes if there's one thing the rules are not intended to do, it's protect the student-athlete. "Nobody's interested in building better human beings," Chambers said. "If they were, the first thing the NCAA would do would be to create a wholesome environment for athletics and produce something good from athletics. Their illogical rules would not let Nebraska play at Utah State or New Mexico or some of these little schools that have no chance, and the only reason they play is because the athletic directors get that guaranteed fee, so they throw their kids to the meat grinder. This kind of unequal competition is one of the most reprehensible aspects of intercollegiate athletics right now, and you find it in football like no place else. That's what shows how insincere and corrupt the adults are who are running this whole operation. If you took the money out of it, the NCAA would cease to exist."

More than 36 million people passed through turnstiles to see NCAA football games in 1989. The Final Four teams in 1990's basketball tournament took home $1.43 million each. The 36 teams that made it to 1990 bowl games split $75 million. Major basketball programs have recruiting budgets in excess of six figures; football programs spend even more. The NCAA wants colleges to recruit smarter athletes. That's great. But in pursuing that noble goal, the organization may find that those athletes can read and understand numbers. That's not so great—if you like the rules as they are.

"Eventually, the athlete is going to be heard," Nebraska's Osborne said. "I think there are athletes out there who feel somewhat used and put upon by these rules. How long it takes to get them organized, I don't know. But we better do something before it's too late."

DALE BROWN

"It ain't easy being a rebel," Dale Brown said, sitting down for a light breakfast of a quart of coffee and more waffles than even his 7-foot-1-inch center Shaquille O'Neal can eat. "And, well, I'm a rebel. When a window's broken, it always seems I'm at the rock pile."

No truer words ever have been spoken. The dean of Southeastern Conference basketball coaches, Brown has twice taken his Louisiana State Tigers to the NCAA's Final Four. But whether his teams were winning or losing, one thing has remained constant during his 18 years in Baton Rouge—Dale Brown has always spoken his mind and ruffled feathers. When it comes to living within the confines of the NCAA's 400-page rule book, Brown agrees with most coaches that it can't be done. What Brown will do that most won't, though, is openly admit he's violated those rules. And he'll get specific. Once he gets going on the topic, save your breath. He is next to impossible to stop. Just turn on the tape recorder and sit back.

"I tried to read the [NCAA] manual," Brown said between

inhaling breakfast and exhaling run-on sentences. "I'm fairly scholarly, but this thing was 400 pages thick. And as I read it, I thought, isn't it funny that I can type on a 3-by-5 card God's Ten Commandments, and I haven't been able to follow those — as clear as they are and as healthy as they are. Now I haven't broken all of them yet, and I hope I don't. But how in the world am I going to learn all of these rules? So I said this is simple. I know right from wrong. My human instincts tell me right from wrong. I grew up with the most pathologically honest woman in the world. My mother. I've seen her return 40 cents and a quarter back to the Piggly Wiggly and the Red Owl when they gave her too much change. So I knew honesty. There are some things we automatically know are wrong. You don't change a transcript. You don't give someone money. You don't get someone to take a player's entrance exam. You don't get them a car. But you don't legislate against human dignity, either. I found my philosophy was incorrect. I was just hired [at LSU] in 1972 and it was my first head coaching job. I had a lot to learn.

"That second year, we had a kid that came here. He had no father and he had an alcoholic mother. I don't want to name the name because I don't want to hurt the kid. He came into my office one day, his face was all swollen up. I asked him what in the world was wrong. He said, 'Coach, my teeth are killing me.' So I said, 'Let me take you to the trainer.' The trainer wasn't in. So, I called a friend of mine who's a dentist. I told him, 'I'm going to send the player out to see you.' I sent the manager to take him out. I found out, number one, that the manager driving him out was an NCAA violation. But the player didn't have a car. He didn't even have a quarter for a bus. Number two, after he got out there, the dentist called me and said, 'Coach, this guy is sick. He's got five major puss pockets in his mouth. It looks like a cherry bomb went off in there. He needs to have help. I can't believe this boy is functioning. These are the worst teeth I've ever seen.' I said, 'Do whatever you've got to do.' The bill comes six weeks later. I take it into the trainer. He says, 'We can't pay this.' I asked him what he meant. 'You weren't here, so I sent him to the doctor,' I said. He said, 'We can't pay for anything to do with teeth.' I asked him why. He said, 'We can pay for a $3,000 knee surgery but we can't pay for the guy's teeth.' Now, I'm dealing in a dilemma. So, I have to call the dentist. I don't deal with the gray very well. I have to call the dentist and say we can't pay, it's an NCAA violation. He said, 'I don't need payment for this. If he doesn't have any money, I do a lot of charity work. I'll just go ahead and handle this.' He said he'd try and work out a payment schedule, but if the kid didn't pay, he'd just show it as paid. I said, 'Hey, ok, that's great.' That was illegal, too.

"That was the first rule I ever broke. It was 1973-74.

"Then, little tiny other things started to come up. I'd want to have a kid to my house for dinner. I invited them all over, four at a time. The athletic director picked up the phone and asked if I was inviting the kids over for dinner. I said, 'Yeah, I was a new coach trying to get to know them, let them meet my wife and have a home-cooked meal.' Well, that was a violation. I couldn't invite those children to my home. That was 1974.

"Rudy Macklin is from Louisville, Kentucky. He came here to Baton Rouge, a long way from home. Not once did Mr. and Mrs. Macklin insinuate they wanted anything. They saved enough money and they would come down once a year to watch their son play. Here, I have these people who I'm very close to. Their son is the star of the team. I cannot take them out to eat dinner. I did take them out to eat dinner. Every year. That's an NCAA violation. I paid for it. It didn't have anything to do with recruiting. I didn't promise them one meal a year when I was recruiting Rudy. It was a kind act that you would do for anyone. Particularly because I have no one I'm closer to than my wife, my daughter and the basketball family. That was '77-'81.

"Then we go to Dallas, Texas, for the Final Four [in 1986]. We stay at this luxurious hotel. Two of my players were standing downstairs. They had a table laid out and filled with all kinds of Final Four shirts and banners and sweat bands. I'm standing there talking to our chancellor at the time. I saw two of our guys walk by and there's a table of shirts being hawked by people. And I hear one player say to the person behind the counter, 'How much are these shirts?' He said, '$14.' I heard him say to the other player, 'How much money you got?' He said, 'I got 6 bucks.' He said, 'You got any shirts for $9?' The guy laughed at them. I said, 'I can't believe this. We're in the tournament and they never even gave them shirts. This is sickening.' I go upstairs and get my administrative assistant and I said, 'I want some shooting t-shirts for shooting practice the next few days.' He said we had some with us. I said they were too old. He thought I was nuts, they were almost new. I said, 'Why can't our kids have shirts, they're selling them.' I said, 'Go buy shirts and put them down as shooting shirts and we'll wear them.'

"So in order to beat the system, we had to go pretend we were buying shooting shirts for the warmups. That, just so we could deliver t-shirts that our organization should have been sensitive enough to have given the kids.

"Now the next day, we're sitting in this luxurious hotel. We're sitting in this restaurant, a five-star restaurant. We're ordering steak and lobster. One of my players that comes from a poor family, they [the family] drive over to watch the tournament. There's about eight of them. I see them come in the restaurant, they're dressed poorly. I see the maître d' take off to push them out of there. So I run over and tell them to come in and show them where their son's sitting. And I'm sitting back down, I'm thinking, this is unbelievable. Here we are, we're going to get a check for $850,000 just for being there. And here's this poor boy's parents and I can't ask them to sit down and have a hamburger, or eat with us. Here they are, driving all that way, staying in a cheap motel about 30 miles from Dallas because they couldn't afford to stay in Dallas. Here I am, eating steak and lobster and I couldn't even feed his family. Now, what decision do you think I made? Was I going to let the maître d' turn them into the streets like peasants or was I going to find a way to feed them?

"Then what really captured it. We go out to play Louisville and I wondered where my wife and daughter were. I knew the coaches got this side [of the arena]. I couldn't find my wife and daughter. An assistant told me they were over there with the LSU people. I look over and way in the corner of the end zone are the parents of the players, my wife and daughter. And it just hit me. It depressed me again. I said, who is sitting in these [half-court] seats. I can tell you who, large corporate sponsors, politicians, the money aspect of the game. And I was thinking who deserves more than the parents of these children to be sitting right there in the spotlight, in the middle. My wife and daughter come second. That was one I couldn't do anything about. But what kind of organization would set its priorities like that?

"I broke this rule. We get our kids' eyes checked. In 1983, three kids needed help—one needed reading glasses, two needed contact lenses. I sent the bill to the trainer. The trainer comes back and says, 'We can't pay for the glasses.' I said, 'What are you talking about? Did you pay for the contact lenses?' 'Yeah.' 'Well, why can't we pay for the glasses?' 'Because the glasses aren't used for basketball.' 'So, we can pay $200 for contact lenses because they're used for basketball, but not the eye glasses the other kid needs so he can read and study? Why didn't we buy the guy contact lenses so he could read?' 'Well, you could have done that.' I had to call the opthalmologist and say, 'I can't figure this out, Doc, but we can't pay for these glasses. You've got to do one of two things. You either got to bring him back in and get him contact lenses, we can pay for those, or you got to jack up the money for the [other players'] contact lenses to pay for the glasses.' I don't know what he did, but we got the glasses."

"Then one day I get a call from Miami, Florida. [Seven-foot center] Zoran Jovanovich went home for Christmas with Ricky Blanton, his teammate. While the two of them were working out, Zoran's knee popped out. They rushed to the emergency room, and, while Zoran was in surgery, Rickey called and made me talk to someone at the hospital about insurance. Because Zoran was from Yugoslavia, they wanted to know if he was covered. I said yes, he was covered by the athletic department insurance policy, but that wasn't right. We couldn't, by NCAA rules, cover him with our policy. You know why? Because his knee did not pop out in practice, it popped out while working out. There's a rule that makes one a violation and the other not. But I had told them to work out over Christmas. I told them to run in the morning and shoot in the afternoon. They were doing exactly what I told them to do except they weren't here. I broke an NCAA rule by even telling the guy, 'Go ahead and operate.' I told them to send us the bill. To solve the problem, our trainer typed up a letter spelling out the workout instructions I gave the players so we could show it was a workout. What were we going to do, let him lay in a hospital room in Miami? That was in 1986.

"I'll tell you another thing we did. We're getting ready to go on a road trip. I cannot tell all my players to wear suits and sports coats—they don't have them. We used to be able to provide a blazer. They won't even let us do that anymore. So I say, dress nice but do not wear Levis or tennis shoes or t-shirts. We're at the airport and I happen to see one of my kids and he's got on a pair of white canvas shoes. I called my assistant over and said to tell the kid to get his butt home. He's not going on the trip. He [the assistant] comes back and says, 'He doesn't own any dress shoes.

Let's let him go this time, and when we get back I'll take him downtown. I've got a friend who owns a clothing store, we'll get him a pair of shoes. I'm sure my friend will help him.' I said, 'Do that.' It was an NCAA violation. Is that wrong? I mean it was either that or embarrass him in front of everybody.

"I've never had a problem knowing right from wrong. I'm not trying to be Robin Hood or anybody else. I've never done anything since I've become a coach that I can't look my wife, my daughter and my Lord in the eye and admit to. I'm not a rule breaker. But I'm certainly going to break rules that are against human dignity. Have I violated some NCAA rules? You're damn right I have. The problem with all of these rules is that they stand against decency. The NCAA doesn't solve the problem; they keep throwing talcum powder on cancer. Now, I know the NCAA says that if I can find a way to do something and call it human dignity, someone else can go a step further. But these things are nonsense. And every time I ask for a ruling from the NCAA, well, they're good at saying 'No.'

"I called the NCAA office. There was like a coldness, an indifference. The most dictatorial, communist, fascist thing about our country has been the very organization that controls [athletics]. What I was always told was, 'We don't make the rules, you do.' There was never any compassion or sensitivity or assistance. I almost felt after I called that I needed to take a shower. I thought, 'Geez, I'm wrong.' They think I'm marching to my own drummer, that I'm crazy or something, trying to change legislation.

"I kept trying to figure out how all these rules were getting passed. I never voted for one. The [NCAA] convention is right in the middle of basketball season. So these rules are being voted on by a bunch of people who don't have to go into these players' homes during recruiting. They haven't been to the ghetto. Some of them do not know how to spell the word 'ghetto,' let alone go there. They don't know what's going on. They live in an ivory tower.

"We need migrant farm worker leader César Chavez to come back and help these college athletes. We have no disability coverage for athletes in most institutions. You get permanently disabled, you come up with a big zero. We should have to continue your financial aid until you graduate if disabled. It's wrong what's going on in collegiate athletics. And while I love college athletics, I'm not going to be a part of the part that is wrong. St. Augustine in one of his books said that we are all morally obligated to violate unjustifiable laws. He wrote, 'An unjust law is no law at all and must be opposed.'

"I guess you could say I'm just following St. Augustine's words. Just because it's a rule doesn't make it right. I believe that. There used to be a rule women couldn't vote. There used to be a rule blacks had to ride in the back of the bus. B.S. Whose rule is that?

"Excuse me, ma'am," Brown beckoned to the waitress. "Can I get another waffle?"

4

LOOKING THROUGH THE HOLES

THE DETAILS

Most coaches agree that making it through the NCAA's minefield of rules is difficult at best. But worse than the rules themselves is the outmoded system the NCAA employs to enforce them. It is an enforcement program that is arbitrary, sloppy and often unfair. As more schools labor through NCAA investigations, complaints about the organization's methods have grown louder. An increasing number of NCAA members are learning that when you combine bad and unenforceable rules with bad and unfair enforcement of those rules, you're guaranteed bad results.   A review of the NCAA enforcement process reveals many serious shortcomings.

■   Despite its supposed commitment to stop cheating, the NCAA spends a paltry 2 percent of its annual budget on enforcement. According to the NCAA's 1989-90 budget summary, the organization invested $1.9 million of its $98.2-million budget to keep an eye on more than 800 institutions, each of which operates multi-sport athletic programs.

■   If justice delayed is justice denied, many schools have reason to complain. No one is quite sure which school has earned the distinction of suffering through the longest NCAA investigation, but Louisiana State University entertained investigators for nearly four years. The University of Florida hosted them for 28 months, the University of Houston was under the microscope for four years and the University of Illinois football program earned a three-year look. "If you hung around the Vatican long enough, I'm convinced you could indict the Pope," LSU basketball coach Dale Brown said, only half in jest. University of Maryland basketball coach Gary Williams, while waiting for the NCAA to conclude its investigations of alleged violations that occurred under his predecessor, likened the delay to "living through Chinese water torture."

■   As an investigation lingers on from months to years, schools find their opponents using the specter of NCAA sanctions in the high-stakes recruiting wars. "What being under investigation does is make recruiting more frustrating," said former University of Georgia football coach Vince Dooley. "You know other schools are using it against you. It just gives them something bad to say about you.

■   And if your opponents aren't using the investigation to chill your recruiting, the NCAA will. When 6-foot-11-inch forward LeRon Ellis was allowed to transfer from the sanctioned Kentucky program, he was leaning toward taking his talents to the University of Nevada–Las Vegas. After his visit to Vegas, Ellis talked to "a couple" of NCAA investigators who advised him not to transfer to UNLV, Ellis told the *Syracuse* (New York) *Herald-Journal*. "Yeah, honestly, we have been watching them," Ellis quoted an investigator as telling him. "[UNLV] Coach Tarkanian could possibly not be coaching." After that conversation, Ellis chose to attend Syracuse over UNLV. "That's the only reason I changed my mind," he said. The investigators' warning came weeks before any official announcement of a UNLV investigation, which seems to be a "leak" of confidential information—something the NCAA swears never happens. But NCAA spokesman Jim Marchiony told the *Herald-Journal* that internal rules allow investigators to warn recruits about schools under the gun, even though such a warning might find its way into print and spoil the NCAA's promised confidential inquiry.

■   Others complain the NCAA has used the media feeding frenzy surrounding corruption in college sports to its advantage, leveling charges that it knows won't stick, but will be well covered in the press. The week before Louisiana State University was to face allegations of rule-breaking in its basketball program, NCAA investigators added three violations to the list of charges. Each named basketball coach Dale Brown, an outspoken critic of the enforcement staff. The news of the added charges played big in sports sections across America. "We got to Kansas City, and are going through the hearing in the morning," Brown said. "The committee worked up until the three allegations that were made against me, then they adjourned for lunch. I went downstairs and there's the chancellor and the two university attorneys. They said, 'Come oh over, we've got good news. Dave Berst just said they're dropping the three allegations on you.' I said, 'No they're not.' When the hearing began again, I requested that those allegations not be dropped against me. The chairman said, 'Coach, maybe you didn't understand. They didn't occur, they never happened.' I said, 'I understand but I want those allega- tions brought up before this committee.' He asked, 'Why?' I said, 'Because I want to prove that that man [NCAA investigator Doug Johnson] sitting across the table who has not looked me in the eye is a liar. These charges were made up and I resent the fact your investigators did that.' The fact I was cleared of those allegations didn't make the media splash that being charged did. They did it to embarrass me."

■   Often, investigations drag on so long that those who committed the violations are long gone before the penalty is served out. Others are left to suffer the consequences. Barry Switzer had a book written and published before Oklahoma finished its probation for rules broken during his tenure. Marist College basketball coach Mike Perry was selling trinkets on Waikiki Beach while the Red Foxes were not permitted to play in the NCAA tournament for violations he committed. Nearly two dozen Southern Methodist University football players trans- ferred and played in bowl games the year after the school's football program received the NCAA's death penalty. And Chris Mills, whose father received $1,000 in an overnight envelope from the University of Kentucky, transferred from the Wildcats program and a year later was eligible to play at the University of Arizona. While the players he left behind in Lexington couldn't play in two NCAA tournaments, Mills could play in the NCAA's big show as early as 1991 at Arizona. "It may have been bad news for Kentucky, but it isn't bad news for Chris," Chris's father, Claud, told the *Los Angeles Times*. "Only the guilty party should be penalized," said LSU's Brown. "If I speed, are you going to pay my ticket because I bought the car from you? If two people are on the team and they take automobiles, their careers are done. Leave the rest of the team alone. If an assistant coach set it up, he's done. A coach's career should end if he violates a major rule."

■   The penalties handed down often hurt other schools as severely as the school violating the rules. When Oklahoma and Oklahoma State were both placed on probation and banned from television for their part in recruiting wide receiver Hart Lee Dykes, the Nebraska Cornhuskers paid a hefty price. Nebraska, which wasn't even in the running to sign Dykes, lost the chance to play its two biggest rivals on television, costing the school an estimated $1 million and the kind of exposure you can't put a price tag on. The same is true of Kentucky basketball rival Notre Dame. "The TV sanctions also penalize schools like us," Fighting Irish coach Digger Phelps said after the NCAA's 1989 thrashing of the Wildcats. "When we're the home team against Kentucky, we also have to lose a TV appearance."

■   As discussed in detail in chapter 2, the NCAA does not allow its investigators to tape-record interviews. Instead, investigators write memorandums after the interviews summarizing the conversations. NCAA officials say taping would be costly and intimidating; most who have been through the process dispute both of those points.

■   As discussed in detail in chapter 5, turnover among the investigators is so high—most investigators concede that they join the NCAA with expectations of staying only two years—and investigations take so long, cases sometimes have involved as many as seven members of the enforcement staff. Each time, a new investigator must try to pick up where the last one left off, creating confusion and delays. This problem further magnifies the lack of accurate interview records since each new investigator must build a case based on someone else's summary of an interview.

■   Although the *NCAA Manual* requires that an investigation be "cooperative," many members say cooperation is a one-way street. If an institution does not bend over backwards to give its records to the NCAA, the infractions committee can cite the school for "violation of the spirit of cooperation." Yet institutions that ask for information from NCAA files early in an investigation are flatly denied such cooperation from the NCAA. "I'm sure you would agree that Woodward and Bernstein wouldn't have wanted to conduct their Watergate interviews each day, then go to Nixon and tell him what they had," NCAA enforcement chief David Berst said. "If they had, they surely wouldn't have had a case."

■   Some have questioned the chummy relationship between the enforcement staff and the infractions committee. The same people that investigate cases serve as staff support for the committee that must eventually rule on the quality and outcome of those investigations. It's as if the police officer that arrested you also clerked for the judge that tried you.

■   Even though the NCAA's investigation can take years, schools are given but a few months to investigate themselves and to prepare a defense. Typically, schools do not see the NCAA's evidence against them until a week or two before the NCAA hearing. It is then, at what the NCAA calls a "pre-hearing conference," that university personnel get their first glimpse at the memorandums NCAA investigators have filed following their interviews with sources. Berst said the pre-hearing conference is purposely set for just days before the infractions hearing so as to limit the time an institution has to rebut NCAA information. "That's done intentionally, so the institution just doesn't go out and try to beat the NCAA's evidence." This one-sided discovery process once was standard fare in the federal court system; but, years ago, presumably from a sense of justice, new federal rules for civil procedure were instituted. "These [new] rules rested on a basic philosophy that, prior to trial, every party to a civil action is entitled to the disclosure of all relevant information in the possession of any person, unless the information is privileged. No longer are civil trials to be carried on in the dark. Use of the new discovery rule is intended to make a trial less a game of blind man's bluff and more a fair contest with the basic issues and facts disclosed to the fullest practicable extent. Victory is intended to go to the party entitled to it, based on all the facts, rather than to the side that best uses its wits." The references to those old federal rules of discovery, which sound frighteningly similar to the NCAA's, come from the book *Laws of Federal Court.* The author: Charles Alan Wright, former chairman of the NCAA's Committee on Infractions.

Even at that late discovery hearing, when it may be too late for an institution to track down the sources of NCAA information, the NCAA does not allow schools to have a copy of the statements that will be used against them. "If what you're really trying to ask me is whether we should give institutions copies of those memos, I'm not comfortable with that idea," the NCAA's Steve Morgan told a reporter. "Because then, the opportunity to control access to that information is lost by us. Being able to control the text of information provided by sources is important to us." If information is power, the NCAA's tight grip on the memos that may help as an institution prepares its defense allows NCAA staff to maintain its control over member schools. The result is to deny schools, coaches and others that basic American right: to face one's accuser. NCAA officials say its enforcement program isn't set up to allow such.

As a result of these and other problems in the enforcement process, no school ever wins its case and no school has ever made a successful appeal.

■   When a school receives a preliminary letter of inquiry, the initial fact-finding stage of an NCAA investigation, there is a 90 percent chance it will be found guilty of at least one charge, NCAA officials say. A review of NCAA enforcement records shows that, after the school receives an Official letter of Inquiry, the second stage of an investigation, there is complete certainty it will be found guilty, regardless of what kind of evidence the school might present on its own behalf. Because the statistics show their conviction is assured before they present evidence, many schools argue they entered the infractions hearing already judged guilty with the burden to prove themselves innocent, rather than vice versa. "They wanted us, and they got us," University of Oklahoma Athletic Director Donnie Duncan said after his school's hearing before the NCAA infractions committee.

■   Although an avenue for appeal exists, few schools use it—and none ever has won reversal of the infractions committee's verdict. In fact, David Berst has been quoted as calling appeals a waste of time. In one case, members of the NCAA Council, which hears infractions appeals, were overheard in a restaurant complaining that a school's appeal brief was too long. So they didn't read it. "I've been a lawyer for more than 40 years, and I've yet to find a trial court that has never been overturned on appeal," said Sam Lionel, attorney for University of Nevada–Las Vegas basketball coach Jerry Tarkanian, who fought the NCAA for 13 years. "Nobody is *that* perfect."

Asked if the long list of questions about the NCAA's enforcement program, combined with the statistically evident futility of fighting charges, might leave schools discouraged and intimidated, Steve Morgan said without hesitation, "I don't know that if the process is intimidating, it's such a bad thing."

Others disagree. Interviews with dozens of college athletic officials show that more and more NCAA member schools are becoming disgruntled. "I think you would find discontent among many of the schools who have been through an NCAA investigation, with a lot of them raising good questions about how it's being handled—the fairness of it," said Ron Mason, vice-president and general counsel of Tulane University of New Orleans. Tulane avoided an NCAA investigation in 1985 by abolishing its own basketball program, amid reports of point shaving, extra benefits for players and participation in organized gambling. "Other folks think you're complaining because you got caught. That's sometimes true. But more people have gone through this now, and more people understand what some of those complaints are."

Former NCAA president John Fuzak said there has never been any rush to change the NCAA's enforcement program because most of the NCAA's 800 members will never know what it is like to go through an investigation. "The majority of the

members are rather well satisfied with the present procedures,"
Fuzak said. "I believe that part of that satisfaction comes from
lack of experience with the procedure itself. They have not—as
have some of the institutions which have been before the infractions committee—suffered through the entire process."

The complaints come from people like Dwight Vines, president of Northeast Louisiana University, who was angered both
by the severe penalties and by the quality of NCAA staff work
that his school received. "The minor infractions that we had
committed brought very, very harsh sanctions to this institution," President Vines told the Associated Press. "We were
disappointed because we were misinformed about what was
going on—not once, but repeatedly. We were told it was minor,
then told it was serious. If I could use one word in characterizing
our dealings with the NCAA, I would say they were unprofes-
sional. Everybody is telling me to shut up. The more you say, the
more trouble you're in. But people need to know that this is how
the NCAA does business."

Northeast Louisiana's women's basketball program was
judged guilty in January 1986 of six NCAA rules violations. The
most serious "violations": recruit Chana Perry received 40-mile
round-trip transportation and a night's lodging in a motel; she
attended a party where she met a "representative of the
university's athletic interests," a contact that is illegal under
NCAA rules; she played one-on-one with an assistant coach; and
she borrowed the assistant's plastic watch to keep track of time
on her official campus visit, later returning it to the coach.

The penalty for these heinous crimes: probation for one
year, no postseason play and reduction of recruiting privileges
for the head coach. Additionally, Perry—who had enrolled at
Northeast Louisiana by the time that charges were made—was
declared ineligible and forced to transfer.

And the complaints come from people like Thomas Day,
president of San Diego State University, and his school's athletic
director, Alice Hill. The Aztecs were slapped with the toughest
Divison I basketball sanctions levied to that date when they were
banned from postseason play for two years, lost two scholarships, and were cut from television appearances in 1984-85. The
penalties stemmed from the NCAA's investigation into the recruitment of disgruntled player David Bradley, who told NCAA
investigators in 1983 that he had been given 5 semester hours of

transfer credits from San Diego City College in 1980 without taking the classes. The NCAA provided no documents. The university countered with testimony from Bradley's coach at San Diego City College and school attendance records, showing that he did attend the classes. Regardless, the Committee on Infractions ruled against San Diego State.

"What happened was the university was guilty and had to prove itself innocent, within a shadow of a doubt," Athletic Director Hill said. "That's not like the court system in this country. The NCAA has to be held accountable. If they're in error, they have to be held accountable."

"Outside of the enforcement staff, I believe in the NCAA," President Day told *Sports Illustrated's* Armen Keteyian. "I had a feeling, after a while, it had nothing to do with Bradley. It was a vendetta [that David Berst had against basketball coach Smokey Gaines]. I'm one of the presidents. Those guys are working for me and I got the feeling like I'm a criminal. Who in the hell do they think they are?"

Others are left with just as many questions. Former University of Kansas basketball coach Larry Brown, who resigned to coach the NBA's San Antonio Spurs just before the Jayhawks were placed on probation in 1988, said investigators in that case continually told him there was "nothing serious" among the violations they had discovered. Suddenly, the case resulted in a three-year probation that kept the Jayhawks from being able to defend their national championship. "When I left Kansas," Brown told *Time* the week after the sanctions were handed down, "I was led to believe that this was no big deal. I now realize that, every time you are investigated by the NCAA, it's a big deal."

At Cleveland State University, officials complain that their appeal hearing before the NCAA was a sham. Cited for 17 rules violations, Cleveland State was penalized with three years of probation, no postseason play for two years, a one-year ban on live television appearances, recruiting limitations and other sanctions.

Cleveland State appealed to the NCAA Council. According to memos the university filed with the NCAA, the night before the appeal, university attorneys had dinner in the restaurant of the Washington, D.C. hotel where the hearing would take place. In the adjacent booth were five Council members, and the attorneys overheard them saying that they hadn't had time to read the 300-page brief the school had submitted for the appeal hearing.

"They, amid much jocularity, stated that it was futile for Cleveland State University to appeal its case and the document we had submitted had not been read because it was too voluminous," wrote Walter Waetjen, who was then Cleveland State president and a member of the NCAA Presidents Commission. "The die was cast before the hearing began. The hearing gave new meaning and definition to the term "star chamber." (He was referring to an old English court infamous for its secrecy and often arbitrary and oppressive character.) "So much for justice."

The NCAA's appeals process requires that the Council consider the university's complaint de novo, meaning as if the matter was being heard for the first time. That increases the need for Council members to pay thorough attention to the reports submitted by concerned schools. "That obviously didn't happen in our case," Waetjen said. "You could tell that simply by the lame and mundane questions the Council asked."

Others have experienced Waetjen's frustration. Even former NCAA president Wilford Bailey, who handled Auburn University's appeal when he served on the university's athletic oversight committee, said he felt "some of the points in our appeal were not really heard and therefore not given adequate weight by the Council."

The NCAA's Steve Morgan said the appeals process and the Council's ability to handle the appeals was a source of concern for many who have tried and failed to win in this, the NCAA's court of last resort. "There has been some concern that the Council was not particularly well prepared to sit and hear those appeals," Morgan said in 1988. "Because for Council members, it happens infrequently enough and it's kind of a sidelight focus for them and they were not sure that they fully understood the procedures."

NCAA staff answers its critics by pointing out that membership in the organization is voluntary. If you don't like the organization, either work to make it better or get out. Save your breath when it comes to complaining.

But that voluntary membership isn't really so voluntary, and the NCAA knows it. In fact, NCAA membership is a must for those schools that want to share in the wealth of college athletics. "NCAA membership is not voluntary in any but a technical definition of the word," said University of Denver law professor Burton Brody. "The members realize that membership is not truly voluntary. Most significantly, the NCAA knows it is not. Clearly, the membership understands that, if you want to play, you must belong."

"When I was a boy, I played ball with the boys who owned the ball, because I didn't [own a ball]," said Wilford Bailey. "If you want to be involved, you've got to be in it. If you drop out, you have to pay the price."

The price is high. The Division I men's basketball championship—the NCAA's biggest money-maker—grossed $49 million in 1987 and $68 million in 1988, according to the NCAA's annual report. Of that, $26 million went to participating schools in 1987, and $29.7 million went to them in 1988. Each Final Four team in the 1990 tournament earned $1.43 million. If a school chooses not to join the NCAA, it can't share in those tremendous revenues. "You don't have an alternative," said former University of Florida president Marshall Criser. "If you withdraw from the NCAA, you close down your intercollegiate athletic program."

Criser knows all about NCAA investigations. In 1985, the Florida football program earned a three-year probation—later reduced to two years—including loss of postseason play, scholarships and live-television privileges, for 59 violations of NCAA rules.

Florida's case came in the midst of a period of rapid growth in activity for the NCAA enforcement staff. Since 1980, the number of cases handled by the NCAA has increased tremendously, from 81 in 1980 to 261 in fiscal year 1988. The growth of NCAA infractions cases illustrates to some extent the degree of complexity in NCAA rules.

"There is no program that is squeaky clean," said George Bisacca, a Connecticut attorney who represents institutions fighting the NCAA. "There can't be, because the rules just govern everything. The rules are so pervasive, that there is no way at a major athletic department that you can go a day without breaking one."

As the volume has grown, the NCAA has directed more resources toward enforcement. The NCAA's budget for enforcement has nearly tripled during the 1980s—growing from $690,082 in 1980 to $1.93 million in fiscal year 1990, annual reports show. Still, even with that growth, the NCAA has never spent even 3 percent of its budget on cleaning up college sports, its most well-known—and, in the minds of many, its most important—function. In fact, the NCAA annually spends less on enforcement than it does on its public relations and promotions department. In 1989-90, for example, enforcement accounted for 2 percent of NCAA spending, but the organization's public relations department swallowed up 4.8 percent of the budget. In 1988-89, the numbers were 2.2 percent for enforcement and 4.4 percent for public relations. Those numbers have remained constant throughout the 1980s. In 1987-88, when the enforcement and compliance departments were merged, the two departments combined accounted for 2.8 percent of the budget while public relations accounted for 4.5 percent.

In fact, over the last three fiscal years of the 1980s, the NCAA spent nearly as much flying members of their many committees around the country first class and putting them up in top-flight hotels and golf resorts as it did on its entire enforcement program. In fiscal year 1990, the organization spent $1.4 million on committee entertainment and $1.9 million on enforcement. The organization even budgeted 70 percent more for its Visitors Center ($3.3 million) than it did for enforcement. "I'd say you could look at that [budget] and wonder exactly what their priorities are," said sports law professor Lonny Rose. "Those figures sure don't look good for them."

The enforcement staff—with 15 investigators now—is up from 7 investigators in 1980. But it is lacking 24 of 25 part-time investigators who were employed by the NCAA until 1987. The NCAA decided to stop using the part-timers—most of whom were former FBI agents who also investigated arson cases for National Fire Associates in Kansas City—after one of the agents slipped a student-athlete a $20 bill for information during the Southern Methodist University investigation.

"That's the kind of thing that our full-time people know better than to do," said Steve Morgan. "It is interesting that the person who did that saw nothing wrong with it. He's a former FBI agent and that's apparently a common practice in law enforcement. I felt that from my perspective this pointed up a concern that we couldn't maintain adequate management control over them [the FBI investigators]. We want to have the highest possible level of confidence that our employees are following our level of conduct."

Despite the added funds and full-time staff, big-time cheating remains a problem in college sports, with little hope that the NCAA can stop or even slow the trend. As part of a five-month study of the NCAA's enforcement program in 1988, the *Florida Times-Union* examined each of the 54 cases that were heard by the NCAA between September 1985 and September 1988. During those three years, every case heard resulted in a guilty verdict, and 20 Division I schools investigated had committed violations serious enough to receive probation and suspension of postseason play. Four of those schools also were temporarily banned from live television. Of the 54 schools, only one—the University of Central Florida in Orlando—escaped without a penalty. Three others received only reprimands. The 50 others received some type of sanction—either removal of a specific privilege for a time, or required staff changes.

That may be just the tip of the cheating iceberg, but the NCAA will never know it. The organization's enforcement program, officials say, is not designed to look for the portion of the iceberg that remains under water. "We're not a police department," NCAA Executive Director Dick Schultz said. "We're not out looking for violators. We initiate an investigation because information comes to us." "We don't have the luxury of starting an investigation simply because someone is suspicious," Berst told the *Kansas City Times* in late 1988. "We usually are acting on information that might already have been in some newspaper. In fact, we're always behind in handling things people are really complaining about."

The NCAA investigative staff that must follow up those leads is composed of novice investigators, whom many coaches accuse of sloppy work. During his investigation of LSU, Doug Johnson violated the organization's rules by taking basketball player Tito Horford off campus to do an interview. Had Johnson stayed on campus to talk to Horford, he would have had to notify the LSU athletic department. The athletic department then could sit in on the interview. By dragging Horford to the Baton Rouge Hilton, Johnson was able to avoid letting LSU staff in on his line of questioning. The result was a reprimand from the infractions committee, said D. Alan Williams, a history professor at the University of Virginia in Charlottesville, who heads the committee. "It was less that he [Johnson] tried to mislead us than that he had used methods that were not acceptable," Williams said.

Part of the problem in these questionable investigations may be due to inexperience among investigators. Of the 1985-86 investigators, only 18 percent still were field investigators in 1989-90. And in the last three years of the 1980s, 62 percent of the investigators moved on to other jobs—often as assistant athletic directors at schools under investigation—or to other positions within the NCAA.

A growing number of coaches, administrators and others have begun openly criticizing the organization's investigative tactics. In 1986 the *Atlanta Journal-Constitution* conducted a poll of 240 Division I presidents, athletic directors and football and basketball coaches:

Question: Do you approve of the NCAA's investigative methods?
40 percent said no, with these responses typical:

"No. They should not give immunity to guilty players to secure information" (former University of Kentucky football coach Jerry Claiborne). "No. They are sneaky and underhanded. They are like the Gestapo" (former Ball State University basketball coach Al Brown). "No. You are guilty until proven innocent—opposite of our legal system. You can never face your accuser either" (former University of Kansas basketball coach Larry Brown). "No. Sounds to me like Walter Byers and his people should investigate themselves" (Harvard basketball coach Peter Roby). "No. They have a tendency to step over nickels to get to pennies" (former Washington State basketball coach Len Stevens).

A significant point about these five responses is that none of those coaches had gone through an NCAA investigation at the time. All of them were reacting based on the horror stories that float through the coaching fraternity. And all five of them were right.

In 1988, then-NCAA president Bailey said he believed that an ad hoc committee, created the year before to examine the organization's enforcement process, would offer changes to make it more fair and less punitive. But Al Witte, a law professor at the University of Arkansas and chairman of the committee, said he "did not anticipate recommending any major changes, either in the infractions committee or the way in which the enforcement staff works."

The committee delivered exactly what Witte predicted—nothing. "The committee met a couple of times in its first year of existence to come to an understanding of where we were and I don't think had any dissatisfaction," said Steve Morgan, who conceded he did not follow up on President Bailey's suggestion that schools who had gone through the process be allowed to air their complaints to the committee. Is it any wonder the committee found no dissatisfaction when NCAA staff members were the only ones called to share opinions? In fact, Cecil "Hootie" Ingram, athletic director at the University of Alabama, said he didn't even know such a committee had been formed. According to the NCAA, Ingram was on the committee.

Bailey and others said they hope that someday the NCAA investigative staff would begin working more closely with universities to investigate athletic programs, sharing information with schools early in the investigative process so institutions can avoid committing further mistakes.

However, Morgan, the top man in the NCAA's enforcement chain, said that isn't likely because some member institutions can't be trusted. Morgan said it would "drastically restrict your ability to prove violations if you immediately notify a violator that you are suspicious or have some credible information. If you're going to err, you have to err on the side of not sharing the information."

Institutions fear the NCAA. The NCAA can't trust them. The ingredients are there, some think, for an upheaval in college sports. "If we have some kind of disaster in the NCAA, the organization will change," said attorney Bisacca. "I hope it doesn't have to come to that."

TAKE THE MONEY AND RUN

The message Willie Anderson received when he deplaned at St. Louis's Lambert International Airport read "Urgent. Call your office. Big news." From the nearest pay phone, Anderson called the football office at Oklahoma State University, where he was the Cowboy's head recruiter.

The secretary on the other end was ecstatic. Hart Lee Dykes, the nation's hottest high school receiver, wanted Anderson to call him at Bay City High School, just outside Houston. Dykes had told Anderson's secretary to get him on the phone by 11:30 a.m. It was already just after 11. Anderson was anxious to make the call, but he didn't want to appear in too great a hurry. Like dozens of other coaches who make their living catering to 17-year-old prima donnas, Anderson was tired of having his chain jerked, as Dykes had done for most of the previous year.

When the phone rang in the athletic director's office at Bay City High, Dykes picked it up. The conversation was rather short but sweet, as far as Anderson was concerned. Dykes announced that he wanted to take his 6-foot-4-inch frame, supple hands and smooth moves to Stillwater. On orders from head coach Pat Jones, Anderson boarded the next flight to Houston, abandoning his plans to sign a running back from St. Louis before going to visit Dykes.

"During the phone call he said, 'The door was open' and he asked me if I was going to take care of him," Anderson recalled later. "I knew what he meant and he knew what he meant. I told him, 'Son, you're going to have to trust me.' I knew what I meant and he knew what I meant. He had spent the whole year telling me what everyone else was offering him. When he first started talking that way, I told him, 'I'm not going to promise you anything because if I do, you're going to get yourself in trouble, get me fired and everything else.' He said, 'Who is going to tell them [the NCAA]?' I said to Hart, 'What the heck, you know we'll do what we can to take care of you.' "

The *Dallas Morning News* later reported that, in a last-minute discussion, Dykes and Anderson agreed the *Parade* All-American would come to OSU in exchange for a car. Then, at 5:05 p.m., February 13, 1985, Dykes strolled into a room where Anderson and his counterparts from Oklahoma, Illinois and Texas A&M waited. The three-sport star announced his choice was OSU, a decision that even caught Anderson unprepared.

"The only letter of intent I had with me had the player from St. Louis's name on it," Anderson said. "I went and found a typing teacher and got Hart's name typed in right quick. We blotted out the other name and put Hart's on it." Anderson, who

Walter Byers, R. Wayne Duke, and Arthur J. Bergstrom, the nucleus of the NCAA during its formative years, gather in Byers's office.

Photo by Alan Carey

Former Marist College basketball coach, Mike Perry, broke NCAA rules, was fired, then helped the NCAA prosecute his former employer.

Illinois player Deon Thomas (No. 50), who starred at Chicago Simeon High School, sat out his freshma year after an illicit tape-recorded conversation with an Iowa coach prompted an NCAA investigation. While the NCAA used that tape against Thomas, it would no tape-record his claims that he was innocent.

Illinois assistant coach Jimmy Collins was alleged to have offered Thomas $80,000 and a Chevrolet Blazer if he came to Illinois.

Rik Smits, a gangly kid from Holland with little basketball experience, was thrust into the national news when Marist College was sanctioned for NCAA violations that he said he still does not understand.

Former NCAA president Al Witte admits the organization's rule against tape-recording interviews, "is the single biggest defect in our enforcement program."

Mark Alcorn was able to watch his Louisiana State basketball team go to the Final Four before he succumbed to cancer. Tiger basketball coach Dale Brown had to break NCAA rules to get Alcorn's teammates to a fundraiser, which paid for his cancer treatments.

Indiana University guard Steve Alford was suspended by the NCAA for appearing in a calendar for charity.

DePauw basketball player Steve Hollar (far left) was forced by the NCAA to repay $632 of the fee he earned as an actor in the movie *Hoosiers.* Hollar, shown here with star Gene Hackman, used "athletic talent" for profit, a violation of obscure NCAA rules.

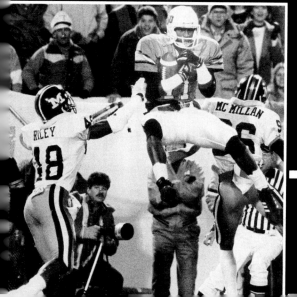

Hart Lee Dykes took gifts from four schools—then helped put all four on probation after receiving immunity.

Dale Brown, whose running criticism of the NCAA brought investigators to the Louisiana State campus, continues to fight against rules that "legislate against human dignity."

University of Miami law professor Lonny Rose (left) chats with David Berst, NCAA assistant executive director for enforcement, at a reception during the 1990 NCAA convention.

The rugged life of an NCAA investigator cost Ron Watson his marriage before he—like most NCAA investigators—quit after 16 months on the job. He is now assistant athletic director at the University of Oklahoma.

Former NCAA president Wilford Bailey of Auburn conceded the NCAA enforcement process leaves many with "the impression almost like the prosecuting attorney, jury, and judge are working side by side."

Former NCAA investigator Doug Johnson said he used the tension his job created "as a motivating factor."

Photo by Greg Cava Photo

Jerry Tarkanian fought the NCAA for 13 years before the U.S. Supreme Court said the organization did not have to treat him with due process.

Nebraska Senator Ernie Chambers won the NCAA staff's "consistent pain in the ass" award for his work on behalf of college athletics.

had also recruited for Clemson in the early 1980s when that school's football program was placed on NCAA probation, swears Hart Lee Dykes is the only player he ever cut a deal with.

"I had a bad feeling," he said. "I didn't feel guilty, exactly, but I knew afterward that according to the NCAA it [the promise] was wrong. But I also knew Hart Lee Dykes would help bring millions of dollars to this university. I knew this was a player Coach [Pat Jones] wanted bad. Throughout the course of the recruiting, it was brought to my attention how important it was to sign Hart Lee Dykes."

Anderson should have listened to his original gut instinct. It would have spared him a great deal of grief. Not long after Dykes began racing down the sideline at Lewis Field, he began racing through the streets of Stillwater in a red $17,000 Chevrolet IROC Camaro. Not long after that, NCAA investigators were crawling all over that city of 40,000 people and Willie Anderson found himself unemployed.

The recruitment of Hart Lee Dykes will go down as one of the fiercest in all of college sports. No one knew how fierce the competition was, exactly, until NCAA investigators convinced the rising star that they would ground him, making him ineligible to play college football and jeopardizing his pro career, if he didn't start to squeal. Dykes told tales about the University of Illinois, Texas A&M, Oklahoma and his own school, Oklahoma State. One by one, each school was placed on probation.

From Illinois, Dykes said he was given $100 by recruiter Rick George. According to the NCAA, the money enabled Dykes to stay in a hotel where he could be protected from rival recruiters. George, who resigned after telling the NCAA that he expected Dykes to repay the $100 "loan," said it was Dykes who asked for the money. The Dykes allegation was the most serious one uncovered by the NCAA in an investigation of Illinois that resulted in 17 months' probation and other sanctions.

From Oklahoma, Dykes told investigators he was offered $1,000 cash by Sooners receivers coach Mike Jones. Jones reportedly showed up at Bay City High and offered Dykes the money in an envelope just before signing day in 1985. According to the NCAA, Jones then called Dykes's older brother, Todd Chambers, and told him about the money. Former Sooners coach Barry Switzer talked with Jones and said, "I believe the coach, not the player." The NCAA went the other way.

From Oklahoma State, Dykes said, came Anderson's offer of a car, a high-paying summer job in the oil fields, a monthly stipend and other unnamed perks. Again, the coach said it was Dykes who stood there with his hand out. "He was less than truthful when he said what he received at OSU was offered to him," Anderson said.

"I talked to him all during his senior year [of high school]," Anderson said. "And he kept telling me he really wanted to come to OSU. But he always wanted to know what I was going to do for him. He would say things to me and I was in awe, to be perfectly honest with you. I came from the East Coast and money just doesn't flow like he was talking about. He said one school offered him two sets of wheels, another offered him a house for his mother and monthly cash payments. I couldn't believe it. I said, 'Naw, you're kidding me, man.' And he said, 'I'm serious as can be.' He just kept saying what the latest offer was and asking me what was I going to do. I kept trying to put it off, but I guess he knew we were going to take care of what we could. What he got from O State, really, was low.

"I do have to say, though, that when he said he wanted a car, I didn't think he meant a car like that," Anderson said. "I mean I hadn't even heard of an IROC before this. The thing was pretty nice."

In the end, the head coaches at three of the four schools—Illinois's Mike White, Oklahoma's Switzer and Texas A&M's Jackie Sherrill—along with several assistant coaches resigned after the NCAA investigated Dykes's allegations. And while each of those schools were losing millions of dollars in television and bowl appearance money for their attempts to sign Hart Lee Dykes, the pampered receiver continued to streak down the sidelines in a Cowboy uniform and through the streets of Stillwater in expensive cars.

NCAA investigators, you see, had offered Dykes immunity from NCAA prosecution of the rules he violated as long as he continued to talk. He didn't have to repay the $100 he had asked George to give him. He didn't have to return the $5,000 in cash or $125 a month ($200 a month his sophomore year) that he received from OSU above and beyond the car. But he was asked to return the IROC, which he did after driving it for nearly two years.

Nobody seemed bothered by the fact that Dykes, a kid who grew up in the housing projects of Bay City, started driving a gray

Mercedes with a sticker price in excess of $50,000 after trading in the IROC. *Boston Globe* reporter Mark Blaudschun, in a May 1989 feature about the New England Patriots' first-round draft pick, wrote Dykes "concedes quietly he has owned [the Mercedes] for a year and a half, leaving unanswered the question of who paid for such a car a full year before his collegiate eligibility was completed."

So here we have Hart Lee Dykes soliciting offers from coaches and turning those coaches in once the NCAA starts asking questions. Then while the coaches are banned from making a living—Anderson cannot coach at an NCAA institution for the remainder of this century—Dykes continues to both play college football and tool around in a Mercedes for the last year of his "amateur" career.

Dykes has refused all interviews to talk about the case, telling reporters that keeping quiet "is in my pact" with the NCAA. But there are plenty of others willing to talk for—or rather about—him.

"Hart Lee Dykes made kind óf a mockery of the NCAA system because he played while everyone knows he received extra benefits that no other athlete should be able to receive," said former NCAA investigator Ron Watson, who was hired by the University of Oklahoma to set up a rules compliance program.

"This young man will always be able to look back at this as if he completely tricked the NCAA," Watson told *Newsday*. "He got to keep the material things that got him interested in a particular school to begin with. If they [the NCAA] are going to strengthen penalties against a school, fine. If they are going to strengthen them against a coach, fine. But I am still of the opinion that we had better do something with the athlete. I think young people in this day and age are very aware that if they have their hands out and accept things, it's wrong. They should be subject to extreme punishment, and I'm talking about banning them from all NCAA play."

Former NCAA investigator J. Brent Clark offered a more generic criticism of the organization's deal-making with athletes. "Typically, of course, these student-athletes are very young, naive, impressionable, and easily intimidated in such a setting [as an interview with the NCAA]," Clark said. "That such young men have intense, almost desperate, aspirations to go to the pros is, of course, a foregone conclusion. The point is, in such a setting

a confused student-athlete is apt to provide unreliable information to a stranger he perceives to be wielding tremendous power
over his life and whom, therefore, he wants very much to please."
Clark said in that setting, an NCAA investigator has the potential
"to bring a case home" without even attempting to intimidate the
athlete. That puts investigators at a tremendous advantage.

The NCAA hierarchy, for whom Watson and Clark once
worked, defend the practice of offering athletes like Dykes a
chance to keep both their eligibility and their illicitly gained
profits. Steve Morgan said such deals with athletes have proved
so fruitful that his staff is "talking about expanding the use of
immunity even more. Your best sources of information may be
the students involved in these programs and those people would
be in jeopardy if they told you what they know because it would
affect their eligibility and their opportunity to participate. There's
not much incentive to tell someone if you're going to lose your
eligibility."

Wielding that eligibility hammer allows the NCAA to
make offers that athletes can't refuse. Former Louisiana State
University basketball player Steffond Johnson, who was asked to
quit the Tiger team and later transferred to San Diego State, said
to LSU coach Dale Brown in a tape-recorded conversation that
the NCAA threatened to end his playing days in San Diego if he
didn't accept immunity and talk. "[NCAA investigator] Doug
Johnson gave me an ultimatum," Steffond Johnson told Brown.
"I had no choice, really. He said if I didn't help him get you, I
could forget about playing my last year at San Diego. That's not
fair, for sure. I felt I had to give him something. He kept saying,
'It's terrible you're going to lose your eligibility trying to protect
LSU because they're not going to protect you.' "

Doug Johnson refused to discuss his work on the LSU case.

NCAA enforcement chief David Berst told the *Atlanta
Constitution-Journal* that the use of immunity "has become a
common tool in cases involving significant extra benefits. It has
to be a situation where we think a student-athlete has knowledge
that would help us all understand what the real problem is at a
particular school," he told the newspaper for a story detailing the
NCAA's offer of immunity to former Missouri basketball players
P. J. Mays and Daniel Lyton. "Or a situation where we can't get
it except through the student-athlete."

Berst and his staff decide which athletes should be offered

immunity, then go to the Committee on Infractions, which later will judge the case, for approval of the immunity offer. D. Alan Williams, chairman of the Committee on Infractions, said he does not recall rejecting a staff request for immunity. "The staff has asked for immunity more frequently than it used to," Williams said in a 1988 interview with the *Florida Times-Union*. "The immunity is limited only for those activities in which that person might be involved which the staff cannot otherwise corroborate on its own. The immunity does not remove the person from responsibility for other actions not related to this. Although I can't think of a time when we prosecuted someone for something outside what they were given immunity for. There's a tendency to say the crook got away when we use immunity. But the purpose of this whole infractions process is to give to the membership a sense of fairness and equal competition. You're not giving immunity to the head coach who is dealing in these kinds of things. You're only giving it to the athlete. That, in my opinion, is the way to go. Happy campers never turn the institution in. Happy coaches, well-satisfied, well-paid players are not the ones who will call us up.

"I don't like immunity," Williams told the Atlanta newspaper. "But it is necessary. It's what I call the John Dean factor. It takes a John Dean to get a Richard Nixon."

Williams isn't 100 percent on the mark when he says the NCAA is "only giving it [immunity] to the athlete." But he is correct when he says the immunity program is expanding. During its investigation of the University of Kansas basketball program, NCAA investigators delivered a written guarantee from the organization's home office to former Jayhawk player Mike Marshall, who had hopes of one day coaching in the college ranks. The letter, from Assistant Director of Enforcement Dan Beebe, assured Marshall that his "identity would not be made available to the public by the NCAA and would not be reported to NCAA member institutions that may inquire when he [Marshall] seeks employment," according to a copy of the letter reviewed by *Sports Illustrated*. In exchange, Marshall provided information about $533 he spent on Memphis State forward Vincent Askew, who was considering a transfer to Kansas. That information proved to be the turning point in the Kansas case.

Many coaches and athletic directors agree with former investigators Watson and Clark that the use of immunity sets a bad precedent. "I think we should get tough on two fronts and immediately fire the coach and at the same time declare the kid a pro and make him ineligible," Texas Christian University football coach Jim Wacker said. "There are kids out there with their hand out. It is a farce that the NCAA will then treat them like they've done nothing wrong. Hart Lee Dykes made this a total joke."

"Who in their right mind can defend immunity?" asked former North Carolina State basketball coach Jim Valvano. "You're going to kids who left the program, who are mostly unhappy, and asking them to come up with something. How can that be a credible source? The most powerful tool you have over a kid playing sports is ineligibility. And now, the whole world's being held hostage by kids who may have been unhappy. Talk about questionable."

"Athletes involved in violations should not compete. Period," said Bob Marcum, former University of South Carolina athletic director.

"There have been 21 notable civilizations that have left an impact on the world," LSU's Brown said. "Nineteen of those 21 have crumbled from within and history will show you that each crumbled in part because it used a snitch system as its means of policing itself. The system doesn't work and that's what immunity is all about with the NCAA. The people that commit the crimes walk away and leave others who have done nothing to suffer? That makes no sense to me."

"It takes two to play that game," said former University of Florida basketball coach Norm Sloan. "It takes a giver and a taker. To punish one of the two and let the other off scot-free is wrong. The NCAA knows it, but is willing to close its eyes to some things in order to catch others. When we were under investigation at N. C. State, I complained to Bill Hunt from the NCAA that he was using people who wanted David [Thompson] to go someplace else for most of his allegations. I said, 'You talked to people who are mad at us, who have an ax to grind with us.' And he said that was the only thing they had going for them. 'We don't have subpoena powers, we have to take unhappy, disgruntled people and they give us our leads.' He admitted that to me."

Ironically, Sloan resigned in 1989 when one of his players used immunity—not from the NCAA, but from federal prosecutors—to tell a U.S. Attorney that Sloan had committed a litany of legal and NCAA violations. Former Gator forward Kenny McClary told federal authorities that Sloan gave him money that he used to buy drugs, arranged through an assistant to sell McClary's season tickets and arranged for McClary to live in an off-campus apartment, among other things.

But when McClary was summoned to appear before a federal grand jury investigating drug use in Gainesville, he changed his tune. According to testimony obtained by the *Palm Beach Post*, McClary told the grand jury that he had lied to prosecutors because he "just wanted to get Coach Sloan fired." It worked. In the face of what was reported to be a sure indictment, Sloan opted for a forced early retirement. McClary said the reason for his vindictiveness was that during his senior year he "didn't receive no playing time."

Anyone wonder whether there might be a few more disgruntled athletes out there willing to tell similar lies to the NCAA in exchange for the opportunity to continue playing under the NCAA's version of immunity?

"Subpoena power, compared to immunity power, is like night and day because subpoena power simply means that the person you want to attend will be there," said law professor Lonny Rose. "Immunity power says that the person who is being offered immunity is being told, 'Talk to us privately and we will not penalize you.' The subpoena power says, 'You will give me records.' But there's no school or school employee that can refuse the NCAA records. That's part of your agreement of membership. The expanded use of immunity makes the NCAA's argument about subpoena power pretty weak, in my opinion.

"With immunity, if you value your position within collegiate athletics, if you value your eligibility, if you value your reputation, immunity is much more important," Rose said. "I can say to you, 'Tell me anything you want and you will not be penalized for it.' You will get a lot more people to talk that way than by forcing people to show up under subpoena for a discussion with an investigator. Prosecutors will tell you, in a criminal context, that immunity is definitely a more valuable tool than a subpoena.

"Let's play this out. Who decides who gets that immunity? The prosecutors. The enforcement staff. The enforcement staff goes to the Committee on Infractions and says, 'We want to give this person immunity.' It is not the infractions committee who says, 'Oh, give that person immunity.' So, it is the enforcement staff who decides who gets it. Does that color what the person given immunity says? Maybe. But, more importantly, isn't that a lot of discretion about who gets immunity vested to the organizational bureaucrats?

"Now, who gets immunity? Athletes. They go to some 18-year-old kid and say, we will not take away your eligibility—your lifeblood, if you will, if you talk. The problem here is that years ago the bribes went from the booster or the coach to the players. Today, kids are walking in with their hand out. Sometimes in the recruiting process today, the kid now goes to the highest bidder and the kid is the one soliticing the bid. They walk in now saying, 'What are you going to give me to attend your school?'

"These are the kids who now are being given immunity, yet continue to have their hands out and continue to go from school to school," Rose said. "We're giving them immunity under the belief that these kids will help us catch the big fish. Well, you know what? I'm not sure who the big fish are anymore, the kids or the boosters. The NCAA's plan to expand the use of immunity bothers me tremendously. That's like saying, 'Go out there and commit a crime, kids, and know that if we come talk to you, you ought to ask for immunity. We've got some of it for everybody.'"

Anderson agreed that all the attention given Dykes's take-the-money-and-run stories may well serve as a lesson to other athletes. "He certainly has made this the way to go," said Anderson, now the director of admissions at Langston (Oklahoma) University and a minister at Mount Zion Baptist Church in Stillwater. "If you're out there reading about Hart and you're a superstar like he was, put your hand out, but always be ready to cut a deal with the NCAA. That's the lesson of the day. Is it wrong, what he did? It is as wrong as it can be. I was wrong, too. I knew not to do it. But people will learn from the fact he escaped without paying any price. And they'll remember."

GETTING COZY

Bruce Webster walked from an outdoor patio into the conference room at a hotel in Duluth, Minnesota, and despite the fact that a refreshing breeze was blowing in off Lake Superior, sweat already was puddling in his palms. When the large wooden doors closed behind him, the future of his University of Bridgeport basketball program would lie in the hands of five complete strangers. As he looked around the room, Webster noticed that the university lawyers looked lonely standing on one side of the room. Closer to the front stood several members of the NCAA's Committee on Infractions, engaging in a little chit-chat with the only other people he recognized, the NCAA's investigative staff.

"I had only been in a court once in my life, to pay a traffic ticket," Webster said. "So when I looked around the room and saw just how many people it looked like we were up against—all the committee members and it must have been eight NCAA enforcement staff—I had a real nervous reaction. It wasn't a good feeling. David Berst was up there, he was the prosecutor, and he looked more relaxed with those people. But I guess he should have. He had been there with them all weekend and he knows them and they know him."

That cozy relationship between NCAA investigators and the committee that rules on the quality of an investigation has concerned many who have passed through the doors to a secret meeting with the Committee on Infractions.

"At the first hearing, we were not really being heard by the infractions committee, but by the enforcement staff," said Walter Waetjen, former Cleveland State University president. "If you look at where the locus of power was, it was with the staff. I felt that increasingly as the hearing went on. When the enforcement staff was established, inadvertently what was transferred to it, which was not intended to be transferred to it, was tremendous power and decision making. They would make accusations about what they said happened. We would have affidavits showing that not to be the case. Yet our affidavits would be ignored by the infractions committee because the committee members said they felt comfortable with what the staff had said. That is capricious abuse of power."

Former University of Florida football coach Charley Pell said it is not uncommon "for those of us that don't become NCAA insiders to feel intimidated by the prospect of taking on the infractions committee and the enforcement staff at the same time. There's a feeling when you're standing there that the guys on the other side hold all the cards," Pell said. "Just the way they talk to each other is different from the way they talk to you. It doesn't take much to pick those things up."

Mickey Holmes, executive director of the USF&G Sugar Bowl, said recently that, while he was commissioner of the Missouri Valley Conference, his two appearances before the infractions committee led him to believe the enforcement staff "had assumed an inappropriate and too far-reaching role in the hearings. They [staff] guided the hearing completely," Holmes said. "They would interrupt the flow, the comments of anybody that contradicted them. It was an intimidating procedure. It isn't any fun when the questioning part of a hearing before the infractions comittee is supposed to be a session with the infractions committee. And staff members are jumping up and down across that no-man's land in the space in the U-shaped tables, jumping up and down and going over and whispering in the ears of the committee members, you know damn well [giving them] questions to ask. I said once, 'Hey, why don't you guys just sit down. You are going to get worn out telling them what to ask.'"

NCAA officials acknowledge that there may appear to be a relationship between the infractions committee and the NCAA staff that investigates cases. But they say it is only because the one-time visitor to an infractions hearing forgets that the staff and the committee work together continuously throughout the year. That explains the use of first names and the occasional inside joke. But, really, it doesn't mean anything, the NCAA says. "There's no doubt the committee has come to know the staff through working with them," said Steve Morgan. "But I think you would be hard pressed to prove that that relationship has ever had a bearing on the outcome of a hearing."

Criticism stems largely from the fact that the Committee on

Infractions, which meets as many as six times a year, has no staff of its own. The committee counts on the enforcement staff to do the committee's leg work. Then the committee—an appointed group of six people from NCAA member institutions—is expected to step back and judge the work of the field investigators presenting the NCAA's case against an accused institution. Even some NCAA officials agree this is a concern.

"I think that the criticism is to a degree justified," said former president Bailey. "You get the impression almost like the prosecuting attorney, jury and judge are working side by side, using the same personnel, office and everything. That perception has been one that's been widely held, certainly by institutions that have gone through the trauma of an investigation. There is no question but that there is a relationship there that can leave the perception that these people are too close."

As would be expected, members of the enforcement staff and infractions committee say the perception is nothing more than that: perception.

"I'm not sure how you change the perception that it's not fair," said former investigator Mike Gilleran, now commissioner of the West Coast Athletic Conference. "The staff knows the committee because we've presented other cases. It is true that schools always felt that it was them against the world. That's unfortunate because it really is not so."

"We have tried over the years to create more and more distance, not officially, but just for perception's sake, between the staff and the committee," Morgan said. That attempt apparently failed. Shortly after the 1988 investigation at the University of Kentucky, investigator Dave Didion, who presented part of the NCAA's case to the Committee on Infractions, and committee member Marilyn Yarborough left the NCAA to get married. Didion has since returned to the NCAA staff. "I can't for the life of me figure out how they found time to socialize," infractions committee chairman D. Alan Williams said, downplaying the damage the marriage did to Morgan's pronouncements that no special relationship exists between staff and the committee.

"We may have dinner sometimes after a hearing, but never before," said Le Moyne College Athletic Director Tom Niland, a nine-year veteran of the infractions committee. "I guess I shouldn't say never because I might be there—the meetings generally start on Friday—on a Thursday night in the hotel coffee shop and one of the investigators might come in and I might have dinner with him. They came here to Syracuse [New York] and we all played golf and we went to Cooperstown after the hearings were over. Some members of the infractions committee played, some investigators played. But certainly I would be astonished if anyone said there was collusion or a friendship on the part of the members in some combined effort."

Whether Niland is correct or not, the sense that staff has an advantage during hearings because of its established relationship with the committee is not a new concern of some NCAA members.

During the congressional investigation of the NCAA enforcement program more than a decade ago, the subcommittee on oversight and investigations of the House Committee on Interstate and Foreign Commerce heard testimony from more than 40 people. In its final report, the committee concluded:

"The most widely perceived problem with the NCAA infractions hearing, however, is not so much what is not allowed in the existing structure, but what is. The perception, voiced to the subcommittee by virtually all witnesses not presently part of NCAA officialdom itself, is that there exists a kind of unseemly alliance, the appearance of an 'inescapable relationship' between infractions committee members and the prosecutorial enforcement staff, giving rise to an unbeatable home court advantage. In other words, it is at least the perception of many that infractions hearings are not conducted by what all affected parties have a right to expect, a neutral decision maker."

Former NCAA president John Fuzak admitted to the committee that the appearance of an advantage for staff had created "a good deal of resentment on the part of individual institutions."

"Looking at the infractions committee, I believe, and have believed, that there is an inescapable relationship between the infractions committee and the investigative staff," Fuzak testified. "Over a period of time, they [the committee] come to know members of that enforcement staff. They come to respect them. They tend to accept their evidence less critically than the evidence put forth by an institution or by individuals in their own defense. I think there were occasions when, in terms of accepting evidence and accepting indicators, they [infractions committee members] tended to accept what the investigative staff said over what was presented from the other side. Committee members must depend upon staff work and that staff work involving the investigative staff puts them too close to being investigator, judge and jury."

The perception is compounded by the manner in which infractions committee members are selected. The members are picked by the NCAA's Committee on Committees, which relies on administrative staff input in making its choices, congressional staff said.

"These people are not impartial," former North Carolina State and former University of Florida basketball coach Norm Sloan said, echoing the complaint in Congress. "They are selected by the NCAA. They work their way up through the ranks to be selected by the NCAA, to be in this position. And therefore, if the NCAA after their investigation says we think these people are guilty, you are being judged now by people who belong to the same organization who just said you are guilty. How do you move from the very bottom up to an important committee? You have to do some things the NCAA likes. Obviously you gotta do things that they like. You have got to be an NCAA man through and through. You can never stand up on the floor and challenge the NCAA and make it to one of the important committees. You can't do that."

Attorneys for Marist College had similar observations. "There is such a reliance by the Committee on Infractions on staff," said Paul Sullivan, Marist's lead counsel. "As far as these people [infractions committee members] are concerned, this is just a part-time honorary position. In the judicial system, the judge is first and foremost impartial. That's not the case with the NCAA. They are selected by the NCAA. They serve at the whim of the NCAA and they rely on the NCAA. They do it subtly. These people depend on staff to do their work. If staff didn't do the work, these volunteers would have to do the work."

College Football Association Executive Director Charles Neinas, a former NCAA employee who testified before Congress, said then and continues to say today that until the NCAA divorces the enforcement staff from the infractions committee, members always will be suspicious of that relationship.

"Why don't they establish, like they do in the courts, a clerk of the court and he or she would work for the judge?" Neinas asked a decade after he first mentioned the idea to Congress. "If the NCAA were to establish someone who could be in that clerk capacity for the committee, then, for appearance' sake if nothing else, there would be a more clear demarcation. The reason I'm given [for rejecting the idea] is that the NCAA operates as an administrative procedure and that gives them a license to do things that you wouldn't do in a court of law. The impression left as long as they continue to refuse the idea is that the staff has an advantage. I don't understand their reluctance to address this."

Neinas said there is little doubt the committee is in need of staff assistance. It is just that the assistance should not come from David Berst's troops. Independent staff, he said, might help make the committee's tremendous amount of work flow quicker and more smoothly. And the amount of work members of the committee must do is staggering.

"I would read probably an average of 40 to 60 hours at home preparing for each case," Tom Niland said. "Which means if you get three or four substantial telephone-book sized packs of material to read—and it's not like reading a novel— you have to compare interviews of coaches and players. You have to read the interviews and you have to read them hard."

"For every eight hours of meeting, you should assume there's another eight hours in the office," said John Nowak, former faculty NCAA representative for the University of Illinois and a long-time member of the infractions committee. "It is not a fun committee."

Charles Alan Wright, University of Texas law professor and former chairman of the infractions committee, said it "was ordinary for there to be 1,500 pages to 2,000 pages of information to read before each meeting. It was very time consuming."

The volumes sent to the committee generally represent the university's response only to the charges it is contesting. Often the NCAA staff and university representatives will meet a week or so before the infractions hearing. It is during this meeting, usually, that the university has its first look at the NCAA's evidence against the school. The staff and school might agree that certain violations occurred and the staff might drop other allegations it can't prove.

"If the staff didn't feel like they [allegations] were accurate, [enforcement director] David Berst would say, 'Fellows, you're trying, but you're not getting there, so just knock it off,' " said former investigator Ron Watson. In other cases, the staff or the committee will dismiss, or "wash," allegations during a Committee on Infractions meeting. "I would say we wash as many things as we find, at any given time," said committee chairman D. Alan Williams.

Those allegations that can't be resolved in the pre-hearing conference often require lengthy presentations before the committee. Ten-hour hearings are not unusual. "Very short means four hours," Williams said.

The Committee on Infractions sets its own schedule, but can meet as often as every other month. During each of the three-day meetings, the committee generally handles three major cases and a dozen smaller or secondary cases. The NCAA pays for the members to fly first class to the meetings, which generally are held in upscale hotels. If a committee member opts to fly coach, the NCAA will pay that person an extra $100 for his or her "inconvenience." The organization covers the hotel cost, including the suite rented for the committee chairman, and pays each member $80 per day above his or her university salary.

After an infractions hearing, the committee meets for several hours and decides what charges they believe have been proved. The meetings are private, although that wasn't always the case. For years, the committee and members of the enforcement staff would retire to a suite in the hotel where the hearing was being held and, after opening up the liquor cabinet, further discuss the case, former investigator Brent Clark said. "It is at this point that the staff made its hard pitch to the committee members in a convivial and totally ex parte session," Clark said. Loud rumblings from within the organization led the NCAA to call a halt to that practice a few years ago.

In considering penalties, the committee does not look to comparable cases for precedent, said Frank Remington, a University of Wisconsin law professor who served on the Committee on Infractions for nine years, five as chairman. "More frequently you try to fit the sanctions in with the kind of violation. The coaches association told us that . . . limiting the number of coaches, taking away grants, reducing visits, grounding coaches, those are the things that hurt the most."

Former University of Florida president Marshall Criser said his experience showed there was a "lack of consistency in the administration of penalties. They get very severe at times and other times aren't as severe. That sends mixed messages to a coach whose job depends on winning or to a student-athlete who's thinking principally about a pro contract."

The NCAA dismisses such criticisms, especially as they relate to the levying of sanctions. Almost every penalty is subject to question by those outside the system, infractions committee chairman Williams said. "If the institution thinks it's too hard and other people think it's too easy on them, then it's probably all right," he said.

Once it has established a penalty that at least the required two-thirds of the committee agrees with, the committee divides up the responsibility for writing the final report. Two members will work on the introduction, describing what violations the committee believe occurred while another member will write the section detailing the penalty. Then the report is sent to David Berst, who rewrites the document in NCAA lingo.

Berst will send each committee member a copy of the final report and the group will conduct a teleconference to discuss the case. "Sometimes we get away and think, 'How did that really work?' " Williams said, adding that it is not uncommon during the teleconference for the committee to change the penalty it had assessed.

After the committee has agreed to a final penalty, NCAA staff calls the institution and asks when the school wants to get spanked. "Sometimes it is not advantageous to get these things on Fridays," Williams said. "Or there may be sometimes when the president is out of town for a few days and he may want to be there when the announcement is made. We give them a window of a few days to get the report."

Former chairman Wright said one problem was that new members of the infractions committee had no training and some, like himself, had little knowledge of NCAA rules before suddenly being asked to cast stones at those who violate the rules. "We learned, I suppose, the same way a newly sworn-in judge learns what the laws are that he is enforcing," he said. "We learned more about them [rules] the longer we were on the committee."

Wright, who served on the committee from 1973 to 1983, said recent changes in NCAA legislation have increased the influence staff has over the infractions process. "The staff actually has a larger role now than when I was chairman," he said. "In the present procedure, with some minor punishments, the staff can impose the punishment themselves subject to the review of the chairman. We did not have such a procedure when I was chairman. I had some reluctance about moving to a system of that sort when I was chairman. I thought the infliction of penalties was something for the committee to do, not for the paid staff to do. The administrative work, of course, they did all of it. But it was purely in an administrative sense. In the same way my secretary types all my letters, the staff drafted confidential reports."

Wright contends that, despite impressions to the contrary, his experience was that NCAA staff has no advantage over institutions during hearings. But that wasn't always so, he said. "There were some cases early on where the staff may have had an advantage," he said. "After all, this is what they do for a living. But I really do believe, and I understand how some might think otherwise, that as institutions became more sophisticated and hired better lawyers, it has pretty much evened out."

COURTING DISASTER

Institutions frustrated by fighting the NCAA through the no-win infractions hearing and farcical appeals process often mutter that it might be best to take the organization to court. Don't bother. The NCAA, like the athletic programs it oversees, hates to lose. The NCAA spends more than $1.5 million a year on legal fees, almost as much as it spends on enforcement alone, often hiring well-known attorneys to defend itself against its own members.

"At the NCAA, if anybody ever threatens lawsuit, you don't care," said Mike Gilleran, an NCAA investigator from 1976 to 1984. "Because the NCAA is not going to be outspent or outworked in a lawsuit. That's entirely different from a league like ours. We have insurance and all that, but we don't want to mess around with lawsuits. We don't even want the threat of them. That didn't bother the NCAA."

That's because the never-ending money supply at the NCAA allows the association to spend as much as $2.3 million a year— as it did in 1981—to beat back legal challenges. According to one former NCAA counsel, the organization banks on its track record being a deterrent to keep cases out of court. "We sort of adopted the attitude that if we'd win most of our cases, it would sort of dampen litigation, " said George Gangwere, who served as the NCAA chief legal counsel from 1972 until his retirement in 1988. "That's sort of what happened to some degree."

"Most of the time, if there were losses, we do appeal," said John J. Kitchin, NCAA legal counsel for more than 15 years. "We feel that we're right. We wouldn't appeal if we felt we were absolutely wrong."

When in 1986 attorney James Rochford of Peoria, Illinois, prepared to file a lawsuit on behalf of four Bradley University basketball players, he had law clerks pore over previous cases in which the NCAA was named. The results of his research: The NCAA had won about 80 percent of the 120 cases in which it had been involved and had appealed nearly every loss to higher courts. "The NCAA is obviously a hard nut to crack in court," Rochford said. Dick Versace, the former Bradley coach now with the NBA's Indiana Pacers, was a little less subtle: "You might do better to take on an oil cartel. They're not as powerful. If you look at the NCAA long enough, you'll find that they pay informants, and if they want to hurt you, they will."

In some cases, the NCAA has spent years and millions of dollars of its members' money fighting those same members.

■   In a fight to retain control of television broadcast rights to college football games, the NCAA spent two years and more than $2 million dollars, eventually taking the case all the way to the Supreme Court. The NCAA lost.

■   In a case that lasted more than three years, and also one it lost, the NCAA fought to have two Canadian hockey players declared ineligible for accepting $60-a-month payments while playing on a club team during their high school years.

■   In fighting to enforce its penalties against University of Nevada–Las Vegas coach Jerry Tarkanian, the NCAA spent more than 10 years in court and nearly $1 million in legal fees.

■   In fighting to avoid paying sales tax on its purchases, the NCAA took its argument that it was an educational institution all the way to the Kansas Supreme Court, costing both the NCAA and the State of Kansas hundreds of thousands of dollars. The NCAA prevailed.

There's no end in sight to the expensive litigation, either. In its 1988-89 annual report, the NCAA attempted to reassure its members, stating "several lawsuits. . . have resulted in substantial attorneys' fees and could result in substantial fees in the future. The majority of the litigation would not result in material losses to the Association."

The television rights case was one of the most celebrated of the NCAA's legal battles. For years, the NCAA had the power to determine which games were televised. In 1982, the universities of Georgia and Oklahoma filed suit, saying the NCAA's clout violated antitrust laws. In 1984, the U.S. Supreme Court ruled in favor of the schools and the NCAA was forced to pay nearly $1 million for the universities' legal costs as well as its own costs, also estimated at $1 million. Still, the NCAA apparently was reluctant to accept the Supreme Court's decision and attempted in editorials it wrote in its in-house publication to claim some victory in the case, according to an October 1984 U. S. District Court order.

"The Court is concerned by the lengths to which the NCAA has apparently gone in its zeal to impress upon its membership that somehow the NCAA prevailed in this action," wrote Judge John Burciaga. "This Court wondered whether the membership was being given a report of a case different from the one this Court heard. . . . I say this in order to forcefully impress upon the parties that the court found illegal conduct on the part of the NCAA; that this same or similar conduct, however veiled, will not be condoned by this court."

When the case was initially heard in 1982, William S. Banowsky, then president of the University of Oklahoma, testified that members were frightened to challenge the NCAA. "As president of a major university, there is very little that I fear more than our relationship with the NCAA. It's what a taxpayer fears in his relationship with the IRS. It's not that the taxpayer may be trying to do something dishonest, it is he fears a power which is pervasive and has such control over his life," Banowsky said. "I wake up every morning knowing that anything in our athletic program might, because of the terrific powers of the NCAA, be on the front pages of the *Los Angeles Times* immediately. . . . I would be less than candid if I did not say that I have been concerned that subsequently, next year, the year after, the year after, when the smoke settles, the NCAA might wish to exercise unusually intense investigative procedures of those institutions which have had the nerve to challenge them in this public way. And in those cases, we are at the mercy, of course, of that system, a policy system which I wish to say that I strongly favor."

It was actually about five years later that the University of Oklahoma's football program came under NCAA investigation.

Banowsky's comparison of the IRS to the NCAA is nearly perfect. Facing the IRS, a faceless, nameless bureaucracy that wields incredible power and seems unbeatable, is every American's nightmare. *Money Magazine,* in a 1990 investigation, showed that when the IRS sent out 36 million notices of additional tax and penalties due in 1989, more than half of the notices were incorrect. But because taxpayers are leery of fighting the IRS, they anted up more than $7 billion in wrongful taxes, *Money* reported. And, like universities facing the NCAA, they took their punishment quietly, albeit no less painfully.

Battling a relentless NCAA requires schools to spend large amounts of time and money to defend themselves. "The NCAA has all the money it needs and all the staff necessary and willing to commit to producing a guilty verdict," said George Bisacca, a Connecticut attorney who represents schools against the NCAA. "If you're a school, this is not something you planned for in your budget. You have to find the money for this."

It isn't cheap. From Iowa State to Florida, from Louisiana State to Minnesota, it is not unheard of for schools to spend $500,000—plus untold hours in staff time—defending themselves against what appears to be inevitable. When the case involves a public institution, that bill often is passed on to taxpayers.

Former Florida president Criser said the great expense sometimes is necessary just so a school can understand how the

NCAA is going to beat them. Florida spent $300,000 on its 1984-85 case, in which the school received a three-year probation (later reduced to two years). The university then spent nearly double that in a 1990 case that resulted in two additional years of probation.

"Part of the money you spend is finding out who the NCAA is interviewing and who they're listening to," Criser said. "They don't tell you that. The president has got to know what's happened, and he isn't necessarily going to find out from the NCAA."

WHEN YOU'RE STARING DOWN THE BARREL

Universities don't survive NCAA investigations. They endure them. And from those who have endured, and from their consultants, come three tips:

First, hire good attorneys and hire them fast. *Second*, if the charges are serious, don't believe the NCAA when it says cooperation will lessen your penalty. *Finally*, don't think you're going to beat the NCAA.

"There was no way we had any chance against the NCAA," said Beryl Shipley, who was coach at the University of Southwestern Louisiana when the NCAA closed down the Ragin' Cajun basketball program in 1973. The shutdown of the USL program came before the NCAA adopted a formal death penalty in 1985. "We gave them everything they asked for, answered all their questions," said Shipley. "Then they killed us. I had a better chance of beating John Wooden's UCLA team than beating the NCAA. You're not going to beat those guys."

Once you've accepted that you will be beaten, bring in a

good attorney to at least help soften the blow. "We didn't include an attorney from the beginning because we believed this was going to be a friendly thing, very collegial," former Cleveland State University president Walter Waetjen said. "That was our mistake. My recommendation would be to any other administrator, don't make that mistake. Get an attorney involved instantly."

Lonny Rose, now a law professor at the University of Miami, was an assistant athletic director at the University of Kansas in 1983 when the Jayhawks's football program was under investigation by the NCAA. He looked around and found little outside help for schools under NCAA investigation, so he resigned from the athletic department and formed SportsMasters, a Kansas City-based company that represents institutions, coaches and athletes in infractions and eligibility cases with the NCAA.

Attorneys who normally deal within the court system, Rose said, find it difficult to deal with the NCAA and its nominal standards of due process. Its proceedings bear little resemblance to the judicial system. Because it is not an arm of the state, the NCAA says it doesn't need to guarantee all the rights you would expect in a courtroom. And if you expect the NCAA to behave like a court, and you attempt to fight the organization as if it were like a legal battle, you lose, Rose said.

"If you've got a tax problem, you go to a tax attorney," Rose said. "If you've got an NCAA problem, schools are learning they need to go to an NCAA attorney. That is a good analogy because this is like taking on the IRS." Do not, Waetjen, Rose and others agree, use a booster who is also an attorney to fight the NCAA or investigate your program. Often the booster is too close to the program to remain objective. Many schools have been heeding that advice.

"Schools are hiring outside investigators to conduct their investigations," said Tom Niland. "They [investigators] seem to be able to come up with a less adversarial role than the folks at the schools. Almost naturally, if I have coaches here and I work with the coaches and I was to conduct an investigation, I'm going to defend them a little harder than would some firm I hired downtown whose job is to present the facts."

Charles Alan Wright, who chaired the infractions committee from 1978 to 1983, said the use of attorneys specializing in NCAA matters has begun to balance the scales of NCAA justice.

Before schools figured that out, Wright said, the NCAA staff had the upper hand during the infractions hearings because they knew the NCAA's procedures and understood its process. "Some institutions would assign the case to a law professor to handle their presentation or a lawyer who never had anything to do in his life with athletics or the NCAA and simply would be out of his depth in trying to deal with staff's presentation of the case," Wright said.

"Practicing attorneys who come to our process, at least initially, try to make it an adversarial judicial proceeding because that's the context they're familiar working with," the NCAA's Steve Morgan said. "Part of what we need to do to help institutions is to get past that knee-jerk, adversarial reflex action and point out to them how the process works. The process works just fine if you cooperate, share information and don't strike a defensive posture."

But a bigger mistake than not hiring an attorney, several presidents and coaches said, is buying the NCAA's assertion that everything will be "just fine" if you do things their way.

The picture of an investigation painted in the *NCAA Manual* is one of open cooperation, with the school and the NCAA staff working together on uncovering the truth. A school's cooperation is to be rewarded when a penalty is assessed. In practice, though, the picture is much different, administrators say.

"I believed the *NCAA Manual* when I read it and it said it was going to be a cooperative effort, we were going to be honest with each other," said Marist College President Dennis Murray, whose basketball program lost an appeal of its two-year probation in 1988. "That didn't happen."

"If you're honest, upright, forthright and out front with what happened, they stick it to you," said Texas Christian University football coach Jim Wacker. "Why would anybody in their right mind want to be honest if that's going to cost them? For every question they ask you, the thing to say is, 'I don't remember' or 'I don't recall.' Everybody knows it and everybody's doing it.

"The word is out. The way everybody deals with the NCAA now is to hire a bank of lawyers, spend a lot of money and deny everything. Make them prove it. They can't, without your help," Wacker said. "Every investigator that has come across this campus has said they know who the cheaters are. They just can't catch them. And the reason they can't is because there are some schools that have mastered the art of denying the truth. That makes them good cheaters in the eyes of the NCAA, I guess, because they're the ones that don't get nailed. That's a sick system, if you ask me, when you can't be honest and live with it.

"The way to beat the NCAA today is lie," Wacker continued. "It doesn't matter if they've got you point blank. There's no disadvantage in lying. Being honest is a disadvantage. I'll never regret being honest. I can look at myself in the morning. But was it totally unfair and ridiculous the way they handled our situation? Yeah. They've always asked for self-disclosure and when we did what they ask we got totally hammered. Obviously, they don't want self-disclosure. I'm not sure the NCAA wants to catch people, the big ones in particular."

The NCAA's David Berst cringed when he heard Wacker's comments. "That's a wrong approach and we'll tell institutions so when we get there," Berst said. "If you let us do it all, we will do it all and you'll suffer the consequences. If you don't get on board and try to understand what your own problems are and treat them yourselves, then there won't be any mitigating factors that will be decided later. And you can expect penalties that will adversely affect your program for years to come. It will not only take away the advantage you gained, it will set you back. That is a fact. And I hope that isn't being lost out there."

To explain his cynical view of the system, Wacker didn't have to look far, simply pointing to NCAA sanctions levied against his football program in 1986 after he had dismissed seven players for accepting cars, cash and clothing. TCU cooperated fully with the NCAA. Yet the Horned Frogs were given a three-year probation, lost 25 scholarships over two years and were forced by the NCAA to return $343,203 in television revenues.

"In the one instance where a school really cooperated, the NCAA came down with the second heaviest penalty in football history," Wacker said. "The NCAA would not have had a case if it weren't for us turning ourselves in. The way they handled that case did not do the self-disclosure argument any good." Added TCU Chancellor William Tucker, "In our judgment, the NCAA missed an extraordinary opportunity to encourage self-disclosure and to begin a constructive process of reform across the land. Some of the penalties [against TCU] are totally inappropriate, we think, because they tend to make victims of innocent players and honorable coaches. We are deeply disappointed."

D. Alan Williams, the current chairman of the Committee on Infractions, defended the NCAA's penalty against TCU. "What they [TCU] had done up to that time was horrible. A lot of those kids took a pay cut to go play in the pros. And that case was close to being broken open [by NCAA staff]." The NCAA's account of the investigation, though, credited TCU with uncovering information that NCAA investigators could not and would not have found.

The University of Maryland, during its 1990 effort to avoid major penalties against its basketball program, expressed similar frustration after cooperating fully with the NCAA. The Terrapins were hammered with three years' probation after being found guilty of 18 violations. "As far as we could tell, cooperation didn't seem to make any difference," Maryland President William Kirwan said. "We felt that the sanctions went beyond what was reasonable given what was done. We conducted joint investigations, we invited NCAA investigators in and worked as a team and we were cited by the NCAA as going to extreme lengths to cooperate. According to their own provisions, if an institution cooperates, that is cause for mitigating sanctions. In our opinion, they did not make any meaningful mitigations."

The NCAA's one-sided requirement of "cooperation" in an investigation has prompted complaints in the past as well. In 1978 the University of Denver's Burton Brody described the relationship as "cooperative only in the same sense ancient Rome's system of capital punishment was cooperative—the condemned is expected to carry his cross to the crucifixion."

The TCU case caused many coaches to weigh the value of self-disclosure, Lonny Rose said. "They [coaches] don't have much guidance from the NCAA right now on how much self-reporting really means," Rose said. "If the violation is serious enough, the fact that you self-reported is almost meaningless. If the violations are minor, self-reporting works. I'm not sure coaches have gotten that message yet."

At Cleveland State, which received three years' probation for violations involving two students—including 7-foot-6-inch Sudanese center Manute Bol, who now plays for the NBA's Golden State Warriors—who wound up never playing for the school. Walter Waetjen said his coaching staff took a stand on the cooperation issue, refusing to sign statements that the NCAA staff had prepared. Waetjen believes part of the reason the NCAA lowered the boom on his school was because his staff's refusal to sign statements was interpreted as a failure to cooperate.

But too often, the NCAA investigator's interpretation of what was said is different enough from what was actually said that the coach's own statement could be used to make the coach look like a liar, Waetjen said. "I think our decision not to sign statements was an excellent decision and I would absolutely recommend it to anyone else," Waetjen said. "The stakes are too high to sign those statements."

Waetjen said that while he stands by the decision made not to sign the statements, the school's abnormally harsh penalty may have been a result. During the infractions hearing, the discussion was bitter. At one point, infractions committee member Tom Niland even poked fun at former Viking coach Kevin Mackey, telling the coach, "Your problem is, you don't know how to cheat very well."

Niland later admitted to a reporter that he had made the comment. "Let me explain what I meant," a somewhat startled Niland said. "Let's say that I recruit illegally a player and it turns out the kid can't play for beans. It's like robbing a bank and there's no money. They got caught cheating for players who never played for them. I call that lousy cheating. I think people who cheat are lousy cheaters if they don't get winning players as a result of it. I think there are people who cheat better than others. I can't recall any incidents. Sure, I think there are people who skirt the rules better than other people."

Schools don't always cooperate with the NCAA. Former NCAA staff members and committee members mentioned two schools in particular that were seen as resisters: Southern Methodist University and Kentucky. In the case of SMU, officials say, the school attempted to portray itself as very willing to cooperate, to the point of asking the enforcement staff to recommend penalties to the NCAA Committee on Infractions.

The staff's recommended penalties? A long probationary period—four years—but less stringent schedule and staffing reductions and no termination of the football program. "The only reason we did that [recommended penalties] was SMU asked us to," said Butch Worley, an NCAA investigator for two years and now assistant to the athletic director at the University of Texas. "I think most schools think the NCAA [staff] still has a lot more authority over that committee than we really do. They [SMU] found out we didn't."

Indeed, SMU is one of the few schools that has drawn the true ire of the Committee on Infractions. Rather than rubber-stamping staff recommendations, the committee eliminated football at SMU for one year and imposed more stringent staff reductions than the investigators had suggested. It was the first time the death penalty was used.

The death penalty, instituted by a 1985 special convention, allows the NCAA to terminate a school's program if the school is found in violation of NCAA rules twice within five years. After the penalty was issued to SMU, it appeared the Committee on Infractions decision may have been justified. It was learned that some SMU boosters, including Texas Governor Bill Clements, had conspired to continue to pay football players despite a previous NCAA sanction.

Committee on Infractions members hold SMU up as the ultimate example of failure to cooperate with the NCAA. "The institution has an obligation . . . to tell the truth," infractions committee chairman Williams said. "Therefore, the institution may not do as Southern Methodist did, deliberately suborn and subvert the whole process. Otherwise, they'll pay the price."

5

THE INVESTIGATORS

RON WATSON

Ron Watson walked to the window and pulled back the blackout curtains in his Ramada Inn hotel room. The sun was just climbing over the horizon, burning off a fog that enveloped the parking lot. If it was Monday, this must be Jackson, Mississippi.

A local television station, tipped off by the hotel desk clerk that Watson was in town, had made his presence the lead sports story the night before. And there on the front page of the newspaper tucked neatly in a plastic wrapper and left outside his room was a short story warning readers that Watson was back. With all this attention, Watson knew the week wasn't going to be easy, but neither was the last time he had come to these parts looking for a little dirt on the beloved Golden Eagles of the University of Southern Mississippi. Watson was one of the least popular men in Mississippi doing one of the least popular jobs in America. He was an NCAA investigator.

"It didn't take long to get the feeling people thought of you as the plague," said Watson, who worked at the NCAA from January 1984 until May 1985. "You ever get the feeling people thought you were the devil? I never really felt like I was well received by anyone. You could tell they would rather be talking with anyone but an NCAA investigator. I didn't like the feeling that everybody was hostile towards what I represented."

But with the eagerness and anticipation of a child headed for the first day of school, Watson set out on his mission. "I just wanted people to be honest with me," he said. "I just wanted them to do what was right. Maybe I was a little naive. No, I was definitely a little naive." Somewhere along that dull and dry 100-mile stretch of State Road 49 between Jackson and Hattiesburg, Watson lost his naiveté. Once in Hattiesburg, home of "the University of Southern," as the school is known in Mississippi, what Watson believed would be a rather routine and simple investigation became anything but.

This was Ron Watson's first case. Armed with his high-lighted copy of the NCAA rule book, a pen, paper and a newspaper article detailing alleged NCAA rules violations, Watson began digging. The newspaper story had laid his groundwork in some detail. Don Palmer, a former star linebacker at Brandon (Mississippi) High School, had decided he wanted out of his commitment to the Golden Eagles so he could play for cross-state rival Ole Miss. When Southern Mississippi refused to release Palmer from his National Letter of Intent, Palmer decided in the spring of 1984 to go public with allegations he had been improperly recruited by Golden Eagle assistant football coach Jerry Fremin. Among the violations Palmer alleged: that Fremin had made more than the NCAA-allowed three recruiting visits; that Fremin had allowed another Southern Mississippi player to use Fremin's car to drive Palmer the 180-mile round trip to his home; and that two boosters drove Palmer's mother to another booster's home, where Fremin and Palmer were waiting. Once at the booster's home, Fremin gave Palmer a baseball cap and a warmup suit and the boosters gave his mother a ham, Palmer said. And boosters, through Fremin, bought three meals for Palmer and his mother.

Watson had a willing witness; now all he had to do was find the evidence to substantiate Palmer's charges and he could get back to Kansas City. The first notch on his NCAA gun belt, it seemed, was going to come quickly. "I went immediately to the young man and got his story verbatim," Watson recalled. "Then I went to each one of the boosters for their particular version. After I visited the boosters, I became quite certain that the young man had pulled my leg. These boosters were church-going, very devout, religious-type people. Their homes were very solid homes with young children growing up in them and I felt like, 'Hey, these people probably are going to be shootin' straight. Maybe they're right, the kid is just upset that he didn't get his way.' "

Perturbed, Watson went back to Palmer, who by this time had been released from his letter and had transferred to Arkansas State University. "Now this was three months after the first time I interviewed him," Watson said. "I was very serious, very stern, trying to impress the importance of telling the truth. In that interview, he gave me almost exactly the same information he gave me the first time. I knew if he was lying, it would be tough to tell the same lies twice. Having gotten fairly secure that he was telling the truth, then I went on campus and interviewed the coach involved. The whole thing started to fall in place. I got his hotel, telephone and credit card records and they seemed to show the young athlete was telling the truth. The four boosters, the guys I thought looked straight as an arrow, were not telling the truth.

"That whole incident shattered a lot of confidence I had in people," Watson said. "How could they sit there and just lie? But for them, it had become more important to protect the name of the school. They were protecting a coach they particularly liked and knew that if he would get caught up in this, if they would admit to some underhanded dealings by this coach, he would be fired. Their concern for the coach more than anything else, I guess, was the reason they felt like they couldn't tell the truth. They were protecting not only the school but a coach they had gotten quite attached to.

"Suddenly, I started to doubt everyone. I just thought everyone was telling me nothing but B.S." That was the apex of Watson's career with the NCAA. He made his case. The assistant coach was fired, the student allowed to play elsewhere. But by that time some of the luster had come off of Ron Watson's image of college athletics, an image that had developed over 16 years as a player and coach. That wasn't all Watson lost during his 16 months as an NCAA investigator. The demands of a grueling job, coupled with the paltry salary the NCAA pays its enforcement staff, changed Watson's life. It wasn't all for the better.

A former lineman at Ames High School in Iowa, Watson went on to play defensive end for the Indiana State University Sycamores. While at Indiana State, he earned bachelor's and master's degrees and married his childhood sweetheart. After a few years of teaching and coaching in Indiana, it seemed life had come full circle when in 1977 Watson accepted a job teaching physical education at Iowa State while also coaching on the football staff. What could be more perfect? A football hero marries his sweetheart, and years later returns to his hometown where his daughter enrolls at his old high school, becomes a cheerleader and spends Friday nights doing cartwheels down the same sidelines her father had stalked two decades years earlier as a local schoolboy star.

But after six years, Watson became restless. It was time for a change. A friend who was reading the NCAA's in-house newsletter, the *NCAA News*, clipped an advertisement out of the job listings. "Wanted: NCAA enforcement representatives." Watson was intrigued. He submitted a resume. The NCAA was equally intrigued at the possibility of adding a coach who had had to live within its many rules to an enforcement staff loaded with recent college graduates. "They really needed someone with an athletic background who'd kind of been through the rules and recruited and interpreted them," Watson said. Twice, Watson was brought in for interviews. Before he left the second interview, the NCAA made an offer. If he was willing to spend every other week on the road—leaving late Sunday night and coming home late Friday—for $22,500 a year, he had the job. "It looked like a helluva challenge," Watson said. He accepted.

As often as possible, Watson tried to route his return flights through Ames, hoping to spend a quick 36 hours with his wife and kids. Making the most of that time proved to be more difficult, even, than trying to catch flights in and out of Ames. "The family pressures—I had two young daughters at the time, 15 and 10," Watson said. "I had moved in January [1984] from Ames. My family stayed behind because my wife had a good surgical nursing job. The two children, I wanted them to finish their four-year school there. My daughter was a cheerleader at Ames High School, where I graduated from, was enjoying it and loved the school. My young daughter was doing great in her elementary school. So I left the family behind and moved to Kansas City. I was flying out so often it was difficult for me to get back to Ames. In that four-month period, before they finally moved to Kansas City, there was a real strain. After having been married for 17 years, this was the ultimate strain. While I was with my family, I thought about the job. While I was on the job, I thought about my family. It became a little bit of a problem in trying to figure out who I was married to when I finally got back on weekends to see them. I would try to see the kids but yet my thoughts were on the job. I knew I needed to go interview some people, so I'd try to line out in my head who I wanted to see, where I had to go once Monday came. I didn't really concentrate too much on the family."

Watson's marriage ended in divorce. "It wasn't all due to [the job], but it did have an impact," he says. "You come home and say, 'Who is this person I'm living with on weekends?' It took a pretty understanding wife. In most jobs, you know you get to come home at 5:00, see the children, spend the evening, eat with them. In this job, they may go for a full week without seeing you at all. And then you may have so many things on your mind that you don't really have quality time with them. Usually the career of an NCAA investigator is a short-duration kind of deal, and a lot of that is due to wives who want them to move into something a little more stable, where there's a little more quality time." Because of the working conditions and the pressure, said Watson, "they [the NCAA] have lost a lot of good people."

For Watson, the pressure got worse on Monday mornings. "It is very lonely out there on the road. If you got quite a few interviews out of the way, you could get back to the hotel room, eat a bite, start dictating if you wanted to, write notes to recall what had happened that day, and make plans, getting the old maps out and seeing where I was going to go the next day. You get up at 6, maybe get in a good jog and a bite of breakfast, and actually start getting near your first interview about 8 or 8:30. You probably would be out on the street working that night up to 10 o'clock. Sometimes it approached midnight before I'd finish."

If a key interviewee ducked Watson during the day, the investigator would stake out his home, hoping to conduct the interview at night. "Usually, you just kind of drive around in an area until you saw lights on in the house or saw a car pull up in the driveway," Watson said. "That was the loneliest times of the job. It was so quiet, you'd already read every newspaper available, you'd already stuffed yourself with a burger at a fast food restaurant. There was nothing to do but think."

Every other week, following five long days' worth of

tracking violations, Watson would return to the NCAA's offices in suburban Kansas City to dictate memos detailing his previous week's accomplishments. Traveling was hard, but life in the office was no picnic, either. Bizarre and inexplicable office policies made life nearly as unbearable in the office as it was on the road.

"You couldn't have coffee or Cokes on your desk, you couldn't hang your own pictures in your office, you were in at 8:30 or you were counted as tardy," Watson said, shaking his head. "If you got so many of them [tardies], they would dock your salary. You'd have your wages docked. We're talking about grown, educated adults. If you weren't in your office at 5 p.m. that was about the same, unless you had a reason to be flying out and had checked out. You had to always pull your shades at night. That was one of those little policies no one really ever understood. You couldn't leave your light on and your door unlocked. Your desk had to be completely cleaned off. The only things you could leave on top of the desk were the stapler, maybe a calendar. But everything as far as your work was put away.

"They also had some kind of crazy rules about you couldn't take days off, vacation days, surrounding a holiday. They didn't want anyone taking advantage of long weekends or something. I remember everyone really bitched about it all the time."

Like many before him and many since, the strain, both financially and personally, drove Watson to leave the NCAA. Tulane offered the car he could drive away in. In the midst of a basketball point-shaving scandal that had attracted national attention, Tulane President Eamon Kelly decided it was time to hire a staff member to keep the Green Wave out of future trouble. He turned to the NCAA, where the poorly paid staff is always ripe for the picking. Watson jumped when Tulane called, offering a $9,000 raise—his NCAA salary had grown to a whopping $24,000 by the time he left—and a new luxury car if he would become the school's assistant athletic director and recruiting coordinator.

Watson recalled, "There were so many school officials I talked to while I was at the NCAA who were flabbergasted at the fact that I had a master's degree and was, I guess 35, maybe 34, when I started there and was making what I was," Watson said. "I was one of the older investigators on the staff and I was probably making between $8,000 and $10,000 less than I would at a member school if I had gone into athletic administration. I had no courtesy car, no golf club membership, all those privileges that sometimes are extended to you at an institution. They were kind of surprised and often would ask me, 'What is the deal? Does the NCAA want to have turnover in enforcement? Do they look forward to having new faces come in and out of there?' Well, my answer to them after a while had to be, 'I guess so because they certainly weren't trying to do much to raise the salary structure.' "

When he made his decision to leave, no one at the NCAA seemed shocked. No attempt was made to talk him out of it. "I got the feeling that they didn't particularly care if there was turnover. They [NCAA leaders] treat turnover like it's a good thing. Isn't that an amazing attitude? It takes two years just to get comfortable in the job. But they felt it brought in fresh ideas. I, and a lot of other former investigators, feel you lose a lot of experience. I've been pretty outspoken about the NCAA's archaic pay schedule and my outspokenness has been well-publicized. Now, if I go back to see the NCAA boys, or the young ladies, that are working in enforcement, I always get a hand shoved out at me to say, 'Thanks, I saw what you said.' I think those people appreciate it when former NCAA investigators speak up because you can't be outspoken when you're on the staff. Not unless you want to leave a little quicker than you might otherwise had planned."

There were a lot of personal positives, Watson said, in leaving. But there was a down side that bothered him. His departure continued the NCAA's trend of rapid turnover among investigators, a problem that causes delays in the enforcement program and increases the potential for a breakdown in the investigatory process. "It [the turnover] is unfair, I think, to a lot of people," Watson said. "The turnover there creates havoc in that they're always in a mode of getting new faces familiar with the process and procedures. Then you have those same new people presenting cases to the committee and they don't feel comfortable right off the bat. So, in effect, I think the member institutions suffer somewhat when we don't have continuity with who is out there trying to enforce NCAA legislation.

"It takes a new investigator a lot of time to learn all the principals involved in the case, of what has been done, what's been said, where we're headed, what still needs to be done. I had a major case at a Southern Conference school that I was pulled off of to help finish a different major case. Then I had to try to go back to the Southern Conference case and, basically, refresh my own memory. Then I left and went to Tulane and it got handed off to another investigator who had no clue as to what I was doing, where I had been. I mean, I left a very thorough portfolio of memorandums and had sketched out what needed to be done. But that's still tough to pick up somebody else's work and get a clue right off the bat as to what you need to do.

"When a guy leaves or he's offered another job and he feels like it's bettering himself or herself, he tries to wrap things up, but you can't do it in two weeks. So that means you turn it over to someone else. That hurts the institutions because their timetable on the infractions calendar suddenly is pushed back. And if an investigation goes three or four years, it loses its potency. The kids involved have left; there's no immediate impact on the people involved. The NCAA is hurt by this, too, because they have to hire new people, putting a strain on the experienced guys who have to absorb what is left over from someone that leaves. And it waters down their chance to get other cases resolved. You know it's kind of a domino theory. Most of the time it's not going in the right direction."

Watson left Tulane in 1988 when Donnie Duncan, who had hired him at Iowa State, again called offering a job, this time as assistant athletic director at the University of Oklahoma where Duncan was athletic director. But Watson still has strong feelings about his work with the NCAA. "It got to me. I love the people at the NCAA. They were, in my opinion, very professional. I think it is sad that the setup encourages people to leave. It's wrong. It's wrong for a lot of people. But it doesn't look like it's going to change any time soon."

A PROSECUTOR'S MENTALITY

For more than 18 months, Walter Waetjen knew there were NCAA investigators on his campus. But he never saw them. Waetjen, then president of Cleveland State University, opened his *NCAA Manual* and read where the investigation of alleged wrongdoing was supposed to be "cooperative." So he waited.

"I was sure if they were investigating us, they'd have the decency to come to the president's office, sit down and tell me what they believed was wrong," said Waetjen, a former member of the NCAA's Presidents Commission, who retired from Cleveland State in 1988 to teach at Cambridge University in England. "It was only when their investigation was completed that they came to my office. That was just wrong. They snuck around for a year and a half before seeing the president of the university. And when the investigator finally came in, he believed in his heart we were guilty. There was no doubt in his mind. His you're-guilty-and-I-know-it mindset offended me."

Waetjen's complaint is common. The NCAA's response is simple: sneaking around is part of the job. So, at times, is being deceptive. It is all part of trying to catch cheats in a system most NCAA investigators believe is designed to handcuff them. And given all the creative things schools have tried to hinder investigations, who can blame investigators if they've become cynical and adopted a prosecutor's mentality?

That mentality is developed out of necessity, some former investigators argue. Few jobs in college sports can promise you first-class travel, top-notch accommodations and hatred everywhere you go. As an "enforcement representative" of the NCAA, you get all that and less . . . much less. Though all investigators have advanced degrees, many in law, starting salaries are in the mid-$20,000 range. And despite those degrees, their credentials are often criticized.

"No way would I ever hire any of the people they've got working for them," said an attorney familiar with the NCAA's operations, who asked that his name not be used. "There's a reason why they're working there, and it is often because they couldn't get a job anywhere else. For what they pay, you're certainly not going to get the cream of the crop from law school. A good law school graduate can come to almost any major city and start at twice the NCAA's salary. Tell me, do you really think these investigators would make a conscious decision to go live on the edge of poverty if they could earn twice as much elsewhere?"

Because of the rigors of the job and the poor pay, the investigative staff suffers from high turnover. Most investigators openly concede they join the NCAA with a plan to stay a maximum of two years. Even Steve Morgan, the NCAA's associate executive director, said he intended to stay only two or three years when he joined the NCAA as an investigator in 1977. "I had opportunities open up for me here before I made it through the two- to three-year period, so I didn't leave, but I didn't remain an investigator either," Morgan said.

Each of the 19 former investigators interviewed agreed that the low wage scale was a significant factor in their decision to leave. "The salary thing is a sore point with every former investigator or present one," said R. Dale Smith, who left the NCAA in 1987 to become assistant commissioner of the Metro Conference. "That's why a lot of people leave. And when people leave, it is very disruptive to a case, no question. It did seem rather inconsistent that they would have all that money and pay investigators so little."

In fact, the NCAA's enforcement staff policies are filled with inconsistencies.

■   Morgan claims the investigators operate under a code of ethics designed to avoid potential abuses of power. Morgan, though, declined to release a copy of the code. Seven former and one current investigator interviewed said they never had heard of the code.

■   It would be a violation of that code for any NCAA investigator not to identify himself when interviewing people as part of an NCAA investigation, Morgan said. "If anybody violates our procedures, fails to represent themselves properly or misrepresents themselves in an investigation, we want to know that," Morgan said. "Anytime we get reports that people have acted contrary to procedures or somehow done something that seems inappropriate, we want to know about it and we want to pursue it to try to determine if it's a real problem." But four former investigators, all of whom have left voluntarily in recent years, said they sometimes didn't tell people they were with the NCAA because they worried that some wouldn't talk to an NCAA investigator. David Didion, a current enforcement supervisor who has left and come back to the NCAA staff several times, said he sometimes calls people to interview them but doesn't tell them who he is. He said he mentions the NCAA "only if somebody asked me." Dale Smith said he did the same. "It is true that you might not volunteer that information because, if you did, some people would be less likely to meet you or talk to you," Smith said. "You had to make that decision yourself and there were times when I did [fail to identify myself], yes."

"I always felt the ethical responsibility to tell them this was Marcia Morey of the NCAA and I assumed we had to be forthcoming and honest," said former investigator Marcia Morey. "Obviously, that wasn't always the case because I heard others admit they didn't do that."

The accusations have been worse. In 1977, an Oklahoma bank president signed an affidavit in which he accused former investigator Ron Stratten of representing himself as a federal agent in an attempt to get bank records during an investigation of Oklahoma State. In the affidavit, the banker alleged Stratten misrepresented himself in order to obtain evidence a private airplane was used in transporting Oklahoma State athletes free of charge. The owner of the plane was Clarence Wright, a former Oklahoma State athlete, who was then president of the Yukon (Oklahoma) National Bank. Stratten later left the NCAA staff and is one of the few former investigators who is no longer involved with collegiate athletics.

■   Although most of the athletes the NCAA staff interviews are black, the enforcement staff has always been virtually 100 percent white. No more than a half-dozen black investigators have worked for the NCAA in the 40 years it has had an enforcement function. Morgan said the NCAA, as a matter of course, does not rely on its few black investigators to interview black athletes. "I don't think we have to use women to investigate women's cases or blacks to deal with black athletes," Morgan said. But Bob Minnix, a black investigator, said he has "often been asked over the years by white investigators to go in and talk to black individuals, to try and change the attitude." Mike Garnes, a black former investigator who left and formed a company that conducts NCAA rules compliance audits for schools, said he experienced similar requests. "More than once I was asked to smooth things out for a white investigator," Garnes said. "Sometimes, because many of the kids that we're talking about are black, white investigators would ask us to try and help them. I know one time, one of the guys went in a home that was in a deprived area, in a ghetto area, and he said a couple of things in asking questions, he approached these questions in such a way that people got offended. It was just his lack of cultural awareness, you might say. There are certain things you just don't say. They [the NCAA] need some serious help in two areas. They need to be sensitive to the needs of not just blacks but women, too. I'm going to tell you, I wasn't too happy with the way they treated some of the women out there. Statements made in meetings sometimes they thought were jokes. I didn't think they were jokes."

■   During the course of an investigation, investigators are allowed to buy meals for the athletes they are interviewing. Yet if a coach or booster were to buy that meal, it would be a violation of the NCAA rules. Former Louisiana State basketball player Steffond Johnson told LSU coach Dale Brown in a tape-recorded discussion that NCAA investigator Doug Johnson took him for a steak and lobster dinner, "then got me half-drunk at a bar" before asking questions about LSU.

■   During their investigations, NCAA investigators fly first class and stay in the best hotel available while chasing down penny-ante extra benefits given to student-athletes, many of whom have never seen a first-class seat or slept in a $100-a-night hotel room. Former investigator Smith said the enforcement staff nearly always flew first class at NCAA expense because "a lot of the information you're processing and handling is confidential. You'll have a little more privacy in first class than you do in coach with a full house," Smith said. "It is rather difficult to work on your papers without having them reviewed by other folks when you're traveling coach."

"Because of the extensive travel demands it's something of a gesture on behalf of the executive committee to help people be a little more comfortable," said the NCAA's Morgan. "Also, we've had some investigators who are large enough that it makes a difference whether they travel first class or coach." Apparently it makes no difference whether student-athletes are large enough to need the space in first class. An NCAA rule prohibits universities from paying for student-athletes to ride in the same first-class cabin NCAA staff are allowed to enjoy.

Several investigators said they never questioned why the NCAA allowed them to fly first class and stay in four-star hotels at the same time that it paid them in the mid-$20,000 range. But they did—at least every other week when their paychecks came in—often question their salaries. For most of those who left, the issue was money. "I think they have to take a hard look at the level of compensation," says Dan Beebe, who resigned from the enforcement staff in 1986 to take a job as an assistant athletic director at Wichita State. "It's one of the toughest jobs you can have. If they want good people and want to keep them, they're going to have to pay a lot more."

Sometimes investigators didn't have to wait until payday to be reminded of their lowly paycheck. Mike Garnes said, "I've had several coaches tell me when I came to investigate them, 'Look, you don't come up here telling me, some $25,000 investigator, coming up here looking at my program. Do you know who you're talking to?' You have no credibility when you come up there. 'Some ole wet-nose guy coming up here making $25,000 a year, asking me some questions about violations. You better get out of my face.' But I guess their [the NCAA's] philosophy is there are so many people out there trying to kick the door in, to get up there, because they don't really know what it's like to be up there, that they don't have to pay. They think they're going to become the next Morgan or the next Berst. So they can afford to keep the turnover as high as they do because there are a lot of good people with good academic backgrounds trying to get in. But it hurts enforcement."

While choosing to ignore the existence of such inconsistencies, NCAA officials do acknowledge the stresses of the job and the problems caused by high turnover. They also acknowledge that, in a world where a single investigation can take three years or more, this turnover becomes critical.

"The turnover was the thing that really bothered me," said Le Moyne College Athletic Director Tom Niland, a nine-year member of the NCAA infractions committee who watched nearly two dozen investigators come and go. "It takes time to learn to be an investigator, and they didn't learn it overnight. The process is bound to suffer as a result. Maybe it was due to inexperience, but I did find places where they didn't ask the questions they should have."

Former investigator Doug Johnson said the rapid turnover also affects the NCAA's ability to properly train its enforcement staff. "When I came in, there were a number of guys there who had been there a while," said Johnson, who worked at the NCAA from 1982 to 1987. "That was a good atmosphere to learn in. That isn't the case lately. I think that, again, works in the favor of the institution. It makes it more difficult on the investigator. With an investigator coming on and off a case, an institution is more likely to have something fall through the cracks."

As recently as fall 1985 nearly everything was falling through the cracks. So many investigators were quitting that only five people were left on the entire enforcement staff. And only one of those five had more than 10 months of training on the job. As a result, said enforcement chief David Berst, "There were a number of things that needed to get done and couldn't get done at that point."

Steve Morgan defended his staff, saying, "We haven't had information really break down [because of turnover]. I think that speaks to the credibility of our enforcement staff. In processing the case, if we have to change investigators—I don't know that anybody ever suffered dramatically from that kind of thing. Our people have satisfied the Committee on Infractions that they're able to accurately reflect the things that they've experienced. Our job is to see that turnover has a minimal impact on the institution."

Some school officials argue the NCAA has failed miserably on that account. "The college suffered from habitual turnover of [NCAA] staff involved in the Marist case," Marist College officials wrote in their 1988 appeal, made after the school's basketball program had been found guilty of 14 infractions. "At least seven NCAA staff members have been involved in this case. This revolving door created confusion, lack of continuity, omissions and repetition, and a substantial delay in bringing this case to conclusion."

When Marist took the offensive, the NCAA struck back, calling Marist's claim that turnover hurt the investigation a "smokescreen." Morgan quibbled with Marist's claim that seven investigators worked on the case. But he couldn't answer the question of exactly how many investigators might have been involved. "Normally, you start out with three, four if you count me, on any infractions case," Morgan said. "I guess five if you have some eligibility question. It's clear to me, though, that if I had sent 150 staffers out there it wouldn't have changed the facts. I quite frankly think that Marist's concern about the number of staff people involved was an after-the-fact attempt to defend themselves as having been treated unfairly. I don't really think it contributed significantly to the way it was handled. I don't know how to say it more gently."

"The concern about how many investigators or people were involved in the case, I don't think is significant," Berst chimed in. "Besides, I think there were six, not seven." Whether there were six or seven, Marist is not alone in voicing concern about the debilitating effect of turnover.

Morgan said that, because the NCAA budget is set by the organization's Executive Committee, which is made up predominantly by athletic directors and faculty representatives, it is unlikely the enforcement staff ever will see a significant pay increase. "Campus budgets are generally tight, raises are small, so these people don't feel they can justify large salaries," Morgan said.

"Who is he trying to fool?" one former investigator, who continues to work in college athletics, said. "Those athletic directors are the ones offering coaches $800,000 for a basketball season. For Christ's sake, [former Texas A&M football coach] Jackie Sherrill was earning what, $1.6 million, before he quit to avoid us. And they want me to believe investigators can't be paid because the Executive Committee has athletic directors on it?"

"I'll tell you," former investigator Beebe said, "it takes six months to a year before you begin to feel comfortable with the job. About the time some people become adequate at what they're doing, they move on."

While money is not among them, there are advantages to

being on the NCAA's enforcement staff. "I think there are other benefits it has to offer, like the connections you make," said former investigator Johnson, who received a hefty pay raise when he moved to Coral Gables. "I wouldn't be here if it weren't for the NCAA."

The same could be said for at least two dozen former investigators, many of whom grabbed five-digit pay increases when they left. That scenario has caused some to question the reason schools may have for hiring one-time NCAA staffers. If an employee of the Securities and Exchange Commission went to work for Drexel Burnham Lambert, Wall Street would be abuzz. Similar revolving-door relationships—where the regulators profit personally from going to work for those they regulated— prompted investigations of multimillion dollar fraud in the defense industry during the 1980s. The potential for abuse when the fox is guarding the hen house has prompted Congress and many legislatures to prohibit government regulators from going to work for those they once regulated. Not so in college sports. So far the NCAA's enforcement department has avoided any accusations of a conflict of interest, but the danger is there.

When the University of Oklahoma hired former investigator Ron Watson as its assistant athletic director for compliance, a position it had just created, it did so just two months after receiving official notice that the school was under NCAA investigation. Was it just a coincidence, some asked, that Watson was close friends with Dan Beebe, one of the two investigators on OU's case? Watson and Beebe, in fact, had teamed up to head the NCAA's investigation of Southern Methodist University three years earlier.

When the University of Miami hired former investigator Doug Johnson, also for a newly created assistant athletic director's position, the rumblings were a little louder. Johnson, in his investigation of Louisiana State University's basketball program, spent hours with Tito Horford, the Tigers's 7-foot-1-inch center from the Dominican Republic. During the investigation, Horford packed his bags and left LSU in the middle of the night. He showed up at Miami, where the school had just revived its dormant basketball program. Johnson was hired not long thereafter at a hefty pay increase. Coincidence? "I never once mentioned the University of Miami to Tito," a defensive Johnson said. "All I told him when he left LSU was to go someplace where they didn't cheat to get him, because if they did, I'd be visiting him again."

Sometimes those associations can cast long shadows over the investigative process itself. When the University of Illinois basketball program was placed under the NCAA microscope in 1989, did anyone question investigator Richard Hilliard's relationship with University of Iowa assistant basketball coach Bruce Pearl? Pearl provided the NCAA with an illicitly taped conversation he had with Illini recruit Deon Thomas. That tape, on which Thomas reportedly said Illinois made an improper offer to get him there, provided the bulk of the NCAA's 10 charges against Illinois. Hilliard and Pearl were college buddies; Hilliard was the student announcer at Boston College when Pearl was the student manager of the basketball team. Further, when the NCAA decided to interview Notre Dame star LaPhonso Ellis about his recruitment by Illinois, the NCAA sent Bob Minnix, a former Notre Dame fullback, to do the questioning. Notre Dame's representative in the room with Ellis and Minnix? Missy Conboy, a former NCAA investigator later hired by Notre Dame.

One investigator who hit the jackpot when he cashed in his NCAA badge was Mike Glazier. A former quarterback on the Indiana University football team, Glazier joined the NCAA in late 1979 after graduating from law school. In 1986, he got a call from Mike Slive, a former lacrosse player at Dartmouth College who had gone to the University of Virginia law school. Slive, after serving as assistant commissioner of the Pac-10 Conference and as athletic director at Cornell University, had decided there was a market for "specialists in NCAA law." He asked Glazier to join him, allowing the pair to profit from their history as insiders. The two set up shop in the offices of Coffield Ungaretti Harris & Slavin, a prestigious Chicago law firm. For the next four years, their $135-an-hour rate raked in more than $3 million in fees from universities, including Illinois, Florida, Missouri, Minnesota, Virginia Polytechnic Institute, Arizona State, Texas A&M, Miami, Iowa State and Oklahoma State.

Although all state public record laws are not alike, available records show "the two Mikes," as Glazier and Slive are known, billed Missouri for more than $190,000, Minnesota for more than $250,000, Virginia Tech for $138,000, Oklahoma State for nearly $500,000 and Iowa State for more than $200,000. The University of Miami even continues to pay them $50,000 a year as outside monitors of the school's athletic program. Those figures qualify Slive and Glazier as rainmakers, attorneys who bring in big money for their firms. "Isn't it a sad commentary on our times when lawyers can specialize in NCAA work?" said former University of Florida president Robert Bryan, whose school paid Slive and Glazier nearly $200,000. In 1990, the two took their very valuable practice to a law firm in Kansas City just down the street from the NCAA's offices, further adding to their reputation as "NCAA insiders."

NCAA officials say they will never be able to pay their enforcement staff well enough to prevent member schools from hiring them as insurance or to stop them from leaving for silk-stocking arrangements like Glazier and Slive. "When they are developed [as good investigators]," enforcement chief Berst said in 1986, "they are very good targets for institutions that want a person who is knowledgeable about NCAA affairs and regulations. We can get good folks and keep them for a couple of years. Then they start asking, 'Why am I getting hammered for this money?' I would like for us not to be that vulnerable. If we can't keep the people we have now for a longer period of time, we have a problem." Of the 11 investigators Berst had on his staff when he made that statement, more than half were gone three years later.

"I do think salaries are a little bit of a problem for us," Steve Morgan said. "I also feel that, while some turnover is going to be part of the job, we need to retain part of the enforcement staff for continuity purposes. Plus people get more efficient after they have a couple of years' experience. It's a fact of life we're going to have to deal with turnover. The members raid our staff all the time for qualified personnel. I have to accept turnover as part of what we do."

NCAA officials concede that turnover, coupled with the enormous workload facing the enforcement staff, cripples the NCAA's effort to stem the tide of cheating in college sports. How strong is that tide? David Berst has continually said that 10 to 15 percent of colleges cheat. "And I'm talking about Division I institutions," he said. "That comes out somewhere between 30 and 40 schools at any one time, on any day you ask, that will be on the list of schools we're looking at because we suspect some intentional wrongdoing. That list of schools changes, but the number remains constant." Former NCAA executive director Walter Byers said just before his retirement in 1987 that his discussions with athletic directors suggest as many as 30 percent of the larger NCAA schools are violating NCAA rules.

But Allen L. Sack, a sociology professor at the University of New Haven, said his research shows that both Berst and Byers are way off base. Sack mailed surveys to 3,500 active and retired National Football League players in 1989. From the 1,182 who responded, he learned that 31 percent admitted taking under-the-table payments from alumni or coaches while in school, and 48 percent said they knew of people who took such money. Of the 115 respondents who attended Southeastern Conference schools, 52 percent said they were the recipients of a booster's largesse. "For me, the results of the survey say that the payment of players is far greater than what the NCAA will admit to," Sack said. "This is not just a problem at a renegade institution or with a deviant player. There's a substantial underground economy that's likely to be unstopped."

Former infractions committee chairman Charles Alan Wright, a University of Texas law professor, conceded as much when he said in 1988 that "the enforcement arm was always overworked. My guess is, it's still undermanned."

The enforcement staff also lacks any formal training. The NCAA's investigator training process, current and former investigators say, is nothing more than reading the rule book, reviewing old cases, then picking up tricks while on the job. "It is more or less a process of learning from experience," said former investigator Dale Smith. "I don't believe there are any secrets to the art of, or the science of, investigating. I went out with more experienced investigators for a time before I went out on my own."

Missy Conboy, who worked at the NCAA from 1985 to 1987, said: "We would have staff meetings every month where we would sit down and talk about investigating. On a daily basis, you'd be talking with your supervisor." In the mid-1980s, the NCAA did begin a little professional training when it started sending investigators to a spy school outside of Washington, D.C. There, interrogators from the Israeli army as well as FBI investigators would spend three intensive days teaching NCAA enforcement staff the art of questioning. "It was really neat," former investigator Marcia Morey said.

With this background, the investigators head out to handle their first cases. On campus, they quickly get a taste of what it's like to be less popular than a referee on Saturday afternoon. What often develops is an adversarial relationship that begins the moment the investigator shows up. Former investigators and coaches alike agree both sides often lose their objectivity. Schools feel they are wronged by an overly aggressive NCAA staff and investigators believe schools can't be trusted and are trying to hide the truth.

"It's like if the IRS walked in to ask you a few questions," Dale Smith said. "There's probably nothing good that can come out of a visit by an NCAA investigator."

Former investigator Doug Johnson said he used the tension "as a motivating factor. I knew I couldn't go out to dinner, because everyone at the restaurant would know I was an NCAA investigator. So I'd order my fast food dinner and take it back to my hotel room. There were times when I felt a little lonely, being out there without my family. But my job was to overcome all those obstacles.

"In enforcement, it's like being a policeman," Johnson said. "The NCAA has a lot of detractors. But policemen have a lot of detractors, too. The Army has its detractors for killing people. Basically, you're in the business of punishing people and that doesn't bring many friends. You're administering justice and that makes you not very popular. When you go to a school, you're out there alone. The first question they ask you is when are you leaving? They offer to help make your plane reservations out of town. There are more than enough hints that they don't want you there."

Johnson, who spearheaded investigations of the University of Florida and Louisiana State University during his five years at the NCAA, said the loneliness "just made me more determined." And he staunchly defended the work of the NCAA staff. "In my mind, if a violation is alleged by the investigator, then there's no doubt it existed. To me, they [schools that dispute the allegations] are being whiners and complainers. I'll challenge any school that felt they had to prove their innocence to bring that information to me and prove the facts presented by the NCAA were wrong. As you probably have guessed, I'm not extremely sympathetic to a school that feels they've been wronged."

That attitude, according to many people associated with the NCAA, is the beginning of the breakdown of the organization's enforcement program. Too often, critics say, investigators see themselves as the saviours of college sports and develop the mindset of a prosecutor. "The investigative staff is like the KGB of college sports," said George Bisacca, a Connecticut attorney who represents schools battling the NCAA. "They believe in enforcing every rule, no matter how trivial. And they believe all that they do is for the good of college sports."

"The NCAA is using lawyers who are trained to think in a desired way to get them to a certain result," said Roy Smith, a Las Vegas attorney who helped in the defense of the University of Nevada–Las Vegas. "These guys are on a mission. They're very good at what they do. A competent lawyer can, through proper phrasing of questions, get a lay person to say the sky is green. That is what these guys do to these athletes."

Lonny Rose, a sports law professor who has defended schools during infractions hearings, said the environment in which NCAA investigators work "almost assuredly" will change an investigator's view of college sports. "If I ran a criminal defense law firm, it would be hard for me to hire someone who was a former police officer who has now gone to law school," said Rose. "They just think differently. These are pretty nice people, but they see the seedy side of college athletics and can become very sarcastic and caustic and single-minded easily. They have this mindset that their job is to root out evil in collegiate athletics and, when that occurs, they are not concerned with the wisdom of the rule, it just simply exists and it is their job to enforce it. The mindset is, 'I am the only person standing between collegiate athletics and anarchy.' "

Professor Jacob Hoefer, chairman of Michigan State University's Select Committee on Athletics, said the same mentality proved troubling during that school's investigation more than a decade ago. "As the whole history of our involvement unfolded, we became convinced that there was in the background, perhaps innocently, but maybe it was the torch that the investigators carried, that, 'I haven't lost a case yet and I am not about to lose this one,' " Hoefer said. "There was guilt until you prove your innocence instead of the reverse, as most of us like to believe. There was this feeling of hostility. There is need for an NCAA-type organization but there may be even a stronger need for them to clean up their act with respect to investigating procedures and the way in which they approach the problem. We were frustrated in the process and in the futility of what we were trying to prove. As a scientist, I know how difficult it is to prove the negative."

Former investigator Mike Gilleran, now commissioner of the West Coast Athletic Conference, admitted that several times during his eight years at the NCAA he "got so close I just lost my objectivity. I had to tell myself to back off." That prosecutorial mindset, if it goes unchecked, can magnify several other flaws in the NCAA enforcement program, such as not taping interviews with those under investigation.

And if the NCAA's investigative staff can shade the statements of those it interviews, some argue, it becomes easier for the staff to build cases. "By the time investigators get out there, there's a feeling they've got to come back with something," attorney Bisacca said. "They have to justify their expenses."

Some critics claim the enforcement staff justifies those expenses by playing "the numbers game," a race among investigators in which the goal is to rack up the longest list of alleged violations possible. NCAA officials deny its existence, but those close to several investigators suggest the game is very real.

"I know members of the enforcement staff," said Lonny Rose, three of whose former law students have gone to work at the NCAA. "I know them well, former and present. The numbers game does matter to them. The fact that they can bring up as many violations as they can is important to them. The fact that the public perception then is much greater—the institution must be real crooked if it has 108 violations and the staff must really be doing its job—is a simple fact of life. It does distress me because it makes something sound much more serious than it is. I'm not going to minimize it. It is serious when we violate the principles of amateurism. The problem is that in reporting it with the numbers the NCAA attaches, it indicts not just the coach and the player, but an entire athletic department, which includes other innocent people, an entire university and maybe even a conference. You mention the Southwest Conference now and people start to laugh. It [the numbers] matters, in part, because it helps justify the amount of time and money they spend looking at some of these schools. No doubt about it."

Charles Neinas, executive director of the College Football Association and both a former NCAA staff member and a former commissioner of the Big Eight Conference, said this "game" is one of the biggest complaints NCAA member schools have with the enforcement program. "One of the concerns I've heard is the practice of using numbers, playing the numbers game. For example, I'm going to recruit you on a weekend and it's one incident. But the one incident results in 10 different rules being violated. But rather than listing it as one incident, it's listed as 10 different rules that have been broken. It runs up the numbers. Suddenly you look like you've broken 100 rules. I think this has even bothered some of the Committee on Infractions members."

Neinas likened the work of an NCAA investigator to Inspector Javert in Victor Hugo's novel *Les Misérables*. In the story, set during the French Revolution, Inspector Javert spends 20 years tracking Jean Valjean, a thief who once had stolen a loaf of bread. "Human nature enters into this," Neinas said. "The point being that the inspector got so imbued by tracking the accused that he lost sight of the offense. It was no longer just a loaf of bread; it was a mission. I think it's only natural that this occurs, but that doesn't make it good. If an investigator is out there interviewing people and they're telling him something he pursues with vigor, when the institution comes back and doesn't reach the same conclusion, that leaves the investigator feeling personally challenged and leads to an adversarial situation. That's why I say the problem is not with the infractions committee. The problem lies with the staff."

Former investigator Morey, however, tried to balance things out, and came away disenchanted. "I did have a hard time reconciling the amount of money the enforcement department spends for what it comes up with," Morey said. She left the NCAA in 1984 because "I was disillusioned with the whole scene. I didn't feel I could really make a difference anymore. It was very difficult to fly first class, stay in a Marriott and then go out and interview a kid who could no longer play football or basketball, he couldn't even read a memorandum and he lives in a one-room, dirt-floor house."

Morey said she spent more than $100,000 in traveling and lodging expenses in her last 18 months. And she said she spent most of her time turning up "T-shirts and trips to McDonald's. Usually, we would go after serious allegations. We wouldn't start going after a McDonald's allegation. But a lot of times once we arrived and did some interviews, it turned out that the $40,000 bank account and the Trans Am didn't exist, but there were these little bennies that were given and those could be corroborated by another source and a lot of times that would come up as the allegation against the school. We would go after the big picture because of limited time and resources, that's where the priority was. But once that couldn't be established or verified, we would have to have a compromise and settle for more of the lesser offenses. It was frustrating, more so than I think anyone realizes. The NCAA enforcement program, as it is currently constructed, is not going to stop cheating. No way."

6

SHOOTING AT THE SHARK

TARKANIAN'S BATTLE

During the summer of 1990, columnists and broadcasters across the country expressed amazement when the NCAA, its hands finally untied from a legal battle that raged for years, decided to slap defending national champion University of Nevada–Las Vegas with a one-year ban on participation in the NCAA basketball tournament. The penalty was levied for NCAA sins allegedly committed at least 15 years earlier, when the players banned from the 1991 tournament were more concerned about losing teeth than losing basketball games. Worse, UNLV already had served two years' probation for these supposed transgressions back in the late 1970s. Still, the NCAA prescribed a second dose of bitter medicine and ordered the 1991 team to swallow it. Many sportswriters admitted that rushing to UNLV's defense was not an easy task. This was Las Vegas, after all. Sin City. Gambling. The Strip. And this was coach Jerry Tarkanian, whose long and legendary feud with the NCAA had left his reputation forever scarred. But, many agreed, this also was very wrong.

"The statute of limitations for armed robbery in most states is five years," *USA Today's* Mike Lopresti, never a Tarkanian fan, wrote. "It apparently is a good deal longer for defying the NCAA. Tarkanian's head finally hangs on the wall at the NCAA offices. So do those of his players, none of them guilty—but all of them sentenced. You measure injustice not by the guilty who are punished, but by the innocent who are victimized."

Added *Orlando Sentinel* columnist Brian Schmitz, "The NCAA has a thankless, tough job. But it is supposed to be fair and credible and, above all, not let personal vendettas get in the way. The case against Tarkanian reeks of vindictiveness."

Los Angeles Times columnist Mike Downey had this to say: "I would really like to see some sharp Susan Dey-like attorney step into a courtroom and sue the pants—or skirts, if there are any, though I doubt it—off that august institution, the National Collegiate Athletic Association, which fancies itself the Supreme Court of scholastic sport. Ordinarily, I'm in favor of protests being orderly and proper. But this is one time when I wouldn't object to seeing these Vegas players stomp their sneakers in court until somebody listens. They don't deserve this. I just don't comprehend why the NCAA felt it had to be this strict. It smacks of petty revenge, of getting even with the university for refusing to fall to its knees and salaam before the NCAA's almighty presence."

It really shouldn't have surprised Lopresti, Schmitz or Downey that the NCAA chose to swing hard when it came to slapping Tarkanian in 1990. It fit a pattern begun the day in 1973 when the NCAA opened its file on the man who remains college basketball's winningest coach. Public records suggest his case was the worst investigation ever conducted by the NCAA, rife with intimidation of athletes, bigotry directed at a coach, slipshod work, "creative" notetaking and untruth by an investigator and vindictiveness by a disgruntled former coach.

Thirteen years after that investigation began, Tarkanian's court case against the NCAA might have forced the organization that encourages fair play in college sports to start playing fair itself. But the U.S. Supreme Court, in a 5-4 decision in December 1988, decided that the NCAA doesn't have to play fair, at least where the U.S. Constitution is concerned. That set the stage for one more round with Tarkanian and the knockout punch that came in July 1990.

The ramifications of the Supreme Court decision for college sports have yet to become clear. But even though most sports fans know very little about Tarkanian's case, one thing stands out: Whether you love or hate him—and Tarkanian is one of those rare figures in sports whose wins on the court and losses off it engender one reaction or the other—even the highest court in the land accepts the fact that Jerry Tarkanian got screwed.

Supreme Court Justice Byron White noted in his minority opinion that it was a "given" for purposes of the Supreme Court's review that the NCAA hearings "provided to Tarkanian were constitutionally inadequate." Although the NCAA asked the U.S. Supreme Court to overturn the Nevada Supreme Court's finding that the NCAA had violated Tarkanian's rights, the U.S. Supreme Court refused even to look at the issue. Legally, White wrote, that left the Nevada court's determination that NCAA hearings lacked due process as the final legal authority on the issue. Justice White, a one-time All-America football player at the University of Colorado and the only former college athlete on the Supreme Court, was much gentler in his description of the NCAA's enforcement program than were the trial judges who heard the Tarkanian case earlier.

Clark County (Nevada) District Court Judge James Brennan, who was the first to hear the case and who ruled against the NCAA, said this in his trial court opinion:

> The case against Tarkanian was incredible. The evidence the NCAA presented was 100 percent hearsay without a scrap of documentation in substantiation. The evidence shows that every fundamental principle pertaining to the plaintiff's due process rights were violated. The Committee on Infractions and its staff conducted a star chamber proceeding and a trial by ambush against the plaintiff. The plaintiff was denied the specific charges against him and the facts upon which such charges are based. The plaintiff was denied the right to present evidence and call witnesses in his behalf. And most important, he was denied the right to be confronted by witnesses against him and cross-examine them. The Committee on Infractions allowed a staff investigator, who, the evidence clearly shows, swore he would get Tarkanian if it was the last thing he ever

did, to act as investigator, judge and jury. The record is replete with lies, distortions and half-truths. The evidence clearly shows Berst as a man possessed and consumed with animosity toward the plaintiff. There is no legal credible evidence to support the findings and action of the NCAA.

Not to be outdone, Nevada District Judge Paul Goldman, who next heard the case, put it this way:

This case presents a classic example of how misperception becomes suspicion, which in turn becomes hostility, which leads, inevitably, to a deprivation of one's rights. In short, the NCAA now seems to say: If you want to play ball, you must join us, obey rules and surrender any claim you may have under the Bill of Rights. This court disagrees with that attitude, as any fair-minded person must. At least one of the NCAA's investigators [David Berst] inspired, authored and drafted—in whole or in part—the NCAA preliminary investigation; the authority to issue an inquiry to UNLV; the Official [letter of] Inquiry; the minutes of the Committee on Infractions wherein the committee's rules appeared; the Confidential Report of the Committee; the Findings and Penalties imposed by that Committee; the Expanded Confidential Report (with the enforcement division's comments) used by the Council on appeal; and the order of the Council and the widely promulgated press releases about the supposed violations of NCAA 'legislation.' In sum, what started out as an association whose members met and acceded to certain lofty goals ended up as the NCAA-bureaucracy which looks upon its friends (sycophants) with feigned pleasure, and its enemies (those who still recognize the U.S. Constitution) with barely concealed malevolence. Regrettably, both the full-time investigators and part-time Committee on Infractions and NCAA Council members acted and thought, not like Caesar's wife, but rather as arrogant lords of the manor. The NCAA, incredibly, sought to equate 'time' with 'due process.' The reasoning of the NCAA was, apparently, that since the infractions committee's and the NCAA Council's presentations were time-consuming, Tarkanian and UNLV were afforded due process. NCAA practices might be considered 'efficient,' but so was Adolph Eichmann and so [was] the Ayatollah.

During the trial, Goldman wrote in his opinion, NCAA lawyers even attempted to argue that this case was out of the jurisdiction of any court. They made that claim after quoting the *NCAA Manual*, which states that the infractions committee's decision "shall be final, binding and conclusive, and shall not be subject to further review by the Council *or any other authority.*" Imagine the NCAA telling a judge that its decision was above the law. Goldman said that assertion was "laughable." He said the clause in the *NCAA Manual* "illustrates the arrogance" of the organization. "Even the NCAA's insistence on the use of the word 'legislation' instead of 'rules' gives us a view of the NCAA's view of itself and its power," he wrote. That arrogance was further characterized, Goldman said, by the NCAA's refusal to abide by his order to stop its daily press releases, which it distributed to national media, during the Tarkanian trial. This "clearly was an attempt to wield its powerful connections with the press to win the case through the media if it couldn't do so in court," he said.

Tarkanian's lawyers attempted to convince the U.S. Supreme Court that the NCAA, which has through its own constitution the power to force a university to suspend a coach or face expulsion from the organization, must provide those it punishes with basic rights, including the ability to face one's accusers. What the court was asked to decide was whether the NCAA is an arm of the state—or a "state actor"—because it essentially has the authority to force a state university to discipline a public employee. If the court had decided the NCAA does carry out actions usually reserved for the state, then the NCAA would be required to treat those whose lives it affects with the same legal rights as the state would.

"If the NCAA wants to have the power that it has and it wants to deal with state schools, it's not too much to ask that [it] afford due process in the manner in which it affects the property and liberty of someone whose rights it may cut off," Tarkanian's attorney Sam Lionel said. "Americans have grown to expect decent and fair treatment and that's not the NCAA's way of doing business."

Tarkanian's long fight with the NCAA began in the early 1970s when he was the coach at Long Beach State. From near nothing, he built a Top 20 program, going 116-17 in five years, with four NCAA tournament appearances. During his third season, the Long Beach 49ers came within one point in the Western Regionals of upsetting UCLA, which was on its way to its seventh NCAA title. Tarkanian did all this by bringing in junior college players, many with academic or personal problems that other coaches wouldn't gamble on. His success with junior college players shouldn't have come as a surprise. In seven years as a junior college coach, he posted a 212-26 record, winning four straight California junior college championships.

During Tarkanian's fourth year at Long Beach, the school's swimming and football programs fell under the scrutiny of NCAA investigators. About the same time, Tarkanian wrote two columns for the *Long Beach Independent Press-Telegram* questioning the NCAA's investigations of "such powerhouses as" Western Kentucky and Centenary College. "The University of Kentucky basketball program breaks more rules in a day than Western Kentucky does in a year," Tarkanian wrote in one 1972 column. "The NCAA just doesn't want to take on the big boys."

Then, in January 1973, he wrote: "The NCAA could take another major step in the right direction by revamping its investigative policies. The NCAA investigated and then placed on probation the New Mexico States, Western Kentuckys, Centenarys and Florida States, while the big money-makers go free. If the NCAA is genuinely concerned about recruiting and other athletic irregularities, it should be willing to take a look at all schools. It seems totally unfair that the NCAA doesn't look at the schools that are making money for the NCAA through television appearances. It's a crime that Western Kentucky is placed on probation but the famous University of Kentucky isn't even investigated, even though Tom Payne's story has come to light."

Payne was a 7-foot Wildcat star, the first black basketball player ever recruited to the school. After his career at Kentucky was over, Payne told reporters that Wildcat boosters had "supported" him in college because he had no money. The NCAA never investigated what appeared to be flagrant violations of the rules in Lexington. Instead, NCAA investigators spent their time chasing minutiae across the state in Bowling Green.

The second column caught the eye of Warren Brown, then the NCAA's assistant executive director. He fired off letters to Jesse Hill, the commissioner of the Pacific Coast Athletic Association, of which Long Beach was a member, and to Tarkanian's boss, Long Beach Athletic Director Lou Comer.

"Enclosed for your leisure-time reading is a copy of a newspaper article which I presume was written by Jerry

Tarkanian," Brown wrote in a letter to Hill dated January 26, 1973. "It always amazes me when successful coaches become instant authorities. As in the case of this article, such instant authorities reflect an obvious unfamiliarity with facts. Tarkanian is no exception in this regard. I wonder whether he considers California State University, Long Beach, in the 'big money-maker' category." The meaning was clear, the threat hardly veiled.

In April 1973, three months after that second column, NCAA investigators expanded the Long Beach investigation to an official inquiry and included Tarkanian's basketball program. It took them nearly two years to accomplish it, but the NCAA eventually placed the 49ers basketball and football teams on three years' probation—including the loss of television appearances for both programs and a two-year banishment of the basketball team from the NCAA tournament—for 23 rules violations.

But by the time the NCAA's Long Beach investigation was complete, Tarkanian was gone. Tired of competing with UCLA for attention in southern California, Tarkanian left in March 1973 to become the coach at UNLV. The NCAA's investigative staff was right behind. Enforcement staff records show that an NCAA investigation of UNLV that had lain inactive before Tarkanian became the school's coach was reactivated March 29, 1973, six days after he accepted the job. And the first entry into the file was a newspaper clip detailing the career move.

Three years of digging at UNLV ended on February 25, 1976, when in its 54-page Official letter of Inquiry the NCAA alleged the school had committed 72 rules violations. After three hearings, the Committee on Infractions decided UNLV had committed 38 violations with Tarkanian named in 10 of them. Tarkanian took exception to each of the 10 allegations the NCAA made against him. And on each, his lawyers delivered sworn statements and documents they believed supported and underscored their position. But the Committee on Infractions found him guilty of all the allegations.

In August 1977, UNLV appealed the committee's decision, as NCAA bylaws permit, to the NCAA Council. No school had ever won an appeal up to that time, and it is a matter of record that no school has won one since, either. UNLV contested the factual basis for most of the allegations for which it was deemed guilty, criticized NCAA proceedings and attacked the credibility of the NCAA's David Berst and Hale McMenamin, the two investigators who had presented the NCAA's case to the Committee on Infractions. "The University has good reason to believe, supported by uncontestable facts, that information provided by the NCAA investigators to the Committee on Infractions was either false, misleading or, at best, grossly inaccurate," UNLV wrote in its appeal.

Tarkanian was given only 20 minutes to plead his case, the university another 30 minutes. And just in case every conceivable advantage had not been given to the enforcement staff, documents show the Council—after UNLV's representatives, NCAA staff and Tarkanian had been asked to leave—invited Berst and McMenamin back into the supposedly closed-door deliberation of the appeal. There, while Tarkanian and UNLV were locked out, the NCAA staff was allowed to "clarify" certain issues, as Berst later testified in Nevada District Court. Apparently this process of clarification worked. True to form, the Council upheld the infractions committee's findings, ignoring the evidence about the behavior of the investigators.

After it had exhausted its appeals within the NCAA's system of justice, UNLV was ordered by the NCAA in 1977 to suspend Tarkanian. The NCAA had never ordered a head coach suspended before Tarkanian, and has not since, according to NCAA spokesman Jim Marchiony. In response to the NCAA's demand, UNLV President Donald Baepler appointed Brock Dixon, a university vice-president, to review the case and spell out the university's options as they related to Tarkanian. After Dixon's in-house hearing, he wrote that the facts supporting the NCAA's charges were "clearly in doubt." He also stated that the NCAA's "standards of proof and due process were inferior to what we might expect."

Dixon concluded, "In almost every factual situation delineated by the NCAA, the university's own investigation has been able to find a substantial body of conflicting evidence, some of which has been heard and considered by the NCAA and some of which has been brushed aside. By joining the NCAA we delegated to that organization the establishment of governing standards and their enforcement as well. We are allowed and encouraged to make our own investigations but this is in no way a substitute for the investigative functions of the NCAA itself. We must live by our commitments to the NCAA, its standards and its machinery. We must accept their findings of fact as in some way superior to our own. In this instance we could wish for standards of due process and evidence far superior to that which we have observed, but given the terms of our adherence to the NCAA we can not substitute—biased as we must be—our own judgment on the credibility of witnesses for that of the infractions committee and the Council."

Baepler immediately suspended Tarkanian. He justified the decision by claiming the university voluntarily joined the NCAA, and as a result essentially permitted the organization the right to punish its coach. Forget the fact the coach was a state university employee and the rights generally afforded other university employees were violated by the NCAA, Baepler said. "The University is simply left without alternatives," Baepler wrote to Tarkanian.

With this mountain of questions about the NCAA and its treatment of him, Tarkanian went to court and sued UNLV because it was the university that officially had removed him. During the hearing, a staff attorney for the Nevada Attorney General's Office testified that the investigation conducted by his office "found no factual basis for the NCAA charges." That said, Tarkanian won an injunction against the university, blocking the suspension.

The NCAA pressured UNLV into appealing the decision, then filed a brief as an amicus curiae, or friend of the court. Eventually, the NCAA joined the lawsuit as a defendant and spent more than $1 million on the case over the next 10 years.

Because Tarkanian's saga included a long and winding trip through the courts and was central to a high-profile congressional investigation of the NCAA, documents in his case that have never been viewed in other NCAA investigations were subpoenaed and made public record. This provided a unique glimpse inside the NCAA's enforcement program. What that glimpse revealed, many agree, was appalling, exposing an enforcement program in which the potential for a multitude of abuses is real. Among them:

Malice.   Former University of Florida basketball coach Norm Sloan testified before Congress that, in 1973, then-NCAA investigator Bill Hunt told him the organization was after Tarkanian. Fearful of retribution by the NCAA, Sloan had to be subpoenaed by Congress before he would discuss the conversation he had with Hunt, which took place just after Sloan's Wolfpack basketball program had come off probation. Sloan even asked that his anxiety about appearing before the committee be entered into the record, lest Hunt think he was "egging on" another investigation.

After he was sworn in by the House Committee on Interstate and Foreign Commerce's subcommittee on oversight and investigations, Sloan was asked by John McElroy Atkisson, counsel to the subcommittee, to recall his discussion with Hunt.

ATKISSON: It was in your office, then, in this personal meeting between yourself and Mr. William Hunt that you discussed Mr. Jerry Tarkanian, is that correct?

SLOAN: Yes.

ATKISSON: Can you in your own words relate to us the sum and substance of that conversation?

SLOAN: I can give you the substance of it. I was rather upset about our probation and was stating it to Bill Hunt and explained why, that it branded me, and [basketball star] David [Thompson] and the university in a manner we could never erase, and I didn't think it was justified. That was—I was kind of going on about it. He said in effect, "Yes, I know what you are talking about. It throws you in"—and he named some schools and named a coach, Jerry Tarkanian. When he mentioned Jerry he became a little emotional, I thought, and said in effect, he said, "We are not only going to get him, we are going to run him out of coaching."

Hunt had a little more trouble remembering exactly what he said to Sloan, but he was careful to avoid telling the committee he absolutely did not say the NCAA was out to get Tarkanian:

ATKISSON: Do you recall ever discussing that case [UNLV] or Mr. Tarkanian with Norm Sloan, a North Carolina basketball coach?

HUNT: I do not believe I have. I do not recall.

ATKISSON: You are saying that you do not recall having had the conversation but not—You do not say affirmatively that you did not have it, but you just don't recall, is that correct?

HUNT: That is correct.

ATKISSON: If you did have it, is there any possibility that you would have referred to either your or other people's desire in the NCAA to drive Tarkanian out of coaching?

HUNT: I really do not believe that is possible.

ATKISSON: You qualified it. You mean it is unlikely?

HUNT: No.

ATKISSON: Wholly impossible?

HUNT: The answer is no.

Bigotry.   David Berst, then an investigator, admitted he sometimes referred to Tarkanian as a "rug merchant," a bigoted reference to Tarkanian's Armenian ancestry. "I have utilized the words 'rug merchant' regarding Jerry Tarkanian, and I have used that term ... I cannot give you an approximate number of times," Berst told a congressional subcommittee in 1978. Berst said his reference—particularly when he told NCAA staff members and members of the infractions committee that Tarkanian could easily be recognized "as the one who looks like a rug merchant" —was really uttered in a curious spirit of "affection."

"Bullshit," Tarkanian said of that assertion. "I haven't heard too many people make that comment and not make it with a racial overtone."

After later admitting in court that he used the derogatory reference for Tarkanian, Berst was chided by a trial judge. "The name of the plaintiff is Tarkanian," Judge Paul Goldman admonished Berst. "The name of the chief justice of the state of Nevada is Noel Manoukian and the name of the governor of the state of California is George Deukmejian. All are Armenian and there isn't a rug merchant among the three."

Berst has refused requests to discuss the UNLV case, his comments regarding Tarkanian and his role in the investigation.

Ironically, Tarkanian's ancestral pride contributed, at least partially, to the strength that allowed him to plow through his 17-year struggle with Berst and the NCAA. In 1917, Turkish forces invaded Armenia and slaughtered two million of its citizens. Tarkanian's grandfather, a village official, was forced to watch Turks behead his son, and then was himself beheaded. Ignoring the pleas of other villagers that she flee, Tarkanian's grandmother sewed gold coins into her daughter's slip and sat her atop a horse along with another child. As the horse reached the top of the hill, the young girl who would become Tarkanian's mother looked back on the village. There the Turks were herding dozens of villagers into a church, bolting the door and setting it afire. The story was told and retold to Tarkanian as he grew up. "We have been fighting a long time," he said. "And we don't give up."

Although Tarkanian rarely speaks of his ethnic background, he said he still is upset by Berst's lack of sensitivity, especially since athletics is one of American society's most truly diverse subcultures. "His comments disappointed me tremendously. It makes you wonder, doesn't it, what you're up against."

Creative notetaking. In October 1976, Berst interviewed New York playground basketball guru Rodney Parker, a schoolyard hoops junkie featured in the book *Heaven Is a Playground,* who was close friends with two players Tarkanian was recruiting. Months earlier, the NCAA had sent UNLV its Official letter of Inquiry, alleging 78 rules violations. Five of those allegations stemmed from Berst's belief that UNLV had paid for Parker and recruit Rudy Jackson to come visit Las Vegas. After receiving its Official letter of Inquiry, UNLV was required under NCAA rules to try to determine the truth of the allegations. While UNLV was plowing through its internal investigation, Berst went back to several key figures, including Parker, to ask if the university was taking a defensive posture while interviewing them. Based upon this interview with Parker, Berst attempted to convince the Committee on Infractions that UNLV was trying to cover up violations rather than get to the truth.

Four times during the infractions hearing, court records show, Berst specifically told the committee that Parker said Assistant Attorney General Lyle Rivera, who handled UNLV's internal investigation, asked his questions in a "general manner." That was done, Berst alleged, so Parker would not have to reveal damaging information that could lead to the finding of a violation and thereby be "put in a bind." To back up this very serious claim, Berst read from a memo he prepared after the Parker interview. Berst's memo, entered into the court record, was central to his allegation that UNLV was violating the spirit of its NCAA membership by trying to hide violations from the infractions committee. By quoting Parker, a credible source, as saying UNLV was not trying to get at the truth, Berst could damage the credibility of everything else UNLV would claim.

"The writer [Berst] specifically asked Parker whether University representatives had asked him who paid his travel expenses to Las Vegas or about being reimbursed by Welch for his expenses," Berst wrote in his memo. "Parker reported he did not think the University's representatives asked him these questions or at least the questions posed were general enough so that his answers did not get himself or anybody else 'in a bind.'" Berst's interview with Parker took place in the New York law office of Lew Schaffel, now the managing partner of the NBA's Miami Heat. What Berst didn't know was that, throughout the interview, Parker was taping their conversation; the tape recorder was hidden in his briefcase. Berst himself made no notes, instead relying on his memory when he typed his memo about the meeting a month later according to his later court testimony.

Here's a look at what actually was said during that meeting according to a copy of the transcript obtained for this book:

BERST: I mean, how, you know, were they trying to slam bang you, or just put it down in front of you and let you help them out, or did they really want to know what the truth was?

PARKER: Well, basically, I think they really wanted to know what the truth was. I just told them, you know, exactly what happened and how it happened. They didn't try to lead me in any way.

Berst also repeatedly asked Parker if UNLV attorneys

were taking shots at Berst or any other NCAA investigator.

BERST: Did they ask you about the NCAA investigator, that being me? It ain't going to hurt me either way. What the hell, life's life.

PARKER: I don't think they were leading in that direction. I mean, I don't think they like you very much, but I don't know about, I really don't know whether, I don't know how they feel about you. I think they were more interested in the facts, the same way you are.

BERST: Did they make you feel like somehow I am a bad guy? In other words, when they talk to you, am I a bad guy?

PARKER: No. No. I know, I know they're interested in the truth, but I don't know if they, you know, I'm not sure how they feel about you. They never said.

Berst even admitted on the tape that it appeared, from his conversation with Parker and others, that UNLV was doing as it was required. "From what I've heard, they tried to find out the facts . . . .What I figured was that they would probably come to you and make a deal for whatever the circumstances are in order to protect the school from getting in a jam," Berst said on tape. "I figured they'd probably got you to sign a statement saying the NCAA is a bunch of bad guys and I put words in your mouth, and that kind of stuff. That's really what I figured probably happened to you, and I don't get that out of this conversation. Sounds like they asked you better questions and tried to figure out whether it was going on or not."

Incredibly, after this conversation with Rodney Parker, Berst stepped before the Committee on Infractions and, relying on notes he made a month after this conversation, four times accused UNLV of hiding the truth and of asking questions in such a way as to keep Parker from being put in a bind. Not once during the hour-long interview, it should be noted, does Parker use the words "in a bind," even though Berst specifically attributed that quote to him.

Parker's involvement with recruit Rudy Jackson was important because the NCAA had deemed Parker a "representative of the university's interest," a euphemism usually used by the NCAA to describe boosters. According to the *NCAA Manual*, a school is responsible for the actions of anyone who "has been requested by the athletic department staff to assist in the recruitment of prospective student-athletes or is assisting in the recruitment of prospective student-athletes." If Parker was a representative of UNLV's interest, that would mean the NCAA rules regarding recruiting with which UNLV had to comply also would apply to Parker. Had UNLV asked Parker to work on its behalf in guiding Jackson to the Rebel camp, and then paid his one-night expenses for doing it as was alleged, it would have been a rules violation. At the infractions hearing, Berst expressly told the Committee on Infractions that, during the October interview, Parker said the reason he accompanied Jackson to Las Vegas on Jackson's official visit was because the UNLV coaches asked him to do so. When UNLV attorneys specifically asked Berst at the hearing if Parker had "definitely said the UNLV coaches had requested he make the trip," a transcript of the hearing shows Berst responded, "Yes." But once again, Parker's tape told a different story. A review of the tape shows that at no time during the interview did Parker make or even imply the statement attributed to him by Berst. In fact, Parker explicitly said that he made the trip to Las Vegas because Jackson, not Tarkanian, asked him to. "Rudy wanted me there, you know, to help him out," Parker told Berst on the tape.

"This is what happens when investigators don't take notes. If he can be so wrong on these facts, he sure can bring his case home by changing the substance of the issues as well," UNLV attorney Mike Leavitt said later. "The one thing all of this proves is that staff statements cannot be relied upon in determining the futures and careers of coaches and athletes."

To underscore its defense, UNLV provided each member of the Committee on Infractions with a copy of the transcript and offered to make a copy of the tape for the enforcement staff. The transcripts were ignored, the copy of the tape never requested.

How did the NCAA punish the man who admitted in court and to Congress that he used ethnic slurs in referring to Tarkanian and who, Rodney Parker's tape proves, was not truthful at least six times in his comments to the Committee on Infractions? It promoted him to the organization's top investigative job.

Ignoring evidence.   NCAA investigator Hale McMenamin, a former FBI agent, accused Tarkanian of asking Harvey J. Munford, a part-time UNLV instructor, to give a B grade to center David Vaughn. McMenamin charged the grade was falsified because, he said, Vaughn never attended Munford's class, "The Role of Black Development in America." McMenamin, reading from a memo never shared with the university, told the Committee on Infractions that Munford told him Tarkanian had enrolled Vaughn in the class "with the understanding that the student would not have to attend class or complete any work." McMenamin said Munford had volunteered the information; it did not seem to occur to him or the committee to wonder why the instructor would admit to a total stranger that he had committed the professional sin of falsifying grades. According to court records, that was the extent of the NCAA's evidence: an unsigned statement from McMenamin recalling his conversation with Munford.

UNLV's attorneys provided the committee with:

■   A sworn affidavit from Munford stating that he had never made such a statement to McMenamin and had never made an arrangement with Tarkanian or anyone else from the UNLV athletic department for Vaughn or any other student to receive special treatment or grades. Munford said that he did tell McMenamin that Vaughn did well in the class even though he didn't feel Vaughn attended as often as he could or should have. Munford also stated that he informed McMenamin that he had worked with Vaughn on his own to help him in the class, and that although most of the class members received As, with no Ds or Fs and only one or two Cs being given, Vaughn received a B, a grade actually below the average of the class. Munford also stated that Vaughn had turned in the term paper required of all students.

■   An affidavit from Vaughn stating that Tarkanian had made no special arrangements with his teacher and that he had attended classes and done the required work.

■   Letters from five students, none of whom were athletes, stating that they saw Vaughn attend class and that it was easy to notice him because he was almost 7 feet tall.

■   A statement from Temma Rosenberg, a student in the class, that she had typed Vaughn's final paper for him and had been present in class when he had orally presented the paper.

Munford's attorney presented the NCAA Council with additional evidence on appeal, including:

■   A polygraph test in which Munford backed up his affidavit by emphatically stating that he had made no special arrangements with Tarkanian concerning Vaughn or any other student. The analysis of the polygraph showed Munford was telling the truth.

■   A voice analysis that supported Munford's polygraph test.

The Committee on Infractions and the Council must have simply ignored all that evidence. Tarkanian was found guilty of the charge by the committee and the finding was rubber-stamped by the Council.

Congressional investigators, after reviewing NCAA records of the charge and UNLV's defense, called the committee's verdict "curious," especially given the testimony of two infractions committee members who said when one person's word is pitted against another's and neither is present so that his demeanor can be observed by the committee, "the issue will be resolved, absent other evidence, in favor of the accused." Former infractions committee chairman Arthur Reynolds said as much when he appeared before the congressional subcommittee: "It is well understood by the enforcement staff that where a violation is not admitted by the institution, the staff must carry the burden of proof and they must satisfy the Committee [on Infractions] that the available evidence supports the finding of violation."

In its final investigative report, the congressional committee wrote: "Curious, then, that when UNLV's basketball coach Jerry Tarkanian was accused of suborning a bogus high grade for a student-athlete in a course it was understood he would never have to attend, on the strength of a statement to the infractions committee by investigator Hale McMenamin of his recollection of conversations he had with the instructor involved, and nothing more, Tarkanian and the instructor were convicted. In fairness, Professor [Charles Allen] Wright testified that he voted against this finding. The other members of the infractions committee appearing before the subcommittee simply could not remember, in this most celebrated of all infractions cases in the history of the NCAA, just how they had voted, though obviously a majority of the panel, evidently unswayed by Wright's own subjectively high standards, did vote for the finding. The subcommittee is astounded that the infractions committee could have resolved this particular issue against the accused, in favor of its own investigator, and with a straight face professed to adherence to any sort of evidentiary standard or sense of burden of proof. We do take comfort in Professor Wright's statement, referring to this UNLV finding, that, 'I do not believe that a finding would have been made in that episode if it came before us today.' "

Tarkanian, though, takes little comfort in Wright's concession to Congress. With great fanfare, the NCAA used that charge of academic fraud to shred his reputation, Tarkanian said, while few people ever heard Wright say the finding was wrong. Despite Wright's pronouncement that Tarkanian would not be convicted of the charge "if it came before us today," the academic dishonesty allegation was the one that the nation's three leading newspapers—the *New York Times, Washington Post* and *Los Angeles Times* —used to explain the NCAA's reason for sanctioning Tarkanian in their coverage of the 1988 Supreme Court decision. "To this day, that one haunts me," Tarkanian said. "Because everyone remembers it, but even the former infractions committee chairman admits it shouldn't have been a charge."

Slipshod investigating.   NCAA investigators accused Tarkanian of arranging for center David Vaughn to stay free of charge at the Flagship Inn in Flagstaff, Arizona. They even provided a date when Vaughn was supposed to have received the free accommodations. But, while attempting to find out if the allegation was true, UNLV attorneys could not locate a Flagship Inn in Flagstaff. In fact, their inquiry with the Flagstaff Police Department showed no motel by that name *ever* existed in Flagstaff. The NCAA staff admitted it had no more information and agreed, after UNLV had spent more than a week and hundreds of dollars checking it out, to drop the charge.

Berst also formally accused Tarkanian of bankrolling a trip for recruit Rudy Jackson and his mentor Rodney Parker to attend the Dapper Dan Roundball Classic in Pittsburgh. In the interview he taped, however, Parker denied UNLV had paid for the trip and Berst admitted he had no reason other than intuition for making the allegation:

BERST: I think there is an allegation in there about them arranging to pay the expenses for you and Rudy to go down to that game. I don't really know that. That just makes sense to me that they would have, but nobody's told me that. The only guy that could know that for sure is you, and you didn't tell me that. That's, you know, that's one I don't know. So when we get to that question, I'll just say, you know, I—it just seemed like a reasonable, logical thing to happen based on other information.

PARKER: I've been going down there every year and they never paid for it.

Lack of due process.   With the school's reputation and Tarkanian's livelihood at stake, UNLV requested the right to bring witnesses to its hearings. Tarkanian himself wanted the right to face his accusers. He believed that if the Committee on Infractions was allowed to listen to what his accusers had to say, rather than what the NCAA investigators claimed they had said, he would be vindicated. In an early exchange of correspondence, NCAA administrator Warren Brown made it clear that witnesses would not be a part of the NCAA hearing process. Even though UNLV offered to pay the costs of transporting witnesses to the hearings, the request was denied by the Committee on Infractions. It was clear that only the "accused" and not the "accusers" would be cross-examined before the committee, prompting two courts to note that "every fundamental principle pertaining to the plaintiff's due process rights was violated by the NCAA."

Nonexistent standards of evidence.   UNLV asked the NCAA to explain what the Committee on Infractions considered acceptable evidence so it could better prepare for its hearing. The NCAA never responded. The question was answered, though, when UNLV attorneys attended the hearing and watched the Committee on Infractions repeatedly accept hearsay from NCAA investigators. The staff's hearsay evidence was accepted while more legally recognized evidence—depositions, affidavits, receipts and other documents—submitted by UNLV was ignored.

The presumption of guilt.   In court testimony given by infractions committee members during Tarkanian's lawsuit, several members of the committee admitted that their long-standing relationship with Berst and other NCAA staff members was the reason they gave more consideration to the staff memos than to UNLV's collection of affidavits and documented evidence.

Harry Cross, a University of Washington law professor and member of the Committee on Infractions, testified that the file boxes full of documents presented by UNLV "did not weigh as heavily as what staff had told us" when he was making his decision. He said the basis for that greater faith in the staff was a "great trust and confidence" that "had developed over the years." Committee chairman Arthur Reynolds, after admitting the staff provided "no evidence" other than its unsigned memos, also said he "gave great weight to their integrity as I had experienced it over many years." And University of Kentucky law professor William Matthews, an infractions committee member, even went so far as to say he had his mind made up against UNLV before the hearing even began. "I did believe that was the case," Matthews said from the stand.

One-way "cooperation."   Having never been through an NCAA investigation, UNLV officials asked the NCAA for guidance in conducting its investigation of the NCAA's charges. Assistant Attorney General Lyle Rivera, assigned by the state to handle UNLV's case, requested a copy of the rules, procedures and policies that governed NCAA investigations. The letters he wrote to the NCAA were enough to fill a file folder. His initial request to NCAA administrator Warren Brown went unanswered. After literally begging for guidance in three additional letters, Rivera finally received a letter from Brown a week after UNLV's original deadline for completion of its investigation. In the letter, Rivera was told to refer to the *NCAA Manual*. However, the *Manual* did not provide any semblance of the guidance that Rivera had requested, and during the course of UNLV's hearings, Brown made an off-hand reference to other operating policies which had been established by the infractions committee and which were "in writing." UNLV attorney Leavitt requested a copy from Brown. Brown confirmed that the written policies existed, but that he would need infractions committee approval to give them to the member school. He then told Leavitt that the committee had approved the request, but that the materials would have to be edited because they contained specific references to other schools. He told Leavitt that a copy of the policies should arrive prior to the university's final hearing date. Leavitt confirmed his request and Brown's response in writing and in a personal meeting with the chairman of the infractions committee. Nothing came. Again Leavitt asked the infractions committee chairman for the operating policies and was told that the editing process required extensive work. UNLV's hearing date came and went. UNLV inquired with NCAA administrator Bill Hunt as to why the guidelines promised by Brown had not been received. Astonishingly, Hunt told UNLV that Brown remembered no conversations with Leavitt regarding the guidelines. "Finally, Hunt wrote that UNLV would not be furnished a copy of the policies and procedures until they were made available to the general membership, long after our appeal, and notwithstanding the fact that we had been promised them five months before," Leavitt said. "To my knowledge, they never came."

Rebuffed by the NCAA in his attempt to understand the enforcement process, Rivera called for advice from an attorney who handled Michigan State University's appearance before the infractions committee. "He told me to not even bother," Rivera said. "I remember his words. He said, 'It's a wretched farce.' When our case was over, I thought, 'You know, he was right. It *is* a wretched farce.' You might as well just go in and lie down. Let them hammer you. Why fight it? By the time you've gotten to the infractions hearing they're going to get you for something. Even if you believe you're right. You might as well get your probation and get it over with. At least that way, there's finality to it."

"It is inconceivable that a member institution of a voluntary organization would be asked to conduct an investigation under a set of rules, procedures and policies which it is never allowed to see," UNLV later argued in its appeal. "If specific means of conducting an investigation are expected, then such ways should be specifically outlined to the university upon receipt of the official inquiry. Certainly true justice is obtained more through education than through surprise."

That was neither the beginning nor the end of the mounting friction between the NCAA staff and UNLV officials. The distrust grew to the point that Berst's own memos indicate he believed he should call the FBI each time he came to Las Vegas because he feared UNLV was going to plant cocaine in his motel room in an effort to discredit him.

Intimidating athletes.   Roscoe Pondexter, a 6-foot-6-inch forward who played for Tarkanian at Long Beach State, was one of nearly two dozen people interviewed by the NCAA who later signed affidavits claiming that Berst and his fellow investigators had either attempted to intimidate them or guaranteed that the investigation would end with Tarkanian's ouster. Pondexter had gone to a junior college for one year before posting a dramatic increase in his College Board scores, allowing him to transfer to a four-year school. Tarkanian did not permit him to play at the beginning of the first year after his transfer because he admitted to having concerns over the increase in Pondexter's scores. During that year, Berst cornered Pondexter twice, each time asking for a little dope on Tarkanian.

"Berst told me that they had enough evidence on me and my test scores to declare me ineligible," Pondexter said in a 1988 interview. "But he said that if I gave him evidence on Coach [Tarkanian] I would be able to leave and go to any other school without sitting out a year. He said he wanted Tarkanian out of coaching and he was going to make sure that happened. He told me that Tarkanian was a man who shouldn't be in basketball. He said, 'Tarkanian is bad for the game. Personally, I don't like the man.' He said, 'I'm out to get Tarkanian.' He later told me, 'I've got you now. I got all the stuff against you. You're dead . . . . Roscoe, if you help me get Tarkanian and Long Beach, I won't submit enough evidence to convict you and you'll still be able to play. I'm going to get Tarkanian if it takes the rest of my career.' This made me feel like I should make up something [on Tarkanian] to keep him [Berst] off me."

Pondexter repeatedly told Berst he didn't know of any

rules violations, and, as Berst promised, he was later declared ineligible. But Helen Gallagher, a hearing officer appointed by a U.S. District Court judge, ruled there was not enough evidence to support the NCAA's suspension of Pondexter and he was ordered reinstated.

Tarkanian and his lawyers were willing to accept that coincidence might prompt one or two people to call with such stories. When the list started growing they knew there was trouble. "Over and over, I kept hearing that the NCAA was out to get me," Tarkanian said. "People would call me and say that they had talked to an NCAA investigator, and that I had better be careful because that investigator was saying right out that they wanted to nail me."

As the investigation dragged on into its second year, attorney Leavitt and the attorney general's office began clipping the affidavits together in what became known as the "Pink File," so named simply because the only file folder label Leavitt had with him during the infractions hearing was pink. Below are but a few of the sworn statements in the file.

■   Arthur Montgomery, a former Long Beach player coached by Tarkanian, who later became chairman of the black studies department at Long Beach State, November 9, 1976: "I was summoned by David Berst to meet with him and [NCAA investigator] Lester Burks about their investigation of violations of NCAA rules by Long Beach State College. . . . Berst stated that they wanted me to assist them in the investigation of Tarkanian because they heard I was unhappy with him and they wanted to 'get Tarkanian.' I explained that I knew of no wrong things by Tarkanian and asked who told them that I had bad feelings toward Tarkanian. They said they would not reveal this information. Lester Burks stated that Tarkanian was exploiting black athletes. Berst said that they didn't have enough on Tarkanian yet, but they really wanted to get him . . . . In another meeting, Berst told me to tell other players that if they gave [the NCAA] information on Tarkanian, the player would get immunity even if the school went on probation. He [Berst] would see that [the players] would get into another college . . . . As I recall, Berst said something like Tarkanian was obsessed with abusing athletes from junior colleges all the way up and that the NCAA had a responsibility to stop this. Tarkanian would be an example to show the NCAA doesn't give up and this would deter other coaches. . . . He said, 'It's the Big Guy I want.' . . . He said that Tarkanian didn't belong in coaching because he abused black athletes and that he'd make sure the NCAA followed Tarkanian wherever he went."

■   Dwight Taylor, a former Long Beach player, February 8, 1974: "An NCAA investigator came to see me and told me that a lot of ballplayers in Long Beach were unhappy and that the NCAA was trying to get evidence against Tarkanian. He told me: 'Why do you want to stay loyal to Tarkanian? All he ever did was screw you. Look at what he did to you. We're out to get Tarkanian and we're going to hang him.' "

■   Robert Espinoza, a former basketball coach at San Dimes High School, April 4, 1974: "On May 5, 1973, at approximately 11:45 a.m. at Long Beach City College while I was attending the Southern California Interscholastic Basketball Coaches Clinic, the following statement was made by [college coach] Jim Harrick: 'An NCAA investigator was on campus talking to Jackie Robinson. . . . When he was down, he said the NCAA was checking up on Tarkanian, and that they were out to get Tarkanian.' "

■   Jimmie Baker, former UNLV basketball player, June 17, 1976: "Investigator David Berst talked with me when I left UNLV [and transferred to Hawaii] and threatened me that if I did not cooperate with his investigation, I would not be able to go to any other school under the jurisdiction of the NCAA."

■   Vic Weiss, a friend and adviser to Tarkanian, May 5, 1976: "When Jerry Tarkanian and Long Beach were under investigation by the NCAA for alleged rules infractions, Investigator David Berst questioned me and examined some of my records. Upon his departure, after finding everything in order, he stated to me: 'This time you had time to doctor the records, but don't worry, some day I am going to get you and your friend.' The friend he had in mind was Jerry Tarkanian."

Small wonder, given the constant theme in these and other statements, that Tarkanian became paranoid about the NCAA. Tired of hearing rumors, Tarkanian decided to call David Berst and discuss them. He made the call over the objections of his wife, Lois, who repeatedly warned her husband that Berst, a man neither of them had met, could not be trusted.

"My instincts told me that Jerry would not get a fair chance with the NCAA," Lois Tarkanian said. "The pieces were beginning to fit together. When Jerry suddenly decided to call David Berst, I couldn't believe it. Jerry kept insisting that Berst was a good guy; I remember him saying, 'I can ask him if they can put you on probation even if they can't find any evidence. There can't be evidence if I didn't do it.' I asked Jerry if he was crazy." Tarkanian said he wasn't crazy. He was just trying to find out if he would be fairly treated in the investigation, of which he had yet to be officially informed.

"I was a little naive," he said in retrospect. "But I had a big decision to make. Jack Kent Cooke, then the owner of the Los Angeles Lakers, was pressing me pretty hard to take the head coaching job there. It was the middle of the 1977 season and we were on our way to the Final Four. The Lakers job had a lot going for it. When you have Kareem, you're pretty sure that you'll win a lot of games. The salary wasn't that high by pro standards— $70,000 a year with increases of $2,500 a year—but no other coach in the NBA had a guaranteed five-year contract. Now I called Berst because I didn't want to run out on what was happening to UNLV. I had seen the negative publicity that came when people thought I ran out on Long Beach State. I wasn't going to let that happen again. If I had been guilty, maybe I would have gone, but I knew I had done nothing wrong. I told everyone I wasn't scared of the NCAA, because once the infractions committee sees our evidence, I'll be cleared. "

Convinced if he left for the pros he would be found guilty in the court of public opinion, Tarkanian told Cooke he didn't want the Lakers job and placed his faith in a "fair" NCAA. That was a decision he today regrets.

"When I and others from UNLV went in front of the infractions committee, they didn't really consider our evidence or listen to us," he said years later. "It was a total ambush. They just were a rubber stamp for what the investigators wanted. It was an awful time, because I knew something bad was coming from the NCAA, but I didn't know what the charges would be. All I could be sure of was that the NCAA was going to say we did something.

"When the whole NCAA thing started, some coaches had told me, 'Shut up. You can't fight them. You'll never win. They have unlimited funds. They'll bury you and they're vindictive as hell. If you speak up, they'll make an example of you. Just keep quiet and eventually they'll go away.' I couldn't keep quiet. It hurt too much and it was so unfair. But those coaches were right."

The reason for Tarkanian's confidence at the onset of the infractions hearing could be found in two large legal-size boxes containing UNLV's response to the violations alleged by the enforcement staff. Each violation had been given its own file and inside each file was evidence gathered by the Nevada Attorney General's Office. Some of the files were five inches thick, filled with statements investigators from the Attorney General's Office obtained from every individual the NCAA named in its charges. The State of Nevada paid to either fly those people to Las Vegas to be deposed or sent an investigator to their home for the same purpose.

"The evidence for our side was overwhelming," Tarkanian said. For example:

Of 10 infractions findings in which Tarkanian was named, one of the most serious was the allegation that he had arranged for a player named Robert "Jeep" Kelley, a highly recruited forward from Pittsburgh, to fly home free in November 1973. The NCAA also alleged that Tarkanian reimbursed Kelley in cash for his return trip.

Kelley had returned to his home after quitting the UNLV team a week before the first game of his freshman year. According to the NCAA, Tarkanian had arranged the trip by telling Kelley to call Frank Denton, the owner of American Tour and Travel Service, a Las Vegas agency that operated gambling junkets. When Kelley called Tarkanian three days later and asked to come back, the NCAA alleged, Tarkanian agreed and told Kelley he would reimburse his return flight whenever he finally showed up at the basketball arena. Although Tarkanian argued that it was "ludicrous" to think he would arrange a free flight for a player to quit his team and then pay for his return, the NCAA insisted the charges were true. The NCAA's evidence? Berst said that he recalled having a conversation with Kelley in 1975 during which Kelley, who later was given immunity from the NCAA without asking for it, complained that he had been unhappy at

UNLV and wanted to go home, but that Kelley then changed his mind and wanted to return to UNLV. He said it was Kelley who told him that Tarkanian had made all the arrangements. No documents. No evidence. Just Berst's unsigned memo of a conversation he had with Kelley. When Berst completed his presentation, Tarkanian's lawyers laid the following evidence on the table:

■ A sworn affidavit from Kelley in which he stated that he did not meet Frank Denton until 1974; that he had sold his season tickets—a practice that NCAA rules allowed at the time—to purchase the commercial airline ticket that he used to leave Las Vegas; that the flight he took home was not part of a gambling junket, but was on a commercial airline; that he was never reimbursed any money by Tarkanian or anyone connected with UNLV; and that his return flight to Las Vegas was paid for by his former high school principal, James Robinson.

■ A deposition from Dr. James E. Robinson, Kelley's high school principal, in which the principal stated that he authorized the school treasurer to write a check for the airline ticket. The money was drawn from a special fund at the school which was established years earlier and was to be used for the benefit of current or former students.

■ A sworn affidavit from Spencer Watkins, Kelley's high school basketball coach, in which Watkins stated that he and Principal Robinson made the arrangements for Kelley's return to Las Vegas and the purchase of the plane ticket.

■ A letter from Garin F. Veseley, Kelley's high school athletic director, in which Veseley stated that he used the money provided by the high school and purchased an airline ticket for Kelley on November 30, 1973, for Kelley to return to Las Vegas, as authorized by principal Robinson.

■ A copy of the Schenley High School payment order requesting the issuance of a check for $135 to be made payable to cash "in payment of traveling expenses, RJK," to be charged to the special account and dated November 30, 1973.

■   A canceled check drawn on the account of Schenley High School, at the Mellon National Bank and Trust Company, made payable to cash in the sum of $135 and dated November 30, 1973.

■   And in possibly the most concrete evidence favoring UNLV, Frank Denton offered the Committee on Infractions copies of his agency's manifests for the time period that Berst said Kelley reported accepting a free flight. Those records showed that the companies with which he was associated conducted no aircraft flights between Las Vegas and Pittsburgh and no flights at all on the dates before, during or after the day Kelley left Las Vegas. There was no way Kelley could have gotten from Las Vegas to Pittsburgh on one of his planes, Denton said.

With that as the proof UNLV provided, the Committee on Infractions nevertheless sided with Berst, and Tarkanian was found guilty of the charge. "The amazing thing," Tarkanian said recently, "is that Jeep has been in and out of prison now for most of the last 15 years. Yet he was so credible that they would use whatever he said to Berst to come after me."

Berst told the infractions committee that Kelley changed his story when he talked to UNLV's investigators because Tarkanian had threatened the former player. This very serious allegation was based on telephone conversations Berst said he had with Kelley. During those conversations, Berst said, Kelley reported receiving repeated calls from Tarkanian during which the coach promised to arrange a professional tryout for Kelley if he denied his previous statements. Berst also quoted Kelley's aunt, Frances Parker, as saying Kelley "feared for his life" after Tarkanian called. But UNLV provided telephone records showing it was Kelley, not Tarkanian, who was making the many phone calls. The information proved that during the six months Kelley reportedly feared Tarkanian, he called the coach collect 26 times. Lonnie Wright, Kelley's closest friend, even signed an affidavit swearing that he and Kelley had dinner at the Tarkanians' home at least three times during that six months and "there was never any tension" between the two. And though Berst told the infractions committee that a frightened Kelley had called the NCAA to report the threats, telephone records show that Kelley was in fact returning Berst's call.

Tarkanian's attorneys turned up numerous other cases

where the NCAA's memos just didn't square with what they found to be the facts. In another instance, Hale McMenamin told the Committee on Infractions that Las Vegas sportscaster Ron Vitto had filmed a practice in which a recruit, Jerry Baskerville, had participated. If true, it would be a rules violation. McMenamin, reading from his notes, quoted Vitto as saying he had broadcast the footage on his "5 p.m. and 10 p.m. sports shows" the night of the practice. McMenamin explained that he didn't have the videotape because the broadcaster was reluctant to talk with the NCAA. That reluctance, McMenamin wrote in his memo, stemmed from the fact that Vitto said he "was born and raised in Las Vegas" and "depended on the university to make a living." UNLV, though, produced an affidavit from Vitto saying he never filmed a practice involving Baskerville. It also proved Vitto was born and raised in Los Angeles and did not move to Las Vegas until he was an adult. The practice when the violation was alleged to occur was on a Sunday. UNLV provided programming reports showing that KLAS-TV Channel 8, the television station for which Vitto worked, did not broadcast his show on Sundays during the year of the alleged incident. Furthermore, regular newscasts on KLAS-TV at that time were broadcast at 6:00 p.m. and 11:00 p.m. Monday through Friday. If the recruit truly did participate in the practice—and UNLV coaches denied that he did—it could not have appeared on television as McMenamin said it did. Faced with that information, the infractions committee told McMenamin it believed he'd missed the mark and threw the charge out. The committee wasn't willing, though, to see similarities in other allegations against Tarkanian.

Tarkanian said that, during the early stages of the NCAA's investigation, he remained puzzled over the source of the NCAA's information. That puzzle was solved when he later learned that Tony Morocco, a one-time UNLV assistant coach who recruited Kelley and was later fired by Tarkanian, had been fueling Berst's fire. Throughout the hearings, Berst repeatedly denied to the Committee on Infractions that Morocco was his primary source. At one point, a transcript of the hearing shows, Berst even told the committee that "Tony Morocco would not be interviewed as it relates to anything."

Tarkanian sensed that Berst wasn't being completely truthful. But it wasn't until the infractions committee handed down its verdict that Tarkanian finally discovered the truth. After reading newspaper accounts of UNLV's hearing, Morocco called Tarkanian, admitted he had agreed out of spite to be the NCAA's source and asked for forgiveness. Morocco then voluntarily called the Nevada Attorney General's Office and offered to give a deposition as UNLV prepared for its appeal to the NCAA Council. Morocco told the attorneys during the deposition that, after Berst sought his help in investigating Tarkanian, he arranged to pick Kelley up at his home, take the former player to lunch and then get him to "talk trash" about Tarkanian. After lunch, Berst arrived and listened as Morocco and Kelley "discussed negative aspects of our stay at Las Vegas." Morocco also swore that it was he, not Kelley, who made the bulk of the allegations against Tarkanian during that meeting, but that he asked Berst to shield his identity by naming Kelley as the NCAA's informant. "The discussion actually consisted of a series of events to which I would make reference and to which Jeep would briefly respond," Morocco said in his affidavit. "I was clearly doing nearly all the talking and Jeep merely responded to my discussions." Morocco said he also arranged for Berst to interview several other witnesses, including Kelley's aunt, Frances Parker, who was livid when Tarkanian allowed Kelley to quit the team as a freshman. "I called Mrs. Parker and made it clear that I had a strong dislike for Tarkanian and the university and very much reinforced her own bitter feelings toward them," Morocco swore. "I strongly encouraged Mrs. Parker's bitterness and suggested that she might want to speak with the NCAA since she felt that Jeep had been unfairly treated by the university and Tarkanian."

Four years later, in his deposition taken as part of Tarkanian's legal battle, Berst acknowledged that it was Morocco who arranged and hosted the hour and a half meeting between Berst and Kelley at the Monroeville, Pennsylvania, Howard Johnson's, where Morocco had taken a job managing a rental car counter after being fired by Tarkanian. Berst also admitted that he had visited Morocco at the Howard Johnson's "5 or 6 times," had called him another 10 times and, not surprisingly, had undersold the involvement of the disgruntled ex-coach to the Committee on Infractions. Asked by Tarkanian's lawyers if he had "interviewed anybody in the UNLV case who told you more about possible violations than Tony Morocco," Berst conceded, "I don't think so."

"Berst needed to make the Kelley allegations stick," UNLV

attorney Mike Leavitt said. "I'm sure he realized that if the committee knew the source was a fired and disgruntled coach who had been let go because he was disruptive to the team, it might have misgivings. So he pinned the allegations on Jeep. And in the process, he fashioned his so-called 'evidence' to conform with his needs."

When Sonny Vaccaro, a childhood friend of Morocco's, heard through the grapevine that Morocco was the NCAA's chief witness against Tarkanian, he decided the NCAA might need a little lesson in history. Vaccaro, who today is Nike's chief liaison with basketball coaches, was caught in an awkward position; it was he who had recommended that Tarkanian hire Morocco when Tarkanian was still at Long Beach. Now Morocco had turned on Tarkanian, jeopardizing friendships all around. Vaccaro decided to write NCAA investigator McMenamin a confidential letter "explaining Tony's background" and warning the NCAA that Morocco shouldn't be considered a credible source. In the three-page letter, Vaccaro took McMenamin through his friend's coaching career—which included brief stops at Trafford (Pennsylvania) High School, the University of Iowa, St. Francis College and the University of Arkansas, before he landed a spot on Tarkanian's staff—and detailed how each of those jobs had ended with Morocco criticizing his former employer.

"Mr. McMenin [sic], as a former FBI agent and knowing what it takes to make a character analysis of a human being, you can follow probably more so than I a situation which exists within this individual which shows his instability, envy and disloyalty wherever he has been," Vaccaro wrote. "As I look back at all of this and my part in helping Tony obtain new jobs and be accepted by new people, I feel a partial responsibility in what has occurred. If my providing this information can in any way prevent one more program or one more human being from being unjustly hurt in the way so many have in the past due to Tony's actions, then I will feel my sharing this was worthwhile."

Berst also asked Lew Schaffel, Rodney Parker's lawyer in New York, about Morocco's credibility. The answer was much the same. "If you're going to base your case on Tony Morocco, I think it would be a shame," Schaffel told Berst, according to Schaffel's recollection of the conversation.

The NCAA disregarded Vaccaro's letter and Schaffel's warning, opting instead to build much of its case around the allegations made by the disaffected ex-coach. Berst, in fact, even increased the friction between Vaccaro and Morocco—who today describe their relationship as "like brothers" —when he mailed Morocco a copy of the confidential letter Vaccaro wrote. "That was a total breach of the faith and trust which I had placed in individuals who had asked for my cooperation," Vacarro would say later.

But even before they knew the source of their troubles, UNLV officials knew those troubles would be serious. Consequently, the night before the meeting with the infractions committee, UNLV President Donald Baepler decided it was time to open the Pink File. Surely the infractions committee would be offended by the growing stack of evidence that Berst and the NCAA staff had acted "in anything *but* an objective and impartial manner," UNLV officials wrote in the note attached to the file. The committee was not fazed by the damning comments and even rose to the defense of the enforcement staff. "It is the committee's opinion that the NCAA enforcement staff has investigated this case in accordance with the high standards of personal integrity required in the processing of all infractions cases presented to the committee," the committee wrote in its final report on the Tarkanian case.

"That's frightening," Mike Leavitt said. "That after hearing all this evidence, the committee said the staff handled itself with the 'high standards of personal integrity' that the committee expects." Another attorney familiar with the case said, "It almost makes you wonder what Berst would have had to have done to dip below the committee's standards."

The Pink File came out again on March 13, 1977, at an unusual special hearing held at UNLV's request. Through questioning of NCAA enforcement staff, UNLV officials hoped to prove Berst had not been truthful when he said Morocco was not a key witness. However, hearing records show, NCAA investigators told UNLV that they had the right to distort the facts concerning their sources of information because of "an unwritten and/or unpublished committee policy regarding confidential sources." The infractions committee supported the position. When Sam Lionel, Tarkanian's counsel, attempted to question NCAA staff about sources of other allegations, Berst told Lionel his questions were out of line and beyond the scope of the hearing. The infractions committee upheld that smug claim as well and prevented further questioning. "[Asking for the hearing] was a mistake, I guess," Tarkanian said years later. "[NCAA Executive Director] Walter Byers did not like it when we did that. He thought that if we disputed things, we were attacking him. So he attacked back. He made it even tougher."

With all hope of winning his battle within the NCAA's structure lost, Tarkanian turned to the courts. He was somewhat more successful there, ending with a track record of 5-1. The only loss, though, was the one that counted most: the U.S. Supreme Court. Law professors, university presidents and coaches eagerly awaited the court's landmark decision on Tarkanian's case. While the NCAA has made some changes to avoid events like those in the Tarkanian case—most notably establishing written guidelines for its hearings and sharing those rules with the accused—the Supreme Court had the opportunity to force other, more significant changes. If the NCAA had lost, legal experts agreed, the court could have required the organization to incorporate into its enforcement program many of the same protections afforded the accused by the legal system. But with its victory, the NCAA's ability to run roughshod over those it investigates without fear of federal constitutional challenge was confirmed. "This case had significance to the NCAA far beyond the issue of whether one coach was or was not going to be suspended by one university," said former U.S. Solicitor General Rex Lee, to whom the NCAA paid a small fortune for arguing its case to the Supreme Court. "The decision means that the NCAA can continue to use an investigative and enforcement system which is more efficient, more effective. If the NCAA had lost, it would have had to use something like trial-type proceedings which would have cost more, been less effective and not served the purposes of the NCAA or individual schools."

Said a somewhat skeptical University of Southern California basketball coach George Raveling: "It appears that the Supreme Court has given the NCAA broad, sweeping and unusual powers."

"It is a very mixed picture as to what they got," said Duke University's John Weistart, one of America's most respected sports law professors. "If you look at the decision just on its face, it appears to be a significant victory for the NCAA. But its practical effect, I believe, is one that the NCAA may come to regret. I appreciate that that's a fairly strong statement. But I think some might pose the general theoretical question to the NCAA of, 'Well, why don't you provide due process?' And the NCAA doesn't have a good answer. In our society, we think there are benefits that flow from providing due process. It is not simply fairness to the person being accused, it also is that due process helps to assure the credibility of the decision as it is made. The issue might become, 'Aren't you a bit concerned that the punishment that you impose might be less believable because you haven't committed yourself to providing a fair hearing with a full chance of cross-examination?' and so on."

Weistart said the changes the NCAA would have been forced to make had it lost would have added greater protection for the accused. "We're talking basically about affording an open hearing in which the evidence is presented in an orderly fashion and there is some right, on the part of the person who is accused, to participate in the proceeding, and present countervailing evidence and cross-examine people who testify against them."

Such protections would be in stark contrast to the current hearing system, which is closed and which does not allow universities to bring witnesses to dispute the NCAA's allegations. The NCAA also would have been forced to be more selective in the evidence it accepts, Weistart said. "I think a problem in the NCAA investigations is the quality of the evidence that they rely on. If the NCAA enforcement procedure has a weakness, it really is on the question of what constitutes evidence. There is a lot of dependence on rumor and innuendo, and the requirement of due process would be very helpful in clarifying that."

Tarkanian said he believes the decision sets up a dichotomy within public universities that have joined the NCAA. "The amazing thing is, if you're a professor, the university has to give you due process. But if you're involved in athletics, the NCAA does not have to guarantee you due process. In essence, what the court said is the NCAA doesn't have to give you a fair hearing. I think it just totally contradicts what our country stands for. I thought every American should be entitled to a fair hearing."

Among the most important repercussions of the Tarkanian decision is that many universities have begun adding a clause to coaching contracts allowing for all severance payments to be canceled if an NCAA investigation turns up violations. Thus, coaches now can be tossed out on the basis of findings made during NCAA hearings—hearings that the Supreme Court accepted as constitutionally inadequate when compared to constitutional due process standards. "The court's decision now leaves university administrators with the task of formulating contract and personnel policies that will automatically incorporate the NCAA investigations, hearings and sanctions of all athletic personnel procedures," a 1989 analysis of the decision in the *Whittier Law Review* noted. "The case is described as a godsend by NCAA lawyers and a mistake by coaches and players."

For his part, Tarkanian said he had simply hoped the Supreme Court would "bring the NCAA into the 1980s and remind it that this is still America. It was the most horrifying thing I've ever been through. I've always feared the NCAA, but I've also always said we need an organization like the NCAA, we need an enforcement staff, and they should be able to enforce the rules. And they should be able to suspend coaches that violate the rules. I'm in total agreement with all that. But you need an NCAA enforcement program to stand for everything that's good—fair play, education. The current one does not. You need a strong NCAA, but you need a fair and honorable one. If they're going to have that kind of power, then the person that they accuse should be entitled to a fair hearing. Is that too much to ask?

"I don't know, after our case, if anyone will ever beat them. We had the facts, and the courts agreed the facts showed this wasn't fair. If the facts can't beat them, I don't know what can. They are so powerful. You have to fight them to appreciate how strong they really are. You go to court and they have unlimited funds."

By the time Tarkanian's case finally was heard in the Supreme Court, Walter Byers, the NCAA's crusty executive director of 36 years, had finally retired. In his first interview after retiring, Byers said that, in his opinion, Tarkanian had managed to "beat the system" by fighting the NCAA. "He's a man who worked the system and beat the system," Byers told Doug Tucker of the Associated Press in 1990. "There is a legal bromide about justice delayed is justice denied. The story of this case proves that."

Tarkanian said that if Byers "considers suffering through having your reputation destroyed and 13 years in court a way of beating the system, then he doesn't know what I've been through. But the only thing I can say is that if the system wasn't so bad under his regime, I couldn't have even beat it through the courts. I didn't beat it for any other reason. If the system had been fair, I couldn't have beat it, to use his words. But he had everything stacked on his side, so I guess that's why he figures if he didn't run me out of coaching, I beat the system.

"The key for me," Tarkanian said, "was that people in the whole state knew the whole thing was wrong. That's not true for most coaches. When the NCAA starts shooting, they turn around and everyone is gone. Here's where the NCAA has got you as a coach. Everyone is so scared today, that the minute the NCAA comes in, the university says, 'Fire the coach.' Then the university goes to the NCAA and says, 'Look, we took care of the problem.' Coaches are the ones who really get hurt in all the added power the NCAA got from the Supreme Court case."

Indeed, Committee on Infractions chairman D. Alan Williams said in 1990 with some pride, "Of the last 13 major cases we've handled, the coaches are no longer in college jobs." And universities like the University of Florida, which fired football coach Galen Hall and basketball coach Norm Sloan in a three-week period during a 1989 NCAA investigation, appear all too willing to comply with the NCAA's desire that they dump coaches even before their guilt has been decided by the infractions committee. Clemson asked football coach Danny Ford to "step down" shortly after it was announced the NCAA was looking into his program. When the investigation was completed, investigators were able to show that one player had received $150 in cash from a coach, but not from Ford. So, Clemson forced Ford to stop doing the work he did best, coaching football, in the hopes that by sacrificing his career, it could be spared greater penalties. To ease Ford's pain, Clemson threw in about $2 million. It apparently worked. The Tigers were given only one year's probation. Six months later, Ford still was out of a job.

"It used to be, they would fire you if you didn't win enough games," Tarkanian said. "But now coaches are getting fired for almost anything. There's a real problem when universities start firing coaches based on the NCAA. Unless the NCAA is going to be fair, and makes its process and investigation fair, it's not fair to fire coaches just because the NCAA comes around. Someday, something has got to change. It's just got to."

DÉJÀ VU ALL OVER AGAIN

Even before the NCAA argued the Tarkanian case in the Supreme Court, it had found cause to jump into another investigation of the Runnin' Rebels. During the summer of 1987, NCAA investigators began crisscrossing the country contacting former players and recruits and combing through UNLV athletic department files as part of a preliminary inquiry. The inquiry dragged on through 1990, hanging over the heads of Tarkanian and his team as they marched to UNLV's first national championship.

At the heart of the investigation was UNLV's recruitment of Lloyd "Sweet Pea" Daniels, a 6-foot-8-inch swingman from New York who was regarded by many as the most talented schoolboy basketball player to come out of the Big Apple since Lew Alcindor. But, as UNLV would soon discover, Daniels's ability on the court was matched only by his uncanny knack for finding trouble off it. When Daniels signed with UNLV in April 1986, he read at a third-grade level and had just dropped out of Andrew Jackson High School in Queens, the fourth high school he had attended. He also suffered from "cultural deprivation" and dyslexia, according to guardian-court documents. One writer described Daniels as having "a jump shot like Larry Bird and a handle like Magic Johnson. The only thing he couldn't do with a basketball was autograph it."

Daniels's dismal showing in the classroom forced UNLV to deny him admission. He then enrolled at Mt. San Antonio Junior College in Walnut, California, during the fall of 1986. After completing 12 hours of athletics-related coursework, he enrolled at UNLV in January 1987 as a full-time student—finally on track to play for the Rebels. Only a month later, Daniels was derailed, when he was one of 54 people arrested in a drug sting operation in Las Vegas. Tarkanian announced immediately that Daniels would never play at UNLV. "He was there, it's on television," Tarkanian said of Daniels's arrest, which was filmed by a TV crew. "It's not like it was a case of mistaken identity." Ironically, while UNLV was being vilified for having recruited the troubled Daniels, the University of Kansas sought his services even after the arrest.   A month later, Daniels, who still was enrolled at UNLV, was identified as one of two people suspected in the theft of five Final Four basketball tickets from an office in UNLV's Thomas and Mack Center; Daniels later returned three of the tickets.

About the same time as the tickets were stolen, stories in *Long Island Newsday* detailed a series of possible NCAA rules violations involving Daniels and UNLV coaches, boosters and other representatives of the school. The stories alleged that Daniels received a variety of special privileges, including cash, a car and a motorcycle, while attempting to become eligible to play for the Rebels.   Many of the allegations focused on Mark Warkentien, UNLV's basketball recruiting coordinator at the time, who had become Daniels's legal guardian. Warkentien's status as Daniels's guardian, although it may seem questionable, had apparently been cleared with the NCAA. Then, apparently, it was not.

After requesting that the Pacific Coast Athletic Association seek a ruling from the NCAA on the situation, then-UNLV athletic director Brad Rothermel was told by the PCAA in August 1986 that the NCAA "would allow a university staff member to become the guardian for a potential student-athlete." Based on that telephone discussion, in which no names were mentioned, Warkentien filed his petition to become Daniels's legal guardian, Rothermel said. The petition received court approval that October.

Remarks about the Daniels-Warkentien relationship by ESPN commentator Dick Vitale a few weeks later, during the broadcast of a game between the University of Arizona and the Soviet national team, raised such a stir that Lew Cryer, who was then commissioner of the PCAA, urged Rothermel to contact the NCAA in writing and specifically mention Warkentien and Daniels. Rothermel did so and received a reply stating that, no matter how the court saw Warkentien's relationship with Daniels and no matter what the NCAA may have told PCAA officials, the relationship would not be exempt from NCAA recruiting rules. By that time, however, Warkentien had purchased an $1,800 motorcycle for Daniels to use while attending Mt. San Antonio. "They [the NCAA] have said we should have specifically identified the student-athlete involved," Rothermel said in 1990. "And we didn't. It would seem like it shouldn't make any difference if your general question and your specific question are basically the same, but it may." Especially if the school asking is UNLV and the player is one of the best ever.

Tarkanian, well known for taking chances on academic stepchildren like Daniels, lambasted reporters who questioned his judgment in Daniels's case. "His situation is no different than Walter Berry's," Tarkanian told the *Los Angeles Times*. "This is what tees me off, the hypocrisy. Berry was not a high school graduate. He was admitted to St. John's without a diploma on a special program they have for New York City kids. Then the NCAA came in and said, 'Hey, this is not sufficient, he can't play.' So they sent him to a junior college, exactly like we did. Their backgrounds are exactly the same. And why it is that St. John's is so nice for giving Walter the opportunity and Lloyd shouldn't have the opportunity?"

Using the Daniels situation as their hook, NCAA investigators again began working to reel in the coach they call the Shark. First, investigators found that Rebel players had made long-distance calls from their hotel rooms while on road trips and had even taken cans of peanuts from the minibars, all without paying for them. That led to the suspension of two players each game for five games during the 1989-90 season. Then, according to Rothermel, came the discovery of "less then $500" in long-distance phone calls made from athletic department telephones by "a half-dozen" UNLV players. NCAA investigators also discovered that Tarkanian's wife, Lois, had paid cap-and-gown rental fees for five players who graduated in 1987. And they learned that when Los Angeles high school star Don MacLean was leaving UNLV's NCAA regional game at Pauley Pavilion, Danny Tarkanian, the coach's son, gave MacLean a ride five blocks to his car, according to Danny's attorney.

But Daniels remained the focus of the investigation; it appeared that the NCAA was willing to pursue Tarkanian into the 1990s with the same vengeance it did during the 1970s investigation that touched off the court battle. In a sworn statement, Daniels claimed he was contacted by an unidentified NCAA investigator in May 1989, when he was at Mary Immaculate Hospital in Queens recovering from gunshot wounds he had received during a drug-related shooting. Daniels said the investigator offered him "an unspecified sum of cash to give evidence of possible recruiting violations by UNLV." Daniels claimed he refused the money and told the investigator he knew of no such violations. In another sworn statement provided to *HoopScoop* magazine, Kevin Barry, a Columbia University graduate and founder of the Give a Kid a Chance Foundation, said that while he was allowing Daniels to live at his home, NCAA investigator Robert Stroup visited more than once. On one of those occasions, at 2 a.m. on August 15, 1989, Stroup told him that he and Daniels would be "great American heroes" if they provided the NCAA with information damaging to Tarkanian, Barry said.

David Berst, Tarkanian's long-time nemesis, said he was aware of the affidavits but declined requests from several reporters to comment on them. "Isn't it interesting that if the allegation is against Tarkanian, they'll go after it like it is the end of the earth," said *HoopScoop* Publisher Clark Francis, who first published news of the affidavits. "But when it has to do with one of their own, Berst manages to sweep it away."

The NCAA's tactics also were called into question during the winter of 1989, when investigator Stroup went to a practice at Dixie College in St. George, Utah, to find Karl "Boobie" James, a point guard who played at UNLV during the 1987-88 season before transferring to Dixie. Todd Street, a student manager for the Dixie basketball team at the time, later told Dixie coach Ken Wagner, who was not at the practice, that Stroup had said he was there to "do an article" on James. "The team was running drills and [Assistant Coach Dave] Rose looked up and there was someone sitting at the top of the gymnasium," said Street, who graduated from the junior college and went on to the University of Utah. "Coach Rose told me to run up and see if we could help him in some way. So I ran up there and asked him what he wanted and he said he was going to write an article about Boobie. He said it at least twice, that he was there to do an article. He didn't say a particular newspaper, but he left no doubt that I was to think he was a reporter. I told Coach Rose it was a reporter and he sent Boobie up there." But when James came back from his face-to-face "interview" with the "reporter," he told Street the man was actually an NCAA investigator. Wagner wrote the NCAA's Dick Schultz to tell him of the incident.

If Stroup misrepresented himself or attempted to mislead

others into believing he was anything but an NCAA investigator, that would be a violation of the NCAA's unwritten code of ethics for investigators. "After I found out, I was a little mad," Street said. "I always thought they had rules that required them to be straight with us. He should have let us know what his full purpose was."

Stroup referred all comment on the matter to Berst, who told the *Los Angeles Times*: "Putting the best light on it, there may have been some form of miscommunication. If what they say is the truth, it may be a matter of somebody [Street] jumping to the conclusion that this guy [Stroup] was there to interview the player for a newspaper instead of interview him for another purpose." Berst could not explain why Street would so vividly remember Stroup saying he was there "to do an article" if the investigator were not trying to disguise his identity.

A couple of months later Stroup came to Las Vegas to interview UNLV assistant coach Tim Grgurich. Grgurich hired attorney Roy Smith to guide him through the question-and-answer minefield. "There were seven of us sitting around a table," Smith recalled. "And here we were all taking notes because they wouldn't let us tape, as you know. Well, after the interview was over, they told us we would be allowed to review their summary of the interview and make any corrections. We were called back to make changes and were appalled at how grossly they had misinterpreted the interview. Their summary, well, it was just off the wall. We said Tim would sign it, but only if they would allow us to attach our transcript to it. They told us it didn't work that way. I mean, there were names mentioned in the summary that neither Tim nor I had ever heard of. They said those names came up in conjunction with other information they had gathered. We argued that nothing that wasn't said by Tim should be included in his summary. Again, they said it didn't work that way. After two hours [NCAA investigator Dan] Calandro finally said, 'We don't care whether you agree with what is in the summary. We're not here to negotiate. You can sign it or don't sign it.' I asked him if the purpose of all this wasn't to get to the truth. I didn't get an answer. It sure seems pretty obvious this isn't about truth, it's about revenge. Once you've read an NCAA investigator's summary, you understand why coaches are scared to death and why everyone facing them needs a good lawyer."

Also, during the university's investigation, UNLV was told by two former players that NCAA investigators had used a microcassette recorder to tape their interviews. "Most of us would love it if they would tape all interviews," said attorney Steve Cohen, who is representing Tarkanian's son, Danny, and Shelley Fisher, a former member of the UNLV basketball staff. "We've asked and asked that they do so. Yet, we're told that's against the rules. Now here they are taping two guys who don't ask to be taped. What, exactly, are the rules?"

Tarkanian said the lesson most coaches have taken from his experience is to "shut up and swallow whatever the NCAA throws at you. They see what we've been through and realize it's not worth the fight. It's cost us hundreds of thousands of dollars to fight them, yet even though courts have agreed we're right, the public's perception has been manipulated by the NCAA. They are so powerful. They control your life if you're involved in intercollegiate athletics.

"There aren't many people who will step up and say what they feel about the NCAA. They have too much to lose. Now, they've already been upset with me. There isn't anything I could say that's going to get them any madder," Tarkanian noted. Which is why he's kept up his criticism of NCAA enforcement, saying the same things he wrote in the 1973 column that started all his troubles. For example, of a 1986 investigation at UCLA, he said: "I'll guarantee you they won't do anything to UCLA. They'll throw them a banquet." And of a 1985 NCAA decision placing Idaho State on two year's probation, Tarkanian said sarcastically: "When you look at it, 30 to 40 percent of high school All-Americans go to Idaho State, don't they? Every year, Idaho State gets all those guys. They don't even have enough money in all of Pocatello to buy one player at Kentucky."

Years later, when he looked at those comments, Tarkanian said, "There are probably some things I shouldn't say. But at least in all of this, I've been able to speak my mind and feel good about it. If it weren't for fear, others could too."

If there is a lesson in the story of Tarkanian's latest go-around with the NCAA and the allegations of questionable tactics used by its investigators, it is this: Although NCAA executive director Dick Schultz may bring a measure of sanity to the organization, the enforcement division under the win-at-all-costs rule of David Berst hasn't changed much since 1973.

PUTTING THE BRAKES ON

Nebraska Senator Ernest Chambers was despondent after reading the full text of the U.S. Supreme Court decision in *National Collegiate Athletic Association v. Tarkanian*. For nearly a decade, Chambers had been fighting to protect the constitutional rights of those involved in collegiate athletics in his state. And now, the highest court in the country had ruled the NCAA didn't have to recognize those rights. Because the NCAA is a voluntary organization, the court said, those who feel wronged by the NCAA can either work to fix it or quit. Just don't come looking for relief from the courts.

The truth, Chambers knows, is that working for substantive change in an organization as large as the NCAA is nearly impossible. And despite the claim the NCAA is a "voluntary association," quitting is really not an option for any university desiring to share in the profit and prestige of big-time athletics.

As he scrutinized the Tarkanian decision, Chambers realized that, although the court said the NCAA did not have to recognize the due process rights guaranteed by the U.S. Constitution, it had left open the possibility that states could guarantee those rights individually. So he drafted a bill to accomplish exactly that.

"The bill simply requires that, in every single stage or facet of action by the NCAA that might result in a penalty against a school for violation or alleged violation of NCAA rules, due process must be applied. The bill further states that due process of law is guaranteed by the constitution of Nebraska and the laws of Nebraska," Chambers said. "And due process, to make it as simple as I can, is a procedure which is fair. You have a right to know what you're charged with, to face your accuser, an opportunity to test the evidence to be used against you through cross-examination, and the things that most people would think of in order to have a fair accusation and a fair opportunity to meet those accusations." Most people, that is, except the NCAA. "I had felt, as had others, that since the NCAA is a national association it would come under the U.S. Constitution, which says a state or agency acting on behalf of the state cannot deny anybody life, liberty or property without due process of law," Chambers said. "Well, the Supreme Court said that is not the case. It said the NCAA, despite the presence of so many public schools, is a private association, so the federal constitutional standard that the states must follow does not apply. That meant that a remedy or a way to give a person fairness would have to be done through state law."

The senator from Omaha joined with Senator Cap Dierks of Ewing in pushing the bill through the 1990 Nebraska legislature. Then the two persuaded Governor Kay Orr, who had vetoed several athletics-related bills in the past, to sign the measure.

John J. Kitchin, NCAA legal counsel, said the Nebraska bill really won't affect the NCAA because the organization already has built due process into its proceedings. "Institutions are given all kinds of written notices about alleged violations and given all kinds of opportunities to present their side of the facts," Kitchin said. "They can have hearings and can have counsel present, if they elect. The NCAA believes in fair enforcement."

That last line brought a laugh from Chambers, whose caustic criticism of the NCAA has earned him their "consistent pain in our ass" award, one former NCAA staff member said.

"The NCAA is an arrogant organization, almost uncontrollable and accountable to nobody," Chambers said. "And since they're in a position to do so much damage to a university or a coach or even a player, they have to be accountable. And right now, without a bill like mine, they could do things the Governor of the state could not do, that the President of the United States could not do, and that is to deny somebody a fair hearing before some kind of punishment is imposed against him. I don't care what the NCAA says, there is nothing fair about the way NCAA hearings are run. In the future, if any of their proceedings move forward as though a presumption of guilt were there, that would be a violation of due process and a violation of this law."

Chambers submitted a draft of his bill to the Nebraska Attorney General who, after deleting several sections, assured him the law was constitutional. If the NCAA violates due process while investigating a school or individual in Nebraska, the organization could be liable for actual damages suffered as a result of the penalty. The next time the NCAA conducts an investigation in his state, Chambers said, he and others will be poised for the chance to apply the law. Chambers also contends the legal interpretation of the new statute could even broaden the potential for legal action against the NCAA.

"The judge," Chambers said, "might do something like this if a case came before him: 'First of all, I want to determine that the rule is a fair one and is fairly applied across the board. Secondly, I want to be sure that the process used to find that a school has committed a violation has been fair throughout. Thirdly, the punishment has to fit the offense, which might mean that mass punishment of everybody for the offenses of one coach or one or two students might be held to violate the due process of other players.' As you can see, there are a lot of ways this bill could turn the NCAA's enforcement program upside down and actually protect people from being run over."

Chambers specifically included a provision in his bill that would penalize the NCAA for punishing a school or individual who might use the law to fight the organization. "What would happen is a court would enjoin the NCAA from punishing anyone, no matter what the outcome of the NCAA's investigation," Chambers said. "And I have yet to see them [the NCAA], as bad as they are, violate a court order. I don't think they would because that would show what they are. It would show what an arrogant, lawless organization they really are."

The attention Chambers's bill drew prompted lawmakers in a dozen other states to request copies of the new Nebraska law. Already, Illinois Representative Tim Johnson of Urbana filed a similar version in his state legislature. That bill, which had 72 co-sponsors, spells out the due process requirements, including provisions requiring the accused to have the chance to face his accuser, forcing the NCAA to tape all statements and providing the interrogated person with a transcript. The NCAA sent Berst and John Kitchin to legislative committee hearings in Springfield to try to kill Johnson's bill. Kitchin even intimated that passing a bill requiring due process could jeopardize the NCAA membership of schools in Illinois.

"It would seem harsh if member institutions were put in a situation where they couldn't continue to be members because the laws of the state preclude them from complying with the rules of the organization," Kitchin said. "This isn't a threat. We're not saying anybody's going to get kicked out. But as a voluntary member, you have to comply with the same rules that bind the other members."

Johnson was unfazed: "Any organization can operate on their own when they don't have to comply with any rules except those they make internally," he told the *Chicago Tribune*. "They can be as unfair as they want. This bill simply guarantees fundamental fairness in areas where lives face dramatic consequences." Johnson's fellow lawmakers were unfazed as well, voting 71-36 to send the bill to the state Senate. The wave of legislation forcing the NCAA to protect individual rights continued through 1990 as bills were filed in the legislatures of Florida, Missouri and South Carolina.

In Florida, State University System Chancellor Charles Reed begged lawmakers not to pass the bill in 1990 for fear of antagonizing the NCAA, which was investigating the University of Florida basketball and football programs during the time the legislature was in session. "The timing is not right," Reed said, never arguing against the bill's merits. "There's some concern that this won't go over well in Kansas [NCAA's headquarters]." Representative Jim King of Jacksonville countered: "If we're scared of some organization we volunteer to be a part of, then that's precisely why this needs to pass. What's wrong with due process? What have they got against due process?" Bill sponsor Senator Vince Bruner, of Fort Walton Beach said he filed the bill "to remind the NCAA that there are authorities out there that they must answer to. For too long, they have not lived by the same rules of fairness that apply to others. It's time that stopped."

Berst, in a warning to Florida lawmakers, called the bill "an inappropriate intrusion into our operation. I don't know how I can say it any more clearly. The few politicians that are seizing the opportunity to obtain a little bit of local support because of the use of the term 'due process' are really doing a disservice to the NCAA and, I think, to the people of the state involved." That prompted Bruner, a former Florida State University football player, to wonder, "Who exactly do these guys think they are? We are elected to govern this state. One of the areas we govern is the state university system. We fund the state universities that fund the NCAA. Who is he saying is intruding here? That's a perfect example of the arrogance shown by this organization that is the reason for bills like this."

Added Senator Larry Plummer of Miami, "I think we ought to smash their arrogance. This is clearly not the organization that was founded by Theodore Roosevelt. They believe that all decisions on athletics should be made by them as ordained by God. It's time to smash them."

Duke University sports law professor John Weistart said the NCAA shouldn't be shocked by the sudden interest state legislators have in passing such laws. "They [the NCAA] have no one to blame but themselves," Weistart said. "If I were one of the NCAA czars, I think I would say that we much prefer a system in which we define within the NCAA the type of hearing we should provide rather than leaving the question up to 50 different states. Once they saw that states had decided to take this on, they should have announced that they would review and revise their process. But they were remiss in not taking the issue on after the Tarkanian decision. I would think that wisdom on the part of the NCAA would have produced a response in which they satisfy all of the requirements of due process and define a hearing that they would provide to people subject to sanctions that would meet the requirements of notice and cross-examination. They should do that for two reasons. One, it makes their decisions more credible. Second, they would forestall regulation in some other form."

Nebraska Senator Chambers said he is glad to see the NCAA feeling some heat. "It is a shame that we may have to do it this way," he said. "But it looks like it will require 50 different legislatures to pass 50 state laws protecting the people of their states from the NCAA. I believe many states will do so because to avoid the issue is to invite trouble."

"If we pass bills in three or four states, you could see a stampede," said Johnson, one of the Illinois bill's sponsors. "As it is right now, the NCAA is a modern-day counterpart to the Third Reich. We [in Illinois] have a long history of what people would call arbitrary and capricious treatment by the NCAA. We need to establish a set of rules to prevent this sort of thing from happening again."

Chambers, Johnson and those who have filed similar bills are not alone in their belief that the NCAA's enforcement program is weighted against the accused. And they aren't the first to argue that the due process rights so ingrained in American justice are ignored by NCAA justice. During 1978 congressional hearings into the NCAA's investigatory process, 11 witnesses said that the lack of attention to the rights of the accused proved the NCAA did not believe in a fair and impartial hearing. "It [the infractions hearing] is not a dispute-resolution system," said University of Denver law professor Burton Brody. "By the time the infractions committee begins an official inquiry, there is no dispute in the sense that our legal system perceives a dispute. The defendant is guilty. The infractions inquisition merely calls upon the defendant to supply additional evidence of that guilt."

Brody's comments were typical of many made during the congressional inquiry, and more than a decade later the issue remains a constant complaint. Presidents and others from schools under investigation believe, without a doubt, that they enter the infractions hearing under a strong presumption of guilt and must work to prove their innocence. The entire system is created to give the NCAA what could be called a home-court advantage. But while trying to win one on the road and prove themselves innocent, schools are not allowed to question their accusers, call witnesses or see the evidence against them until just a week or so before the hearing. The result is an impressive track record for the NCAA: In the nearly 40 years of NCAA enforcement, no one can remember a school that appeared before the infractions committee that was not found guilty of at least one rules violation.

Protocol for an NCAA hearing calls for NCAA investigative staff to make an oral presentation to the Committee on Infractions. The school then is permitted to present its side. Typically, say members of the Committee on Infractions, schools present notebooks full of information to the committee, filled with transcripts of taped interviews, sworn statements and a variety of other documents. The NCAA staff presents nothing but its summary of the case, reading from its own memos, and calls no witnesses.

"This is a big part of the one-sidedness," said sports law professor Lonny Rose. "What does the infractions committee see before the case? It sees the university's response to the published NCAA charges. It never sees the enforcement staff's file. It never sees the people who talked to the enforcement staff. There are no witnesses, there is no confrontation of witnesses. There's no way to judge the credibility of witnesses. There's no one under oath. Nothing that we have put into the traditional legal atmosphere to have the guarantee of truthfulness exists in the NCAA machine.

The NCAA argues that this is collegial, right? Therefore we don't need oaths. We don't need robes. We don't need the flag on the wall. That's tough for people who face that group to swallow."

Committee chairman D. Alan Williams said too many critics "think we have more power than we do. We have no authority to call witnesses." Further, Williams contends it would be "too expensive" to bring witnesses to a hearing even if the committee could require their attendance. As a result, the infractions committee is often asked to adjudicate guilt based on conflicting statements gathered by investigators from the NCAA and member schools.

Because it is a nongovernment organization, the NCAA does not have subpoena power to force people to testify or be interviewed by NCAA investigators, Williams said. But that is tempered somewhat by new NCAA rules that require anyone involved with a member institution—coaches, players and even boosters—to "cooperate fully" with investigators or risk being banished from participation in intercollegiate sports. The *NCAA Manual* provides that "in the event that a representative of a member institution [including boosters] refuses to submit relevant information to the Committee [on Infractions] or the enforcement staff upon request, an official inquiry may be filed with the institution alleging a violation of the cooperative principles of the NCAA bylaws and enforcement procedures." The threat of taking away something so important to those people is "a compelling force," David Berst said. Combine that with the NCAA's growing use of immunity for athletes—allowing them to keep their eligibility if they tattle on the coaches or boosters who provided them handouts—and the absence of subpoena power becomes less of an issue than it may have been a few years ago.

The NCAA readily concedes that it begins most investigations as a consequence of newspaper or television stories detailing apparent rules violations. David Berst and Steve Morgan must have forgotten that none of those reporters is blessed with any more subpoena power than the NCAA. Yet, as the Kentucky case showed, it is not uncommon for reporters to do a better job of proving violations than the NCAA staff.

John Weistart said the NCAA's constant complaints that it does not have subpoena power bothers him for at least one reason: They've never asked for it. "If they wanted to be truly effective, they would come up with an arrangement with state legislatures which would give them the power to compel people to cooperate with them," Weistart said. "The easiest thing to do would be to go to Congress or various state legislatures and ask for subpoena power. One would think the state universities would have an interest in agreeing to that subpoena power because it would ensure that culprits would be found and blame would be allocated in a way that is fair as opposed to unfair. If you don't have all the witnesses, you end up making allegations which might not be substantiated. The fact that they've never requested subpoena power, in my mind, means they shouldn't be using the lack of subpoena power as an excuse for bad enforcement."

That lack of subpoena power can work against the school as often as it does the NCAA investigator, said former University of Florida president Marshall Criser, now a prominent lawyer in Jacksonville. Criser served on the NCAA Presidents Commission and experienced the NCAA hearing process in 1984 and 1985, when Florida received a three-year probation for football rules violations. "The NCAA process suffers from not having penalties for perjury or subpoena power," Criser said. "So, sometimes, they get incorrect or incomplete information. They take testimony without transcripts that later are distilled into an investigator's notes. Someone faced with that statement has no idea of the context in which it was said. They [infractions committee members] are getting an investigator's composite summary. And what is lost in translation may be information helpful to the institution.

"I don't question their integrity," Criser said of the NCAA staff and the Committee on Infractions. "It's just not a process that lends itself to due process or a full and complete hearing. There's no judge or jury, it's just a committee, relying on summary statements with no right of cross-examination."

But Steve Morgan, the NCAA's associate executive director for enforcement, said due process rights have increased in the NCAA system "so everybody has a chance to speak their piece and be heard. "We've got notice requirements to all the coaches identified, the student-athletes identified, they get full notice of the allegations before the hearing," Morgan said. He said that the NCAA wants the accused to feel they have rights, but doing so may slow an already snail-like process. "As you play these things out and try to build in more and more due process, it slows down the process. That could be as bad as it is good."

The denial of the opportunity to face your accuser is especially frustrating for attorneys representing individuals—not institutions—who risk losing careers as a result of an NCAA investigation. University of Illinois assistant basketball coach Jimmy Collins was accused by the NCAA of offering recruit Deon Thomas $80,000 and a Chevrolet Blazer to enroll at Illinois. The NCAA based its charge on a conversation Thomas had with Iowa assistant coach Bruce Pearl. Unbeknownst to Thomas, Pearl tape-recorded the phone call.

When Pearl sent the tape to the NCAA, Collins's head was on the professional chopping block and Thomas risked losing his collegiate eligibility. Yet when attorneys for both Collins and Thomas asked Iowa officials and the NCAA for permission to interview Pearl, the request was denied, leaving the two to try and fashion a defense without ever having talked to the man whose actions put them on trial. "It is true we may have received nothing more than a patronizing interview, but at least we'd get to look our accusers in the face and ask some important questions," said Mark Goldenberg, Collins's attorney. "That's important to us, even if we don't get the answers we want."

To make matters worse, many of the accused are denied the chance even to face the infractions committee. Dixon Pyles, an attorney for Mississippi State University, said this flaw in the enforcement procedures is especially damaging to non–NCAA members, such as boosters, who stand to have their reputations destroyed but cannot appear to defend themselves. NCAA rules require that, if the committee finds a booster to have violated NCAA rules, it can force a school to ban the booster from further participation in athletics, even though the booster's defense may never be heard. Boosters cannot attend the hearing, the NCAA's Rich Hilliard said, because "it is an institutional hearing and only institutional personnel can be admitted."

"Punitive sanctions may be imposed upon private citizens by simply labeling them as representatives of the member institutions and then coercing the member institutions into summarily taking the punitive actions which were unilaterally and indirectly imposed by the NCAA," Pyles said. "No proper procedures are set forth in the *NCAA Manual* for the purpose of determining the truth or falsity of charges lodged against a nonmember person accused of violating the association rules and who may be subjected to punitive sanctions. These nonmember individuals are not served with written specific charges. The nonmember individuals are not given an opportunity or time to prepare a response or defense, and they are never afforded the opportunity or right on their own to appear, to be confronted by and to examine accusing witnesses, or to present evidence in their own behalf. In short, the nonmember chargee is afforded no opportunity or right, on his own, of a full, fair hearing regarding any accusations made against him."

During the hearings, Committee on Infractions members may question administrators, coaches or students in attendance. Those not there are represented only by the summaries NCAA investigators write after their interviews. "The procedure, which I think was a relatively strange one, was we got no [written] information from the [NCAA] staff" before the meeting, said former committee chairman Frank Remington. "I never understood it." Remington said most staff evidence was verbal. "There was very little physical evidence on the part of the staff."

That imbalance of physical evidence presented to the committee has led some to question who bears the burden of proof in an NCAA hearing. Committee members and NCAA staff say it is the staff's responsibility to prove the charges. "The burden is not on the institution, the burden is on the staff," D. Alan Williams said. "The staff has to prove that this thing happened."

"In a criminal case, the reasonable doubt standard is used. You have to prove your case beyond a reasonable doubt," said Doug Johnson, an NCAA investigator for several years who now serves as an assistant athletic director at the University of Miami. "But this isn't a criminal court. In an NCAA case, it's a preponderance of evidence, just more likely than not, 51 percent to 49 percent, that what you allege happened. That places the burden on the investigator to get over the 51 percent mark."

Others, however, said the university bears the burden of proof. "You are guilty until you prove you are innocent," said Mickey Holmes, executive director of the USF&G Sugar Bowl and former commissioner of the Missouri Valley Conference. "When you walk into the hearing, you are going up against insurmountable odds and those odds are that, no matter how hard you try to prove your innocence, no matter how much you send to the committee to show you are innocent, they are going to get you on something."

This long-standing perception is a result, many say, of comparing what the committee has in its hands when the hearing begins with what it issues as its eventual finding. Before the hearing, committee members see the university's response to the published NCAA charges and a short summary from the enforcement staff. They never see the enforcement staff's file. They never see the people who talked to the enforcement staff. There are no witnesses. There is no confrontation of witnesses. There's no way to judge the credibility of witnesses. Yet the enforcement staff *always* walks away with some portion of a victory.

NCAA officials explain this by arguing that they win 100 percent of the time only because they don't take schools to the infractions committee woodshed until they have enough evidence to prove their case. "I think that [conviction rate] really is reflective of the good work done by the enforcement staff and the fact that, if we don't have a case, we don't try one," Steve Morgan said.

"I think it [the conviction rate] reflects a system that is stacked," Senator Chambers said when told of Morgan's quote. "From the moment they step on your campus to the time you lose your appeal, the NCAA is in a no-lose situation. And for too long, we've all sat back and let them work that way. It has got to stop. And I'm looking forward to being the one putting the brakes on."

EPILOGUE

In what may be the cruelest irony of all, the infractions committee's 1990 decision to ban the Runnin' Rebels from defending their national title prompted Tarkanian's two high school recruits to reverse their commitment to UNLV. Ed O'Bannon, one of the three best players in the country, and the recruit Tarkanian touted as his greatest ever, and Shon Tarver, another blue chipper from California, decided not to take their talents to The Strip.

Instead, the two chose to play for UCLA, the school Tarkanian claimed in his 1973 newspaper columns was cheating while the NCAA looked the other way. The Bruin coach who inherited this windfall of talent is Jim Harrick, who as a high school coach in 1973 complained to David Berst that Tarkanian had broken rules to sign forward Jackie Robinson. Harrick had coached Robinson at Morningside (California) High and had hoped to take him to Utah State, where Harrick would be an assistant coach the next year. "He [Robinson] and I were going to make a decision about his college choice for three years," Harrick told Berst in a telephone conversation Berst illicitly tape recorded. "All of a sudden, I'm out of it. I hope you don't think I'm bitter. I'm really not." Later that same year, Robinson signed an affidavit claiming that Harrick suggested to Robinson that he concoct allegations against Tarkanian, thereby nullifying his commitment to UNLV. "He [Harrick] said I could still go to Utah State," Robinson swore in his statement. "[He said] 'Just tell that man from the NCAA that Tarkanian gave you $5 or something like that.' He shows me a letter of intent filled out for Utah State and he said, 'Sign this and we can have [NCAA investigator Lester Burks] take care of the rest.' " Robinson refused Harrick's request and went on to star at UNLV. Although Harrick lost that recruiting battle and his allegations never stuck, his attempts to help the NCAA take down Tarkanian finally paid off in 1990. The addition of UNLV's erstwhile recruits O'Bannon and Tarver allowed Harrick to turn a rather average haul into one of the nation's best recruiting classes.

7

BUILDING A BETTER BEAST

It may have been fine, when the NCAA first established its enforcement program in the early 1950s, to ignore little details like fairness. Or accuracy. Or common sense in applying the rules. After all, that was a time when Executive Director Walter Byers was selling the television rights to the NCAA basketball tournament for a mere $550 an hour, the very best coaches were lucky if they earned $10,000 and the lure of top-dollar professional sports contracts hadn't caught the attention of every high school athlete.

But, as Bob Dylan so eloquently put it, "Times, they are a changin.' " Today, just getting into the 64-team basketball tournament can earn a school nearly $300,000, a figure that likely will increase as the NCAA looks for ways to divide profits from its new $1-billion television contract. Coaches have become America's highest paid higher educators (to use the term loosely) with several earning $1 million a year and more. And what prep star who can run a perfect post pattern or hit a 20-foot jumper isn't thinking about the riches of the NFL or NBA?

The stakes are different now. They're higher, much higher. That's not necessarily positive, but it's real. And as the stakes have grown, so has the incentive to cheat. There needs to be some force out there to take away that incentive. There needs to be an NCAA and it needs to enforce its rules. But just as there is a correlation between higher stakes and increased incentive to cheat, there also is a link between higher stakes and the need for better enforcement. Too many people have too much to lose today for the NCAA to continue living by past standards.

From those who have worked within or against the NCAA comes this 10-point plan for bettering the organization's enforcement function.

1. Tape-record interviews by investigators.   There's absolutely no excuse, as we head into the 21st century, for the NCAA to ignore this point.   The NCAA's refusal to tape interviews because it would "frighten" student-athletes is ridiculous. Again, that may have been true in the 1950s, when Byers adopted this position. But kids are more sophisticated now. A high school star will do more interviews in the week before a big game than Byers did in his entire 36 years at the NCAA. They're used to rambling while the tape's rolling. And the mark of a good questioner is his ability to put people at ease, even with a recorder running. Every real investigator at any real agency uses tape recording today to ensure accuracy and to ensure that the material received is in a useful form. Just ask the IRS, FBI and U.S. Attorney General's Office, all of which confirm that taping is key to their handling of an accurate investigation. Hey, the NCAA can just waltz down the street from its lavish offices to the Overland Park (Kansas) Police Department, where Lieutenant Keith Faddis said tape recording "allows us to capture the interview as it really took place and that's important." In fact, police aren't just using tape recorders anymore, many are using video recorders. It doesn't impede anything, those agencies report. The NCAA's insistence on the status quo weakens the entire process and casts a long shadow over the quality of its investigative work. With lives and livelihoods at stake, it is high time the NCAA recognize the need for increased accuracy. It is no longer sufficient for the organization to rely on an investigator's memory and pen-speed. In fact, to do so is dangerous—dangerous for the investigator, dangerous for the NCAA.

The NCAA's Steve Morgan, when asked in 1988 to identify a conference that was aggressively and effectively policing its membership, pointed to the Pac-10. One of the strengths of the Pac-10's program is tape recording, said David Price, a former NCAA investigator who runs the Pac-10 enforcement office. "It makes a more complete record, without question," Price said. "You simply cannot take notes, at least I can't, as thoroughly as the taping. It also allows you to be able to follow through more quickly with questions that are pertinent. Whereas when you're taking notes, you sometimes have to finish the notetaking before you can go on to the next question and you lose an important germ of an idea. It is just more accurate and that's what we want. I suppose we've all been in places where we've thought we heard something and later found that the person said it a little differently or thought he said it a little differently. When you go back, if you could play a tape, you can get the precise question and the precise answer as opposed to just the notetaking."

Louisiana State University faculty representative Billy Seay and others say the NCAA enforcement staff should follow in the Pac-10's footsteps. "Notes developed from conversations you have had are pretty poor reflections about what might have taken place," Seay said.

A 1988 survey of NCAA members by the *Florida Times-Union* showed a majority agreed it was time this outdated idea go out the window. The newspaper surveyed all 795 NCAA member schools and received 229 responses. The survey had a margin of error of plus or minus 6.5 percent. Of those who responded, 79 percent said NCAA investigators should be tape-recording interviews. Most were unaware that the organization's policies prohibit the practice.

"In fact, taping should go both ways: not only should the NCAA be required to tape-record but so should the university," said University of Miami sports law professor Lonny Rose, who has represented schools and written and lectured on the reform of NCAA enforcement. "I know the NCAA is concerned that information would then be leaked to the media, but I think you could shore up leaks by considering all this to be litigation. And accordingly, except with very minor exemptions, state open-meetings rules might not apply to active litigation of cases. Even states that have an open-records act exempt the litigation process and so it's not disclosed until the litigation is over or filed. Once the litigation is over, it's a different story. So I think those interviews have to be recorded but I think universities should be required to record them, too, because ultimately when I get to the infractions committee we don't want to have a contest over whose story is accurate. If there's a question you have the transcripts, you play the portion of the tape to the infractions committee—let them judge as to whether or not it was said or not said. And if you want a transcript, either side can make a copy of the recording and anybody can have a transcript made at their own expense. Every person interviewed should be entitled to either a copy of the tape recording or a transcript of it. It is just plain fair."

2. Pay the NCAA enforcement staff as professionals, then expect professional work in return.   NCAA officials are proud of their ability to attract candidates with advanced degrees, many in law, to the enforcement staff. That's likely not to change, since being an NCAA investigator sounds a whole lot more exciting than it is. But while attracting bright talent is important, keeping that talent is even more so. Unless there is a drastic overhaul of the pay scale, investigators will continue to throw their empty hands up and leave every two years or so. The losers in that scenario are many: the school under investigation, the recruits waiting to learn the fate of their chosen university, and even NCAA staff. The quality of an investigation—despite NCAA officials' comments to the contrary—has to be damaged by constant investigator turnover.

The *Times-Union* survey showed broad support for bettering the enforcement process by bringing continuity to the investigative staff. Seventy-three percent of the respondents said investigators should be paid more and, of those, 59 percent said investigators should earn an extra $10,000 or more annually.

"The hiring and retention of the enforcement staff must be with a view to professionalism," said Professor Rose. "The level of pay that these people are suffering under is ridiculous. Now, I just don't want to throw money at them and say pay them more. They need to be qualified for higher pay. Many of these people are experienced administrators, coming from jobs that are paying more money, many of them are law graduates who could, if they choose to, get a law position that pays more. Without suggesting that the people they have there now are not the people they should have, you get what you pay for. And with the NCAA, that's not much."

Duke University law professor John Weistart said the NCAA's $1.5-million average annual legal bill should indicate how important it is for the organization to have the very best enforcement staff available. "If you pin down the amount paid for legal fees in connection with NCAA infraction proceedings, it's clear that that number just absolutely exploded in the last few years," Weistart said. "That means the NCAA needs to be equipped to deal with good lawyers from the other side and that means they're going to have to make these jobs more high-status, more permanent. And that's going to mean more pay. There's so much at stake, I mean you're talking about literally millions of dollars—tens of millions of dollars if you're talking about the death penalty. More important, you're talking about the basic credibility and leadership of the university. That's serious stuff."

3. Increase staff size.   Berst is fond of joking that he has "never held out hope that we will work ourselves out of a job here" because cheating is prevalent. With only 14 or 15 investigators on staff, Berst would be more honest if he just said the NCAA is lucky to catch what it does. Enforcement, in the minds of most people, is the NCAA's most important function. Sure, the organization wouldn't exist were it not for the success of its many championships. But even Executive Director Dick Schultz concedes the public perception is that college sports are rancid and they're looking to the NCAA to clean it up. Some coaches—none that will go on the record—will admit that breaking NCAA rules is a risk worth taking. With an overworked, undermanned NCAA enforcement staff, the odds of getting caught are slim. And the truth is coaches will get fired more quickly for losing than they will for cheating. One way to change that would be to establish an enforcement division that did more than wait for newspaper or television stories to break before jumping in. If the NCAA's enforcement function was proactive instead of reactive, the profit from cheating might diminish.

For example, how about conducting an investigation of each of the top four football teams and each Final Four participant immediately after their victorious season is over? Talk about taking away the incentive to win. That also would expose more big-time universities to the investigative process, eliminating charges of selective enforcement while, at the same time, expanding the pool of schools that understand what it is to suffer through investigation by an enforcement program that is so inherently flawed. Right now, the idea is not feasible. The NCAA staff, as Berst said, "still has too much to do. We're always behind."

Before any such plan could be workable, the NCAA must

make a more serious commitment to enforcement. It cannot pretend to police an 800-member national organization with barely more than a dozen investigators. And it cannot believe that spending just 2 percent of the organization's budget on enforcement is adequate. To put fear in the hearts of rule-breaking coaches and athletes, the NCAA must expand its enforcement department, increase the enforcement budget and then focus its energies on serious offenses, not petty crap.

4. Once the NCAA hires good staff, invest in proper training. As it stands now, a new investigator spends a couple of weeks reading the *NCAA Manual*, then is put on the beat. Sometimes he or she travels with more experienced investigators for a short period, other times not. If the organization wants to go about enforcement in a serious fashion, it should establish a rigorous training course for the staff, teaching interviewing techniques, accurate memo writing (at least until tape recording is adopted) and common sense. Lonny Rose said several athletics administrators have suggested an idea that makes great sense—establishing what is tantamount to an apprenticeship program for new investigators, as is done in other professions.

"In terms of staffing, in every case there would be a senior and a junior investigator," Rose said. "The senior is in charge and the junior takes time to learn. That's the way they do it in police departments, its the way they do it in the FBI, it's the way they do it at the Securities and Exchange Commission, it's the way they do it at the IRS, and the seniors—because they are senior level and get paid more—provide the continuity."

NCAA enforcement chief David Berst, a baseball coach at tiny MacMurray College in Jacksonville, Illinois, before joining the NCAA in 1972, concedes he didn't have the training to be an investigator when he came on board. The closest he came to "investigating" was scouting crosstown rival Illinois College. But Berst claims to have "grown into the job" and apparently feels that approach is acceptable for today's investigative staff. It is not.

5. Begin joint and parallel investigations with universities. This is not a new suggestion. But Berst and his boss, Steve Morgan, have almost always turned thumbs down on the idea. College Football Association Executive Director Charles Neinas, a one-time NCAA employee and commissioner of the Big Eight, has been calling on the NCAA to adopt the idea for more than a decade. Even former NCAA president Wilford Bailey of Auburn agrees that the NCAA should abandon its two-tiered investigative approach.

Currently, the NCAA sleuths around for months—and often years—asking questions of players, boosters, former recruits and others. When NCAA investigators are done, they send the school a list of charges and tell the school to go back and interview all those same people to see which charges it agrees occurred. This process is both cumbersome and painfully long. If NCAA investigators were to call the school's designated investigator before an interview and instead invite him or her along, the investigation would proceed more quickly and with less disagreement, Neinas said.

"The NCAA enforcement staff is concerned, as it was explained to me, that the institutions, if they were involved in an early stage of an investigation, might try to stonewall the case," Neinas said. "I disagree. My opinion is based on personal experience. If an institution wants to stonewall a case, they can do it at the end as well as the beginning. I was of the opinion that 90-plus percent of the schools under investigation would want to expedite the procedure. When it's public knowledge and is hanging over your head, you might as well try and get it resolved as quickly as possible, and the parallel investigation idea would expedite that. Additionally, you have some witnesses who will tell the NCAA one thing and the school another. What would happen is you would have the NCAA staff plus an institutional representative interviewing people at the same time so you don't get into a situation where you argue over which statement should be accepted.

"Let's say you're representing the institution and I'm representing the NCAA and I have questions for Joe Jones and we're there questioning him together," Neinas said. "If you think that I'm leading the witness, you can ask your own question and vice versa. If there is need for clarification, we can both hear it. After all, the NCAA promotes their enforcement operation as a cooperative effort between the institution and the organization, right? When I was at the Big Eight Conference we used this model. In nine years we had four major cases, the most notable of which was an Oklahoma case in 1973. I reported to the president of the

University of Oklahoma on Friday, April 13, that we were investigating. The conference processed the case in August. It was a major case, OU got two years probation and sanctions. The point is, when I reported to the president, he was angered by the fact that it had happened, but he pledged his cooperation and anyone who did not cooperate with our investigation would be directly answerable to him. There were 14 allegations involved, the university after the investigation pleaded guilty to 12, pleaded no contest to the 13th and opposed the 14th. It took us four months to take care of a major investigation. You know how long that would have taken the NCAA? We had another major case at Oklahoma State. The thing that is interesting there was the Big Eight Conference had access to people who we would not have been able to get any cooperation from except that the president of the university asked them to cooperate. That absolutely helped us get to the truth better and quicker.

"The NCAA is a voluntary service organization," Charles Neinas said. "The enforcement program is a necessary evil. The thrust of my suggestion is to expedite the investigative process so that both parties benefit and hopefully eliminate the situation where you exchange affidavits and argue over whose to accept."

Another advantage to this idea is it would, to a certain extent, eliminate the complaint schools now have about being unable to face their accusers. As it stands now, the NCAA may interview someone who provides damaging information. But six or eight months later, when it is the university's obligation to interview its accuser, the person may just drift away.

6. Make drastic changes in the infractions committee and the means by which its members are chosen.   Ideas here abound. Marist College President Dennis Murray recommends an outside panel of paid professionals to hear infractions cases, instead of the current committee composed of representatives from NCAA member schools. "The thing that has to be done to create a legitimate system of enforcement is some clear lines of demarcation between the rules of the [NCAA] staff and the people that hear those various cases," Murray said. "I think you have to have independent people who are professionally paid and who have a clear distance and no working relationship with the staff."

Duke University sports law professor John Weistart goes one better. "One of the first things I would do is work on the credibility of the people who make the enforcement decisions. I think the reason the system doesn't work is that the infraction committee members are too anonymous, so I would go to a system in which I used completely outside decision makers. My first choice would be to find people of high public visibility, the Peter Ueberroth-type people, people who carry clout. Retired Supreme Court justices, Lewis Powell for example, who would carry or bring to the job known credibility. The idea is to take it outside the organization, independent decision makers, and preferably again people of high public standing with preestablished reputations for high ethical behavior.

"If you do that, you eliminate the question that there is too close a relationship. For example, in the case against the University of Illinois, [Illinois professor and former infractions committee member] John Nowak had to disqualify himself for obvious reasons. But the truth is, the taint of that is never gone. Are we confident that when the decision makers decide that they're going to stick it to the University of Illinois or not that they don't think about John Nowak at all? And what's going to happen when he comes back in the room? Again, I would not want to accuse any of those people of improper behavior. But this is a question of how believable and how impressive are the decisions that they make. Those decisions could be more believable and impressive if people outside the organization were making them."

Lonny Rose suggests a complete overhaul, but without reaching outside the organization in a search for decision makers. "In order for the infractions committee to be really representative, in order for it to know what's going on in the field, my view is that people should be on there for two- or three-year terms, with maybe one renewal at most. Right now, there are six of them, their terms are three years and they can be reappointed for up to nine years. It really should be made up of seven people. Any fewer and you really run the risk of two or three people just controlling everything. Any more and you run into problems like the U.S. Supreme Court where you get nine different opinions from nine different people. It should be made up of two athletic directors, one coach, one university administrator, one student-athlete and two faculty members that are not associated with athletics. They could be law professors, business school professors, anthropologists—mainstream faculty. If the theory behind the organization of the NCAA is that this is a institution of higher education, what better place to put educators than on the infractions committee?

"Now, they're chosen by the NCAA Council, which we all know is controlled by a couple of people and the executive director," Rose said. "And the Council then is who you would appeal a finding to. That has to change. The infractions committee, then, should be appointed by the Presidents Commission. Very frankly, part of the problem with the infractions committee is that they are many times perceived as merely an extension of the power structure of the NCAA. So this has to be some neutral body, it has to be done with a view toward representation of a variety of interests and the Presidents Commission is a vehicle for doing it. And when it comes to hearing cases, they should be done by divisions. There is no point in having Division II people deciding Division I infractions and Division I people deciding Division II infractions. If everyone is represented, the athletic directors, the coaches, the university administrators, the student-athlete, the faculty, you would be well served to have more than one infractions committee. Division II people do not have a sense of what it's like in Division I. The game is different there. And Division III is totally separate. So let's treat everyone fairly by allowing them a jury of their peers."

7. Give the infractions committee its own staff.   This, too, is an idea the NCAA has heard before. During the 1978 Congressional investigation of NCAA enforcement, several witnesses testified that the relationship between the infractions committee (the judge) and the enforcement staff (the prosecutor) was far too close. The enforcement staff handles everything from the infractions committee's hotel reservations to the drafting of letters and press releases for the committee. As one of its 18 recommendations for improving the NCAA, Congress suggested the infractions committee end the practice of using the enforcement staff as the committee staff.

"Because of this close working relationship between the enforcement staff and the Committee on Infractions, it is not difficult for an institution to conclude that its case has already been weighed and judged before even receiving the official inquiry containing the allegations," Mickey Holmes, then commissioner of the Missouri Valley Conference, told Congress. "Because of this close relationship, I feel the enforcement staff and the Committee on Infractions communicate freely before, during and after a hearing and before adjudication."

Holmes, who today is executive director of the USF&G Sugar Bowl, still believes his is a valid suggestion. "The infractions committee has to have its own staff," Holmes said. "Whether they're in the NCAA offices or not is really not important. The fact is they have to be separate, physically separate from the enforcement staff. Now from a logistical perspective it makes sense to have the staff at the NCAA headquarters, but they have to have an independence. That's most important."

Rose said that staff can serve several important functions. "It [the committee staff] must be run by what I call a staff counsel who advises the infractions committee and who is responsible to the infractions committee only. And that person has a staff of secretaries, of researchers. We're talking maybe three or four people to prepare and disseminate the findings, to coordinate the activities of the infractions committee with the public relations arm of the NCAA, but to work for the infractions committee. And accordingly, the people who run the meeting are the infractions committee, not the enforcement staff.   Right now all the audio taping of the infractions hearings, for example, are run by the enforcement staff. All that should be done by the infractions committee and its staff and not by the enforcement staff. As the university people walk in, so should the enforcement staff."

When Congress suggested the NCAA provide a separate staff for the infractions committee, the NCAA ignored the recommendation, claiming it was too expensive. With the vault open wide and a $1- billion television contract between CBS and the NCAA signed, that excuse no longer works. It's time to make this change.

8. Similarly overhaul the appeals process.   First, appeals should not be heard by the same body that appoints the infractions committee. If the NCAA Council, which selects the infractions committee, were to overturn the committee's verdict, the Council also would seem to be questioning the judgment of the very people it appointed—not a practice to be indulged in frequently. Additionally, current practice is for appeals to be heard de novo, or from the beginning of the case. That is absurd, if only because it is an impractical waste of time. A university should be able to select the points which it believes the infractions committee misunderstood or ignored and appeal only those points. If the Council agrees with the university, then it could alter the penalty in some way.

One suggestion is that the NCAA establish a three-person committee to hear appeals. The 44-member Council has a full agenda each time it meets. An infractions appeal, which is not among the Council's regular functions, just adds to that. Turn that appeal process over to a smaller, less unwieldy body and everyone would be better served.

9. Change the process of granting immunity.   Many coaches — from Notre Dame's Digger Phelps to UNLV's Jerry Tarkanian — believe immunity should be thrown out altogether. If a kid knowingly accepts a benefit outside NCAA rules, he should be banned from college sports, they argue, because it takes two to tango. That's one way to make kids think before accepting something they shouldn't, the coaches say. Unfortunately, turning back the hands of time is nearly impossible; the NCAA's offers of immunity are increasing, not decreasing. That in mind, there should be limits to the practice.

"Now, when the enforcement staff decides it wants to give immunity to a witness, it must request permission from the infractions committee," Lonny Rose said. "I and others believe there needs to be a representative of the university at that hearing in case the university believes it should argue against it. It shouldn't be just the enforcement staff running to the infractions committee and giving a one-sided presentation. The problem is that the immunity is granted at a time when the university doesn't even know that it's going to be charged. There could be some very good reasons that a university could argue against immunity. A university could say, 'Wait a minute, you shouldn't give this student immunity because in reality our investigation shows that this is the person who solicited the bribe. This person has an ax to grind. Let's test the credibility of this person, really test the credibility before you give him immunity.' As it is now, the infractions committee doesn't have any of this information; they simply have the enforcement staff coming by and saying they have to offer immunity or a kid won't talk. That's why even the committee chairman admits he can't remember turning an immunity request down. There may be some very good reasons to turn them down, but the committee won't hear that side of it.

And once he's given immunity, well shoot, a kid will say any-thing. I mean, immunized witnesses don't necessarily tell the truth in courts of law. Well, what's their motivation? Their motivation is to get immunity. And you know what? They're going to say anything to get the immunity. They're going to the investigator and say, 'Hey, you want dirt? I'll give you dirt but you can't penalize me.' What's the alternative? I don't give you the dirt, you find out about it and I lose my eligibility. So I'm the kid and I want to be the first one in the door. Should he now be able to drive away in his car? And if the NCAA says yes, shouldn't the university at the very least be able to argue that point?"

10. Obtain the power to subpoena witnesses.   The lack of subpoena power is the NCAA's excuse for nearly all the abuses of its enforcement program. Because it doesn't have the ability to compel people to testify, Berst often claims, the NCAA is hand-cuffed. Anyone who wants to tinker with the enforcement pro-gram is only trying to tighten those handcuffs. Baloney.

Page 359 of the *NCAA Manual* carries this warning: "In the event that a representative of a member institution refuses to submit relevant information to the Committee [on Infractions] or the enforcement staff upon request, an official inquiry may be filed with the institution alleging a violation of the cooperative principles of the NCAA bylaws and enforcement procedures [a major violation]. Institutional representatives may be requested to appear before the committee at the time the allegation is considered."

Using that threat, NCAA investigators have forced nu-merous coaches, athletes and administrators—anyone connected with the member school—to cough up everything from old phone bills to bank records to car payment slips. Every school that has gone through an NCAA investigation will attest to the strength of that clause. If you fail to "cooperate" with the NCAA and refuse to provide those records, you can be slapped with the most serious of NCAA infractions. For a coach, it can result in banishment, for an athlete, loss of eligibility.

Pretty strong stuff. Still, the NCAA complains that is not enough, mostly because a key group—boosters—falls outside the realm of NCAA punishment. That "cooperative principle" clause doesn't require Joe Bob Booster to open his records, and that handcuffs the NCAA.

John Weistart said the NCAA needs to stop moaning about subpoena power and do something about it. "They ought to arrange to give themselves a subpoena power," he said. "You know they've talked about that but they've never done anything about it, which makes me a little bit suspicious. They could do that in a couple of ways. One is they could go to state legislatures and just ask for it. Another is that it's perfectly possible for the NCAA to link its procedures with the procedures of local law enforcement people and suddenly they'd have subpoena power. That really makes a substantive difference. If those potential NCAA witnesses were threatened with time in jail if they didn't answer, then I believe you'd get a much more thorough, a much more complete investigation." Weistart surmised the NCAA has avoided seeking legislative subpoena power because legislatures might require the organization to abide by certain due process requirements in exchange. "They've always preferred not to face those issues."

"But there are some other things the NCAA can do to give itself subpoena power, as well," Weistart said. "It can give itself an extensive subpoena power by simply requiring each university to sign contracts with everyone—it could even extend to alums, that to be a member of the booster club, to be involved in athletics in any way, you must sign a contract that says you will cooperate with the NCAA and the NCAA has the authority to go into court to force you to cooperate if you don't. And if you fail to cooperate the university could be sanctioned, and you will be automatically disassociated from the program. It's like a contempt citation.

"Or try this. When a school goes under investigation, the NCAA could require the institution or the booster club or whatever to post a substantial bond that would be forfeited if someone doesn't cooperate. The idea is used in other places—that's what states are doing now with athletic agents, making them post bond, and if they violate rules they lose money under the bond. That's a powerful incentive to cooperate, if the university is going to lose big money."

Lonny Rose suggested the NCAA could get subpoena authority through the civil courts. "Suppose a school wins and takes postseason money, then the NCAA says we're going to investigate you and if we find something we're going to ask for the money back. And so the NCAA files an action in court which is in essence a restitution action: 'Give us the money back we gave you on the theory that you acted appropriately. If you didn't act appropriately, you have to pay us back.' As part of that lawsuit the NCAA could subpoena as a witness the person who assisted in or aided and abetted the infraction. So there are numerous ways for the NCAA to get the ability to subpoena records. They just haven't tried any of them."

None of this is intended to suggest that the NCAA should adopt all the trappings of an American courtroom. There certainly is a difference between an NCAA administrative hearing and a criminal trial. But there are very good reasons why courts have gone far in protecting the rights of the accused, of guaranteeing due process, of ensuring that one is presumed innocent until proven guilty. By protecting those rights, the courts have increased the credibility of court decisions. When someone is judged guilty after being guaranteed all of those rights, the verdict is more believable; the public can rest assured the accused was, in fact, guilty. A similar credibility, if they ever had it, has been slipping away from the NCAA, as more and more schools have suffered through its one-sided enforcement program. The whispers of concern are turning to screams. The NCAA would be well advised to weigh the benefit of added credibility against the difficulties it might incur if it began respecting individual rights. As in the court system, the scales should tip toward credibility. An improved NCAA, with a fairer enforcement division, will carry the clout and credibility necessary to make potential cheaters think twice and, at the same time, increase public confidence in its decisions.

If the NCAA does nothing, it shouldn't be surprised if more state legislatures—possibly even Congress—begin passing the "due process" bill Ernie Chambers shepherded through the Nebraska legislature. In August 1990, 32 U.S. congressmen, in fact, sponsored a bill similar to the one passed in Nebraska. Hearings on that bill were scheduled for later in the year. U.S. Representative Tom McMillen of Maryland suggested that Congress needed to go even further. McMillen, a former college and pro basketball star, called for a congressional investigation of the NCAA, its finances, enforcement program and tax-exempt status. His hope was that Congress would delve even further into the NCAA than it did in the late 1970s. "What bothers me is they take draconian steps against a university," McMillen told *USA Today* in August 1990. "[But] they're only PR victories. They're not doing anything to reform collegiate sports. The only people punished are the kids who weren't there when the violations happened. What the NCAA is doing is un-American. They should give every citizen the due process they're entitled to in this country." Politicians, like nature, abhor a vacuum. Any bright politician can recognize this vacuum and the political popularity that might come in filling it. Any bright NCAA leader should recognize it is better to solve this problem before legislatures or Congress solve it for the NCAA.

Should the NCAA choose to discard this list of 10 solutions, it must develop a list of its own. When Congress completed its investigation of the NCAA enforcement program in 1978, it passed along a list of 18 recommended changes. One of those changes rejected by the NCAA, to the surprise of many, was a suggestion that the NCAA create a blue-ribbon study committee to explore the organization's enforcement procedures, looking for ways to improve the process. Now, more than a decade after it was proposed by Congress, serious consideration should be given to creating just such a group. There are, obviously, a great number of people with a great deal to say about how they or their university were treated by the NCAA. Doesn't anyone wonder how all of those people could be wrong?

Let John Weistart, who has given many hours of thought to the problem, chair the committee. Add Lonny Rose and another attorney who has worked within the NCAA system. Throw a former infractions committee member on there, maybe a former investigator who is not afraid to speak his or her mind, and a university president. The panel—which must be appointed in an honestly independent fashion—should then invite former athletes, coaches, boosters and administrators at schools who have felt the enforcement department's sting to tell their stories. Some very positive ideas may grow from that testimony. That kind of postexperiential insight is beneficial, both for the school and the NCAA. Former University of Florida president Marshall Criser telephoned then-NCAA president Wilford Bailey a year after Florida's football program was pounded for rules violations in the mid-1980s, and offered a few suggestions, most of which are included in this list of 10 solutions. Bailey phoned the NCAA's Steve Morgan and asked him to at least listen to Criser's comments, many of which Bailey believed had merit. Morgan didn't follow through. Shouldn't the NCAA be begging members for suggestions that might help rid its enforcement program of bad practices? Its reluctance to do so is as puzzling to Criser as it was to Congress. "I still believe very strongly that the first step is to appoint an outside commission to look at the entire process," Criser said years later. "I don't expect the rules of a court of law, but you're imposing multimillion dollar penalties and affecting the careers of coaches and players. These are big decisions and should be treated as such."

Then it should be the committee's responsibility to bring any recommended changes to the NCAA membership. NCAA bylaws require that any modification of the organization's procedures must be sponsored by eight member institutions. But fear of the investigative staff virtually assures that eight untainted schools never will combine to recommend substantive changes to the enforcement program. Let the blue-ribbon committee sponsor those modifications, and the chance of passing real and meaningful improvements to the enforcement process exists.

There are two forces within the NCAA that also could marshal such a change effort. Many who hope for a new and improved NCAA believe the increasingly active role of college presidents and the pressure of a relatively new executive director can be steps in a positive direction. To date, it's not clear whether either will result in change.

The darkening black eye college sports has given higher education led presidents from several major universities, among them UCLA, Arizona and Wake Forest, to focus their attention on problems within the NCAA. To do so, they felt they had to take control of athletics on their campuses. In 1985, those presidents called for a special "integrity" convention. But the effort to take control floundered for most of the next five years as one NCAA convention after another resulted in little or no substantive change. Then, their backs against the wall, the presidents won several significant victories in 1990. First, the convention passed a Presidents Commission–backed proposal requiring universities to report athletes' graduation rates. The vote could only be considered a minor victory, though, because Congress was on the verge of passing a law requiring the very same thing.

Then, the 1990 convention discussed the presidents' proposal to shorten the basketball season and reduce spring football training. From the outset, the battle lines were drawn: this was the athletic directors vs. presidents, those who have to balance athletic department budgets against those who are trying to restore the credibility of the university system. A motion was made by the athletic directors to defer the entire proposal for study. After intense debate, the deferral motion was defeated, but only by a 20-vote margin, 383-363. Presidents breathed a sigh of relief, and some even felt that victory was in hand. Nebraska President Martin Massengale, chairman of the Presidents Commission, even left the convention to fly to Chicago. But the athletic directors began twisting arms and getting people to change votes. Tennessee Athletic Director Doug Dickey complained, "We're talking significant dollars if we cut the number of basketball games."

Two hours later, several athletic directors submitted a proposal to delay action on the season-shortening proposal and refer it to the NCAA Council. With many presidents out of the room, the motion to refer passed 170-150. During the debate, the Presidents Commission was strongly criticized. "The Presidents Commission needs to do what it does best, and that is macromanage," said Donna Lopiano, women's athletic director at the University of Texas. "Leave the micromanagement to the various expert groups. We will bring back solutions."

Those presidents who stayed were visibly angry. Thomas Hearn of Wake Forest threatened to resign from the commission, noting that "any of us who have spent two years working to get these proposals have to be disappointed." Hearn said that the failure to act decisively on the proposal was "morally unacceptable." Then Hearn, University of New Orleans President Gregory O'Brien and Arizona State's Lattie Coor began to pressure athletic directors who they believed voted against the desires of their respective presidents. An hour later, when it seemed that enough votes could be changed, a motion to reconsider the referral vote was made by Coor. The same proposal now was before the convention for the third time on the same day. Outside the convention hall, Hearn and other presidents told reporters if they lost this battle, the day of the president was gone.

Finally, the presidents succeeded, 165-156. "To be blunt, the presidents needed a win in Dallas," Mansfield University

President Rodney C. Kelchner wrote in the *NCAA News*. "Our credibility within the NCAA was at stake. We were better organized than ever before and we had to be. The margin of passage for the reforms was earned only after the most intensive lobbying efforts I have ever seen. We have been on the sidelines too long."

But how long will it last? Many wonder whether presidents will maintain their vigilance. Will presidents stay involved long enough to take control of the athletic tail and stop it from wagging the university dog? Some predict not. "They [presidents] tend to want quick answers and you don't solve the complexities of intercollegiate athletics overnight," said Jim Delaney, commissioner of the Big Ten. "Yes, presidents are involved, but the truth is, they really don't have the time to be involved."

Bo Schembechler, former University of Michigan athletic director and head football coach, put it more explicitly. "Unfortunately, you're dealing with people who don't understand," he said. "We [athletic directors] are trying to straddle the fence here because you still want me to put 100,000 in the stadium and the reason you want me to do it is because you're not going to help me financially at all." Schembechler later resigned his position to become Detroit Tigers president. In some parting shots, he said, "In the next five years, school presidents will completely confuse intercollegiate athletics directors and then say, 'You straighten this out.' About [the year] 2000, it may be back on track."

For an ally in this fight, it seems both sides are pinning their hopes on new executive director Dick Schultz, who came on board in 1987. His arrival was heralded as the beginning of a new era, in more ways than one. With Byers as its executive director, the NCAA had a certain distant image. Ric Bucher of the *San Diego Union* once described Byers's NCAA as "a medieval castle located high on a precipitous summit in an uncharted region of the Midwest." Byers, Bucher wrote, "had a draconian mystique. He was pictured as a faceless man in druid's robes, ensconced in the castle's most remote quarters, dust rising from the pages of an enormous tattered tome as he searched through it for some obscure regulation with which to terrorize the university of his choice."

Then along came Dick Schultz. In an organization where everyone is listed by full first name and middle initial, Richard D. Schultz prefers to be just plain Dick. For 35 years, he was a coach and an athletic director, qualifying him as "one of us," many within the organization said. A well-respected administrator as athletic director at the University of Virginia, Schultz said he was not looking for other employment when an NCAA search committee asked him to interview for the powerful executive director's position. He told the committee he believed the NCAA was viewed as too clandestine by outsiders. Without pointing the finger at Byers, Schultz said the next leader had to be different.

He has delivered on that promise. His first year in office, Schultz averaged 14 days a month on the road; Byers seldom traveled. Schultz set up interviews with reporters at the drop of a hat; getting Byers to talk was like pulling teeth. Schultz has told the NCAA's 160-person staff that his is an open door; most employees cowered at the thought of riding an elevator with Byers.

Schultz has, many agree, begun to put dents in the walls of the castle Byers built. But one area he said he sees no pressing need to reform is enforcement. "There aren't any changes I see at the present time," Schultz said in a lengthy interview on the subject. "I've really stayed pretty much out of the enforcement area."

In his first three years as executive director, Schultz had spoken to or been a member of a whole host of commissions, committees and study groups from coast to coast, each of which bandied about a similar list of suggestions for solving the problems of college athletics. Many of the ideas include adding sanity to the exploitative rule-making process, making freshmen ineligible, and decreasing the incentive to cheat by changing the payout structure of the basketball tournament.

John Weistart said that last suggestion is key to curbing the abuses of college athletics. He said the whole ethical structure of amateur athletics will always be subverted as long as the NCAA fails to address the economic realities of college sports. Until players in revenue-producing sports share in the wealth they produce and the financial rewards given schools are less dependent upon athletic success, the desire to cheat will remain. "The question the NCAA should be asking is, 'Why is it that pro sports don't seem to be spending as much time and energy on enforcement as the NCAA does?'" he said. "Why is it that enforcement is such a problem for the NCAA? I would say that if the NCAA changed the structure, the economic structure of college sports, which is usually the incentive for cheating, that would be the single biggest step toward better enforcement. If they do anything less than make a radical change in the financial side, they may just be rearranging deck chairs on the *Titanic*. It really does come down to controlling expenditures for athletics and profit-sharing. If you do those things, you reduce the incentives to cheat because right now these incentives are just extraordinarily high. If you ignore those points, the whole problem will continue and we could write this book 10 years from now without many changes."

The Knight Foundation Commission on Intercollegiate Athletics, an independent group of 21 national leaders, in 1989 began a study of the problems of intercollegiate athletics and ways to rein in college sports. The commission co-chairmen, William Friday, president emeritus of the University of North Carolina, and the Reverend Theodore M. Hesburgh, president emeritus of the University of Notre Dame, have sworn this "will not be just another commission" and will result in major initiatives. The two also promised that the commission will follow through to see its initiatives enacted. The group invited coaches, athletic directors, parents and student-athletes to meetings, each providing their perspective on what has turned college sports sour. The commission, which includes eight university presidents, U.S. Representative Tom McMillen and several other corporate and athletic personalities, planned to release its final report in 1991. The power that sits on the Knight panel epitomizes the national concern over college athletics. Why? Because corruption in college sports is an embarrassment to the entire system of higher education.

Through its first five meetings, the commission focused much of its attention on issues like freshman eligibility, the impact of athletic dorms, revenue sharing, length of playing and practice seasons and giving coaches more security through tenure. While college sports will benefit from improvements in all these areas, the truth is there will always be someone willing to step over the line seeking an advantage. The NCAA needs to be there when that happens.

John Weistart said the NCAA's hesitance to adopt significant changes, in enforcement as well as in other areas, is likely to continue as long as the organization is making big money and the popularity of college sports is skyrocketing. "I think a compelling argument could be made that the NCAA doesn't really want to stop cheating," Weistart said. "It is very happy with the status quo. For proof, just you look at the structure of its enforcement program and [the NCAA's] small commitment to enforcement. It certainly seems that a relatively modest, ineffectual enforcement mechanism is acceptable to many within the organization."

If the NCAA refuses to make changes and better its enforcement program, maybe Weistart is right. Maybe the NCAA really doesn't want to catch all those who "cheat." Maybe the NCAA is lamely carrying out an outmoded, overextended, but vindictive enforcement program to soothe the public conscience, to appear as if it is cutting toward the heart of what is wrong with college sports while really just doing a little cosmetic work. If so, it isn't working. The public is increasingly disgusted by what's happening in college sports.

It's time to try something new.

A CHRONOLOGY OF SCHOOLS PENALIZED BY THE NCAA

1952

University of Kentucky
Bradley University
Midwestern University

1953

Arizona State University
Michigan State University
University of Notre Dame

1954

Kansas State University
Border Intercollegiate Conference*
Seton Hall University
North Carolina State University
Western Illinois University
University of Miami
City College of New York
University of Portland

1955

University of Cincinnati
Bethune-Cookman College
Virginia Union University

1955 cont.

University of Oklahoma
University of Dayton
St. Louis University
Wichita State University
Baylor University

1956

Texas A&M University
Mississippi College
University of Kansas
University of Florida
University of Louisville
Auburn University
University of Washington
University of California–Los
   Angeles
North Carolina State University
Ohio State University
University of Southern
   California
University of California–
   Berkeley

*University of Arizona, Hardin Simmons University,
Texas Tech University, West Texas State University

1957

University of Omaha
Montana State University
West Virginia University
Indiana University

1958

Memphis State University
Wichita State University
Southern Methodist University
Seattle University
Auburn University

1959

Gustavus Adolphus College
University of Cincinnati
University of Mississippi
Arizona State University
University of Wyoming
Hamline University
Montana State University

1960

University of Oklahoma
University of Tulsa
Indiana University
University of Kansas

1961

University of North Carolina–
Chapel Hill
Loyola University (Louisiana)
University of Arizona
Tennessee Polytechnic Institute
East Tennessee State College

1962

Whitworth College

1962 cont.

Humboldt State College
University of Utah
New Mexico State University
University of Colorado
University of Missouri–
Columbia
McMurry College (Texas)
University of Florida
University of Dayton

1963

Hardin-Simmons University
University of Omaha
Millersville State College
Wichita State University

1964

University of Iowa
Centenary College
University of Houston
Washington State University
University of Alabama
University of Kentucky
Prairie View A&M College
Slippery Rock State College
Michigan State University
Western State College (Colorado)
University of Miami
United States Naval Academy

1965

West Texas State University
Southern Methodist University
University of Texas at Austin
University of Arkansas

1966

University of Houston

1966 cont.

University of Richmond
Texas A&M University
University of Tennessee–
  Chattanooga
Purdue University
Bradley University

1967

University of Texas at El Paso
University of South Carolina
University of Tulsa
Waynesburg College
Central College
University of Illinois at Urbana-
  Champaign
Mississippi State University
University of Nebraska–Lincoln

1968

University of Southwestern
  Louisiana
Wichita State University
Pan American College
LaSalle College
St. Bonaventure University
Florida State University
Utah State University

1969

Centenary College
University of North Carolina
University of Texas at El Paso
Texas A&M University
University of Minnesota–Twin
  Cities
University of Maryland–
  College Park
San Jose State College
Marshall University

1970

Florida State University
Yale University
Villanova University
University of Massachusetts
St. Norbert College
Jackson State College
State University of New York at
  Buffalo
Southern University and A&M
  College
University of Tulsa
University of Jacksonville
Kansas State University

1971

Northwestern Louisiana State
  University
Westminster College
  (Pennsylvania)
Memphis State University
American International College
University of Notre Dame
University of California–
  Berkeley
University of California–Los
  Angeles
North Carolina Central
  University
Montana State University

1972

Westminster College
  (Pennsylvania)
Illinois State University
Livingston University
University of Minnesota–Duluth
Samford University
University of Kansas
Eastern Michigan University
Duke University
Bloomsburg State College

1972 cont.

California State University–
  Sacramento
North Carolina State University
St. John's University (New York)

1973

Howard University
Western Kentucky University
New Mexico State University
Doane College
Pan American University
Livingston University
University of Nebraska–Omaha
University of Southwestern
  Louisiana
University of Colorado
University of Oklahoma
Louisiana Tech University

1974

Cornell University
California State University–
  Hayward
California State University–
  Long Beach
University of Arizona
University of Illinois at Urbana-
  Champaign
McNeese State University
Florida State University
Cornell University
Southern Methodist University
Western Kentucky University
Wichita State University
University of Maryland–Eastern
  Shore
Augustana College
DePaul University

1974 cont.

Gallaudet College
DePaul University
Ohio Valley Conference*

1975

University of Nebraska–Lincoln
Seton Hall University
University of Nebraska
Canisius College
Kentucky State University
Mississippi State University
University of Wisconsin–
  Milwaukee
Clemson University

1976

Southern Methodist University
Michigan State University
University of Minnesota
Florida A&M University
Midland Lutheran College
West Texas State University
California Lutheran College
University of Denver
University of Hawaii
University of Nevada–Reno
University of Minnesota

1977

Portland State University
Western Carolina University
University of Houston
University of Montana
Texas A&M University
University of Hawaii
University of Redlands
Western State College
University of Nevada–Las Vegas

*Eight institutions: Austin Peay State University; Eastern Kentucky University; East Tennessee State University; Middle Tennessee State University; Morehead State University; Murray State University; Tennessee Tech University, and Western Kentucky University.

1978

Oklahoma State University
University of Idaho
Ohio State University
Grambling State University
University of Alaska–Anchorage
Howard University
University of Idaho
University of Georgia
Kansas State University
University of Cincinnati

1979

Western State College
Auburn University
Southeast Missouri State
 University
Memphis State University
East Carolina University
San Jose State University
University of San Francisco
University of Missouri
Westmont College
West Virginia Wesleyan College
Oklahoma State University

1980

Arizona State University
Oral Roberts University
University of Colorado at Boulder
University of New Mexico
University of Toledo
Auburn University
Hampton University
U.S. Military Academy
University of Oklahoma

1981

Arkansas State University
California State University–
 Pomona

1981

Texas Christian University
University of California–Los
 Angeles
University of Miami
University of New Haven
University of Oregon
Wichita State University
Oregon State University
University of San Francisco
University of Wisconsin–
 Madison

1982

Clemson University
Oklahoma City University
St. Louis University
University of Georgia
University of San Diego
University of Southern
 California
University of Southern
 Mississippi
Western State College of
 Colorado
Wichita State University
New York Institute of
 Technology
University of Southern Florida
University of Texas at Austin
State University of New York at
 Cortland
University of Wisconsin at
 Madison
West Virginia University

1983

California State University–
 Fresno
University of Arizona
University of Kansas

1983 cont.

University of Wisconsin at
  Madison
Florida State University
North Carolina State University
Virginia Polytechnic and State
  University
Jackson State University
University of Washington
Wake Forest University
West Virginia University

1984

Oregon State University
San Diego State University
University of Akron
University of Alaska–Anchorage
University of Illinois at Urbana-
  Champaign
Middle Tennessee State
  University
Alcorn State University
Austin Peay State University
Florida State University
Southern University and A&M
  College
Western Kentucky University

1985

Alabama State University
Idaho State University
Southern Illinois University at
  Carbondale
Southern Methodist University
Tennessee State University
University of Florida
University of Georgia
University of Southern
  Mississippi
Cheyney University of
  Pennsylvania

1985 cont.

Arizona State University
State University of New York at
  Plattsburgh
University of Central Florida
Austin Peay State University
California State University–
  Northridge
San Francisco State University
American University
Tennessee Technological
  University

1986

Alabama A&M University
Texas Christian University
University of Mississippi
University of Nebraska
University of South Florida
University of Tennessee at
  Knoxville
University of Texas at El Paso
University of Wisconsin at
  Madison
East Carolina University
Mississippi State University
Oral Roberts University
University of Iowa
University of Nevada–Las Vegas

1987

Alabama State University
Brooklyn College
Eastern Washington University
McNeese State University
Southern Methodist University
Texas Tech University
University of Bridgeport
University of South Carolina
University of Texas at Austin
University of Utah

1987 cont.

Virginia Polytechnic Institute and
  State University
California State–San Luis Obispo
Louisiana State University
Southern Illinois University at
  Edwardsville
Tulane University
University of California–
  Los Angeles
Westchester University
  Pennsylvania
Kenyon College

1988

Arizona State University
Cleveland State University
Marist College
Texas A&M University
University of Cincinnati
University of Houston
University of Illinois at Urbana-
  Champaign
University of Kansas
University of Minnesota–Twin
  Cities
University of California–Berkeley
University of Kentucky

1989

Adelphi University
Eastern Kentucky University
Grambling State University
Memphis State University
Oklahoma State University
Southeastern Louisiana University
University of Kentucky
University of Oklahoma
West Texas State University
Georgia Institute of Technology

1990

University of Maryland–College
  Park
Houston Baptist University
Robert Morris College
Florida A&M University
State University of New York at
  Plattsburgh
Marshall University
Clemson University
North Carolina State University
Upsala College
University of Florida
University of Illinois at Urbana-
  Champaign
University of Missouri